W9-CIM-110

Praise for
Holy Roller

"An extraordinary book. Few Christians would have the courage to cross the cultural boundaries that Julie Lyons has. Even fewer mainstream journalists would have the guts to write with such naked honesty. To read *Holy Roller* is to be amazed by what God is doing in the forgotten corners of our country. This book marks the debut of a major new voice in American Christianity."

—ROD DREHER, *Dallas Morning News* columnist
and author of *Crunchy Cons*

"*Holy Roller* is a gutsy look into the strengths and weaknesses that are exposed when cultures collide. You will find Julie's raw and honest insights both entertaining and helpful as she opens a window onto the passion and chutzpa of black Pentecostal spirituality. Read it and break down some barriers."

—LISA BEVERE, speaker and best-selling author of *Fight Like
a Girl* and *Kissed the Girls and Made Them Cry*

"Julie Lyons is a devout Christian who edited mostly heathen writers at an alternative newsweekly, the *Dallas Observer*. This church lady makes no effort to convert readers, so Jews, Catholics, Protestants, and pagans can enjoy this book the way they relish viewing Anthony Bourdain on the Travel Channel: *Holy Roller* is a journey to unfamiliar places conducted by a skilled raconteur."

—MICHAEL LACEY, executive editor of Village Voice Media

"This book draws us to the reality of a God who is obsessed with the heart of humankind regardless of race, education, or the location and size of a church building. In *Holy Roller*, we hear a pronounced call to unprecedented spiritual discernment and the transforming power of the Holy Spirit."

—Evangelist JOYCE TERRELL, founder of Oasis
of Miracles Ministries

"Julie Lyons deftly explains the inner workings of black Pentecostalism. Her book is loaded with helpful spiritual insights."

—JULIA DUIN, religion editor of the *Washington Times* and author of *Quitting Church: Why the Faithful Are Fleeing and What to Do About It*

"*Holy Roller* takes you for a ride through a corner of life most of us will never see. More than that, it's about one woman's relationship with God and the unexpected journey that grows out of that relationship. Lyons has given us a spiritual autobiography worth reading from cover to cover."

—ALEX TIZON, a Knight International Fellow and Pulitzer Prize–winning journalist

"Julie Lyons's personal journey of faith is a powerful story of redemption, a testament that one man or one woman can make a lasting change in communities that have been forgotten. For those who have given up on the Christian community to make a difference among those who need it most, this book is a must-read."

—JESSE HYDE, managing editor of the *Miami New Times*

HOLY
ROLLER

JULIE LYONS

**Finding Redemption
and the Holy Ghost
in a Forgotten
Texas Church**

HOLY ROLLER

WaterBrook
Press

HOLY ROLLER
PUBLISHED BY WATERBROOK PRESS
12265 Oracle Boulevard, Suite 200
Colorado Springs, Colorado 80921

All Scripture quotations, unless otherwise indicated, are taken from the Holy Bible, New International Version®. NIV®. Copyright © 1973, 1978, 1984 by International Bible Society. Used by permission of Zondervan Publishing House. All rights reserved. Scripture quotations marked (KJV) are taken from the King James Version.

Italics in Scripture quotations reflect the author's added emphasis.

All stories in this book are true. Some names have been changed to protect the identities of the persons involved.

ISBN 978-1-4000-7495-2
ISBN 978-0-30745-789-9 (electronic)

Copyright © 2009 by Julie Lyons
Interior photographs © 2009 by the Lyons family and © 2009 by Robert Conner, DFW Digital Photography

Published in association with the literary agency of Daniel Literary Group, Nashville, Tennessee.

All rights reserved. No part of this book may be reproduced or transmitted in any form or by any means, electronic or mechanical, including photocopying and recording, or by any information storage and retrieval system, without permission in writing from the publisher.

Published in the United States by WaterBrook Multnomah, an imprint of The Doubleday Publishing Group, a division of Random House Inc., New York.

WATERBROOK and its deer colophon are registered trademarks of Random House Inc.

Library of Congress Cataloging-in-Publication Data
Lyons, Julie.
    Holy roller : finding redemption and the Holy Ghost in a forgotten Texas church / Julie Lyons. — 1st ed.
        p. cm.
    Includes bibliographical references.
    ISBN 978-1-4000-7495-2 — ISBN 978-0-30745-789-9 (electronic)
  1. Lyons, Julie. 2. Body of Christ Assembly (South Dallas, Dallas, Tex.)—Biography.
3. African American Pentecostals—Texas—Dallas. I. Title.
    BX8762.5.Z8L96 2009
    289.9'4097642812—dc22
                                                                        2008054073

Printed in the United States of America
2009—First Edition

10 9 8 7 6 5 4 3 2 1

SPECIAL SALES
Most WaterBrook Multnomah books are available at special quantity discounts when purchased in bulk by corporations, organizations, and special-interest groups. Custom imprinting or excerpting can also be done to fit special needs. For information, please e-mail SpecialMarkets@WaterBrookMultnomah.com or call 1-800-603-7051.

To my mother:
You awakened my conscience.
You inspired my faith.
You gave me a vision for justice.
You taught me to love.

Contents

Working the Crime Beat

I was driving on the wild frontier of gangsta-land, a place I'd learn to navigate by the sites where people got murdered. South Dallas always stayed crazy, and I was just getting used to the experience—the occasional *kak-kak-kak* of semiautomatic-weapon fire, the graffiti tags of the Trey-Five-Seven (.357) Crips, the distinctive choreography of drug dealing, with crack rocks passing invisibly from hand to hand in furtive motions that I came to recognize from afar.

I was twenty-seven years old, white, and quite conspicuous in black South Dallas the evening in late April 1990 when I set out to find a different kind of story for the *Dallas Times Herald*. Since starting a job two months earlier as a crime reporter, I'd been getting to know the roughest parts of the city, places like this. It was nothing like the small Wisconsin town where I grew up.

I'd tell myself I wasn't scared, but I think I was driving too fast to know for sure. This time I wasn't chasing flashing lights toward Bexar Street, hoping to get there before the witnesses and walking wounded had melted away in the dark. Instead, I was looking for the scene of a miracle.

There would be no crime-scene tape marking the spot. It was just me in my little car, prowling the streets and looking for a spiritual outpost. I had no idea what it would look like; all I knew was there had to be a church in this part of the inner city where people came searching for a supernatural breakthrough. I had decided it would be impossible to live in this crumbling, seemingly godforsaken territory without clinging to some shred of hope that things could get better. I was determined to find the place people go when despair drives them to seek a miracle.

I turned a corner and entered a neighborhood with all the familiar signs: slender boys with darting eyes, standing like pickets on the corner, beckoning to people in cars that were slowly passing through. I steered around potholes and broken glass in the street and looked past the drug sentries for evidence of light and life in the neighborhood's churches. You'd find Baptists on one corner and Holy Sanctifieds on the other, with a House of Prayer for All People wedged in between. They stood as silent witnesses while hell swarmed all around them.

The truth is, I really didn't know *what* I was looking for. I just knew I couldn't leave South Dallas until I found it.

All this began with a lie, a made-up story idea that I pitched to my editors at the newspaper. See, there are these preachers in the ghetto who pray for crack-cocaine addicts, and people are supposedly getting miraculously healed. And oh, I know a bunch of these preachers.

The best you could say in my defense is that I thought about the story so much that it became real to me. Before moving to Dallas, I had lived in Belfast, Northern Ireland, where the Troubles erupted regularly into firebombings, shootings, and retaliatory acts between working-class Catholics and Protestants. I had gone to the province of Ulster to write the story of a terrorist who found God and was now trying to lead his former enemies to reconciliation. I learned while living in Belfast that among certain types of Christians, inexplicable things were almost commonplace. You just had to know where to look.

My previous work as a crime reporter at the *Seattle Times* had led me to believe that miracle-working preachers could be found in any major city. In Dallas in 1990, the crack epidemic was leaving a trail of wreckage—of neighborhoods gone to hell in a swath of murder and ruin. Thanks to my experiences in Belfast and Seattle, I had come up with a simple theorem: where desperation multiplied, there you would find God.

At the *Dallas Times Herald* we were always looking for new angles to pursue in reporting the crack-cocaine story. I needed something bigger than yet another shooting, drug raid, or body found in the street. Why not make my mark at the paper by uncovering the miraculous?

Here, then, was the problem: I didn't know any preachers who fit this description. There is a game that newspaper reporters play: you invest as little work as possible before pitching a story to your editor. That way, if your editor rejects the idea, you haven't wasted too much effort. I mentioned my story idea of supernatural healing, and to my surprise and secret horror, the editors seized on it immediately. They scheduled the story for Sunday A-1. I had just a few days to find my mythical ministers and write a lengthy feature story about them in time for the early edition, the "bulldog."

That's why I was cruising aimlessly through South Dallas. As evening moved quickly toward night, I was way more scared of my editors than I was of the ghetto. I passed dozens of churches without stopping. If the lights weren't on, I kept rolling. I eventually turned onto a one-block street, Brigham Lane, and saw two churches, one on each corner. The first seemed inconsequential, with a sagging roof and handmade sign. But at the other end of the block stood a tidy, brick-walled structure. I noted the affiliation: Church of God in Christ. Black Pentecostals. Holy rollers. I aimed for the far corner.

I had my music cranked, a soca artist from Tobago named Shadow, who had an insidiously hummable tune, "Tabanka." It has something to do with the sickness you feel when you're hopelessly attracted to someone. I craved the melody and syncopation of my beloved Caribbean music. All the plastic parts of my little Honda were rattling with the heavy bass line, and the noise helped to bury my nervousness.

I was driving past the scruffy-looking church when something intensely spiritual happened. I don't know how else to say this: God was in the car with me. I could feel his presence, a palpable thing that made my senses light up even amid the dissonance of blaring soca. I might have been a tough-minded crime reporter, but I had recently reconnected with the faith of my childhood, and I was engaged to be married to a man who was a devout Christian. I was far from figuring things out but eager to investigate anything that might shed more light on questions about God's work on earth.

Is that really you, God? I thought. What else could I think? I turned the music down and pulled my car to the curb.

You want me to stop here, don't you? I said to myself and, I suppose, to God as well. Just then a girl popped out the front door of the dilapidated church. As the girl skipped down the sidewalk, I got out of my car, reporter's notebook in hand, and stopped her just short of the house that stood next-door.

"Do you believe in healing prayer?" I asked without introduction.

"Yes!" she said enthusiastically. She was brown-skinned, with pigtails, or so I recall. I don't remember very clearly anymore. I guessed she was about ten, but back then I wasn't good at estimating children's ages.

"Does your minister pray for drug addicts?" I asked.

"Yes!" she answered again.

"Are any getting healed?"

"Yes!"

I asked her to point out her pastor to me. At that moment a black man wearing a suit jacket and tie stepped outside the church's front door. Several church members were visible in the dim yellow light of the tiny foyer behind him. A thought flashed in my brain: *Oh God, don't let him be one of those overbearing egotistical preachers.* I'm not even sure where that objection came from—probably from a bad experience I'd had in my years as a reporter.

I walked over and introduced myself as a journalist. The pastor was Fredrick L. Eddington Sr. He was tall and I am not, and I remember he bent down slightly as he listened to me.

"Do you pray for crack addicts?" I asked. Might as well get right to the point.

"Yes," the pastor said.

"Are they getting healed?"

The pastor paused for a moment. "Some of them are," he said. We chatted some more, and I got the impression he was choosing his words carefully. Still, our conversation was casual. To listen to Pastor Edding-ton, you'd have thought we were discussing the weather or the Dallas Cowboys. But we were talking about *miracles*.

This wasn't at all what I'd expected. The pastor came across as hum-ble, gentle, plain spoken. And he didn't seem the least bit surprised that a young white woman—a stranger who clearly didn't belong in this neighborhood—had suddenly materialized out of the darkness.

I was looking for a feature story to run in the Sunday paper. What I was about to discover was a passionate, self-taught man who would introduce me to a world of spirits, healing, prophecy, and warfare waged to the death between invisible forces of good and evil. To Pastor Eddington these things were not superstition, legend, or overwrought emotion. This was reality, and over the next few months I would see it for myself.

Months later, talking with Diane Eddington, the pastor's wife, I inquired about the girl who had come skipping down the walk in front of the church, telling me that healings took place there. I asked the First Lady to point out the girl so I could thank her, and Diane told me there was no such girl. I thought back to the night I had found this church. The sun had just set, it was a neighborhood where the crackle of gun-fire was often heard, and a young girl was the only person on the side-walk. I realized that no parent would dream of allowing her child to be out alone at night. Not only that, but no one who attended the service that evening had seen a girl matching the description I gave.

So who was the girl I talked to? Diane had an answer.

"Oh," she said, "you was just seeing an angel."

A News Tip from God

It happened exactly two times: I heard the call for a Signal 27 on the police scanner—meaning a dead body had been reported—and I got there before the cops. This time I was standing in a field staring at the body of a middle-aged black man. He lay curled on his side, as though napping, still clutching a 40-ounce in a brown paper bag. Amber-colored liquid was visible inside the bottle. A gunshot had interrupted the man's last drink.

I stood there, stunned. This killing had just happened, I was alone, and I had no idea where the murderer might be. That's when a Dallas police officer walked up. He gestured to my feet with a nod. "Um," he said, "I think you're standing on his brains."

I glanced down but was too creeped out to take a closer look. I stepped back and slowly circled the crime scene, edging farther and farther away. The victim had a gunshot wound to his temple, and in the grass next to his body, blood had pooled with the color and consistency of chocolate syrup.

This was around 1990, wild times in South Dallas. The inner city reeled from crack cocaine–fueled violence, and bodies were dropping just about every day. These were the days of running gun battles with the police, barricaded drug houses, and Jamaican gangsters toting Uzis and TEC-9s. The city recorded 442 murders in 1990, 500 in 1991— still an all-time record—and much of the mayhem occurred within the few square miles known as South Dallas, west of the Texas fairgrounds and just south of I-30, which bisects the city.

The man I had seen lying curled on his side was maybe forty years old. Months after the murder, his body still lay unidentified and unclaimed in the morgue. How a grown man could be wiped off the face of the earth with no one's taking notice, except the person who happened to find his corpse, baffled me. But in parts of this city, violent, meaningless death had become an expected part of life.

The near-daily slaughter dated from around 1986, when crack cocaine hit Dallas. The drug was brought to town by Jamaica-born gangsters based in Brooklyn, New York, who learned how to cook cocaine powder and baking soda into crack rocks. When a rock is lit and smoked through a glass pipe, it delivers an extraordinarily intense but short-lived high, and as little as ten dollars could buy the thrill. The cheap price opened the market to people who had never been able to afford powder cocaine, the glamour drug of the eighties.

Crack spread through South Dallas like a flesh-eating virus, infecting minds, bodies, and spirits and destroying whole neighborhoods. In Dallas's black residential areas, the drug took out a family member here, an acquaintance there, even bishops, schoolteachers, and college administrators. I became intimately acquainted with the carnage through my work as a crime reporter at the *Dallas Times Herald.* Working the night shift, I would sit in a grubby room in the bowels of the main police station downtown, not far from the spot where Jack Ruby shot Lee Harvey Oswald, listening to a police scanner and paging through stacks of offense reports. When I heard a dispatch code for bullets or dead bodies, I'd hop in my car and, more often than not, head to South Dallas or East Oak Cliff, run-down areas where drug-related violence had found a home.

Jamaican gangsters would rent units in low-income apartment complexes—usually through girlfriends or a crooked building manager who shared in the drug profits—and open "traps," which is what retail crack-cocaine outlets were called back then. In parts of South Dallas, men and women would line up in the street outside a crackhouse like they were waiting to board the giant Ferris wheel at Fair Park. The posses knew how to market their product, to the point where they'd offer buy-two-get-one-free deals, even distributing flyers pointing out the location of new traps: "$20 rock, $50 rock—apartment 110."

Customers were welcome, of course, but anyone suspected of being a threat to the crack trade was in jeopardy. A homicide detective told me about finding the body of a teenager whose hands were nailed to a table. One of his knees was shot up. He had been tortured and killed either by his Jamaican bosses or a rival dealer.

Teenage boys from South Dallas would work as crackhouse lookouts for fifty to one hundred dollars a day. Local youths also worked as salesclerks, shoving crack vials through a window or door to users and spending hours every day and night in apartment units devoid of furniture. There was nothing glamorous about this life. The Jamaicans would come by a few times a day in their silk leisure suits, BK shoes, and gold-trimmed Benzes to scoop up cash and drop off fast food for their American slaves. When cops raided the traps, they would find dirty mattresses and piles of empty fried-chicken boxes.

Within a few years many of the apartment complexes resembled bombed-out ruins, with walls and ceilings still standing but with the doors missing, the residents gone, and the windows broken out. It was as though the ground were cursed and the structure couldn't bear the weight of the degradation in and around it.

As all of us "cops reporters" knew, there were still good old boys serving on the Dallas police force who referred to victims of black-on-black violence as "misdemeanor murders." I looked at things more simply, knowing that any murder victim was a human, no matter who he was and under what circumstances he was killed. I felt as though writing a few inches of text about the victim assigned a modicum of dignity to his life. That's why I saw it as a duty to penetrate the worst parts of town in search of the backstory. I was good at knocking on doors in dicey places and getting people to talk to me. Or perhaps it was just that I was the only person who was willing to do it.

I wasn't brave, and I certainly wasn't street-smart. My naiveté led to a number of funny-creepy moments, like the afternoon I got chased by a drug dealer. I had been sitting in my car outside his crackhouse, and when he appeared, I stared him down. I knew that what I was doing was foolish, but the drug trade and the destruction it caused in so many lives made me angry enough to do stupid things. I drove away, and the dealer chased me in his car until he realized I was heading toward a police station.

Another time I was walking through the worst low-income housing complex in South Dallas—a place where I once interviewed a penny-ante crack peddler while he licked powder cocaine off his fingers—and a little girl walked up to me. I was probably the only white person for blocks, and the girl wondered what I was doing there. She asked, "Aren't you scared?"

I was scared at times, but not often. My closest friends joked that I had a death wish, and given my past brushes with depression, there was more to that theory than they realized. But I was also a Christian, and I had a strong sense of calling in my work as a crime reporter. Somehow, I knew that God would protect me. And he always did.

Years into the drug epidemic, the editors and reporters who worked on the *Dallas Times Herald* metro desk were still looking for new wrinkles in the crack-cocaine saga. Drug-related murders were so common they lost much of their shock value. Many of the homicides, particularly those in poor black neighborhoods, were reported in short, hundred-word news briefs. Often, we didn't even bother to run a follow-up story a day or two later when the victim had been positively identified.

With violence the rule and not the exception, it seems odd that cruising through cracked-out Dallas didn't frighten me a lot more than it did. On the night I started looking for a miracle-working church, I headed into the heart of the city's most violent neighborhood without even a mobile phone for protection. (Some of the other crime reporters kept guns at hand. I never owned one.)

You might take issue with this, but I know that in my first night of hunting for a place where crack addicts could get healed, God directed me to The Body of Christ Assembly. I had never before had a close black friend or attended a black church. Yet today I am a black Pentecostal Christian in every way but one. I can't ignore the extraordinary care that God took in steering me to one tiny church in South Dallas.

When I interviewed Pastor Fredrick L. Eddington Sr. for my story, I was immediately won over by his sincerity and humility. A few days after I located the church, we met for an interview at the pastor's modest home in Fort Worth. I perched myself at one end of a couch, he at the other, feet planted in thick green shag carpet. He introduced me to his wife, Diane, who stalked through the living room several times during our conversation. My first impression was that she didn't approve of me. I wouldn't find out until many months later that Diane is legally blind and that she processes the world differently from most, through spiritual receptors. What she lacks in natural vision she possesses many times over in supernatural insight.

I wouldn't have blamed her if she had been suspicious of me. At age twenty-seven, I was a mess. Far from knowing who I was or how exactly God fit in my life, my mind was swirling with ambitions and schemes and a good deal of sexual confusion. I didn't yet know that God sees through the mess to what is inside us, that he seeks to touch the deepest impulses of the heart. The truth that I saw most clearly at that moment was that I was a selfish brat, and a bit of a flake besides.

In my interview with Pastor Eddington I gathered the material I needed. It was a firsthand account of faith, prayer, and God's work made visible in the supernatural deliverance from crack addiction experienced by several desperate people. I talked to members of his church, The Body of Christ Assembly, and they told me their stories: a one-time drunk who had completely lost her desire for alcohol, a couple of former crack addicts now living clean, productive lives. In a variety of ways, I was told that God is present in the services at this church. People get healed. Drunkards and crackheads walk through the church doors high and leave free of their addictions. I called another pastor to get the requisite "other side of the story," which amounted to a mild dismissal of healing prayer. The article ran on the front page, leading off with a photograph of Pastor Eddington, who at the time had a peculiar handlebar mustache with curlicues at the ends.

I never told anyone at the *Dallas Times Herald* how I found the church, and I'm glad no one asked. Try telling your editor you got a news tip from God.

Readers were enthusiastic about the story and sent donations and kind notes to the church, encouraging Pastor Eddington to carry on. The story provided some hope in the midst of an unprecedented wave of inner-city violence. Yet in my rush to compile what I needed for an A-1 Sunday story, I missed the heart of Pastor Eddington's message. Yes, he had seen miracles, but that really wasn't the point, he said. God was doing something bigger than healing crack addicts. He was showing himself strong for suffering people living in one of the hardest places in the country.

As I scribbled down Pastor Eddington's words, I didn't see the bigness of what he was talking about: "The Lord told me he was going to send me on a mission of love. Wherever there is a lot of depravity, sickness, and disease, there is a great harvest. I noticed there were a lot of churches in South Dallas, but there was no harvest."

He was talking about the days back in the mideighties, when he had a dream to start a church on a godless street. He was employing a bit of Biblespeak to tell me that a completely different approach was in order. The churches in South Dallas weren't taking God at his word, but Pastor Eddington saw no other way to live. If God is God, then why shouldn't we assume he will act like God, demonstrating his power when we ask for help?

Pastor Eddington suggested that love was the answer to the struggles of down-and-out South Dallas. In the ministry he had dreamed of starting, he would love people with actions and not just words. He would reach out to children and hug them; he would stand up for single moms; he would visit people in their homes and in jail; he would pray with hurting people. He'd get behind the men who had a desire to live right and support their families; he'd stand like a brother with any man or woman who wanted to be freed from addictions. And he'd do these things whether it brought in bigger donations and more members, or not.

This man's straightforward talk carried such conviction that I couldn't help wanting to be a part of what he was doing in South Dallas. Despite my own conflicts and character flaws, I was straining to hear God's voice in everything I did. I'd been taught as a child that you hear God speak through the Bible and through the counsel of Christian friends—and also through supernatural means. In Pastor Eddington's home, as he shared his dream with me, I could sense God's presence in the room.

Not long before this, my husband-to-be had suggested I find a church in Dallas that we could attend after we got married. Within a few days of my visit with Pastor Eddington, I called Larry and told him, "I've found it. I've found a church for us to join."

On my first visit for a Sunday service at The Body of Christ Assembly, I was struck by a number of things. The first and most obvious was that I was the only white person there. Before I did my *Dallas Times Herald* story, I harbored the notion that in a city as ethnically diverse as Dallas, I would find ethnically diverse church congregations. Boy, was I dumb. Churches were white, black, Latino, or Asian.

Pastor Eddington's congregation was black, but even though I was the only white person present, I found that the members welcomed me warmly, as if I'd been attending for years. The second thing that stood out was that going to church was not just a religious custom for members of The Body of Christ Assembly. These Christians came to church with an expectation that God was there and that he would meet them at any moment.

The sermon—"the message"—was a rhythmic, textured, nonlinear discourse that seemed to go on for a long, long time. It would build to what black Pentecostals call "humming," when the climax of the message is sung as well as preached. Oh, and the pews were hard. I have a hard enough time sitting still even in the best, most comfortable circumstances. Here I got restless. On my first visit the service had gone well past two hours when I decided to leave. It seemed to me that the pastor was just then getting limbered up. Back where I grew up, we started giving the preacher dirty looks if he went past his allotted hour and fifteen minutes—and not for the sermon, for the entire service.

I came back to The Body of Christ Assembly at the end of the week for the Saturday prayer meeting, and there I met Doris Spencer, a friendly woman who told me about being delivered from alcoholism. "Honey, God is real," she said, as we sat on the church stoop, stomping on fire ants. "You might can't see him, but he is real."

Larry and I got married three months later, and at the first church

© Lyons family collection

Julie and Larry Lyons on their wedding day in 1990

service we attended as a couple, Larry started crying uncontrollably. He said he felt like he'd come home. He could physically sense the presence of God's Spirit—the Holy Spirit—and it brought tears. My husband had a radical streak in his faith, and he took to the free-flowing atmosphere of a Holy Ghost church, where there was no program of service, and it was understood that the presence of God could elicit all kinds of responses, from shouting and jumping to weeping and lying facedown on the floor.

Larry and I were casual members at first. The truth was, I hadn't attended church regularly since I was a kid, except for a six-month stint in Belfast. It would take me a good while to commit myself to the black Pentecostal regimen, which consisted of long services, long prayer meetings, long everything, usually done at deafening volume. Sometimes I felt swallowed in noise; I wasn't sure even God could cut through the racket to be heard. But my internal conflicts and mental dissonance had more to do with me than with the customs of a black church.

My work as a crime reporter was taking a toll. No one event did it; it was the accumulation of ugliness, of constantly being exposed to the very worst humanity has to offer.

The tipping point was a particularly grisly crime that involved the shooting of five teenagers. In a squalid South Dallas apartment that served as a crackhouse, five black teenagers were herded into a bathtub and machine-gunned down. One, a fifteen-year-old boy named Juniores Ray Mahan, died there, his blood swirling in the water with that of his friends. I reported on part of the story, and in an awful turn of events I ended up informing the teenager's mother that he was dead. I got to her home before she had been notified by the medical examiner's office. I remember this mother standing on the stairway outside her apartment, smelling of drink, clutching a framed eight-by-ten school photo of her freckled son, her face seized in a scream. Only no noise came out.

I apologized profusely, and I started to weep as I walked back down the stairs to the street.

Three of the other four kids in the bathtub were critically injured but survived; one girl had ten bullet wounds. Another girl climbed out of the tub and was walking around unscathed. She had escaped the gunfire by lying underneath the pile, playing dead.

The incident that came to be known on the street as the Bathtub Massacre wasn't even the most horrifying crime I wrote about. In South Dallas, most families could name at least one casualty of the crack-cocaine epidemic, usually more. In everyday conversation you would hear people mention a family member or close friend who was strung out on drugs, how things had gotten so bad that he'd sell his mama for crack. You'd see cracked-out survivors wandering the streets on stilt-thin legs, filling in the time between hits, and you'd hear about the cream of young manhood locked up in prison on decades-long sentences, destined to spend their productive years in a cage. A whole generation in South Dallas just basically disappeared.

I covered the story of a twelve-year-old girl who was murdered in a filthy South Dallas crackhouse, supposedly for refusing to have sex with a drug dealer. My usual routine when I covered a crime was to talk to the cops and get whatever information I could, then to locate the homes of family members, knock on the door, ask questions, and try to flesh out the victim's life. (Surprisingly, people were usually willing to talk right after a loved one got killed.) This time, I strolled up to a decaying home near Jamaica Street, and I found the girl's portly grandma holding forth from a tattered stuffed chair on the screened-in porch.

"Jesus is coming again soon," she drawled, hands folded across a faded housedress, acting for all the world as though she were accustomed to tragedies such as this. "We are surely living in the Last Days." As I listened to Grandma perorate on Sodom and Gomorrah and the End Times, I noticed a stream of human beings moving listlessly in and out the front door. I heard fragments of conversation, and I was shocked—every single person, who Grandma said were family members, appeared to be either mentally ill, retarded, or strung out on drugs. Grandma seemed to be playing with a full deck, but no one else was.

Church families were in no way spared from the drug epidemic and its consequences. Herthen Eddington Jr., Pastor Eddington's oldest brother, was found shot to death in his Cadillac in 1988. The crime was never solved. Rumor has it that he'd tangled with Cuban drug lords who were then engaged in a deadly battle for supremacy with the Jamaican gangs.

The killings got worse in 1991, and the number of people sucked into the crack trade seemed to be increasing. Even I, a mousy white girl from the Midwest, would frequently get flagged down by crack sellers. One obvious addict signaled that she was willing to perform a certain sex act for me; it made me want to puke.

In South Dallas in 1990 and 1991, it seemed that the entire area was in the grip of evil. Drug dealers, addicts, gangs, prostitutes, predators, and honest citizens alike. It was easy to question whether God had given up on this part of the world.

And the despair became personal. I had seen too many corpses; interviewed too many grieving friends, relatives, and parents; heard too many stories about unrestrained evil. I envisioned myself blowing my brains out innumerable times. I was a Christian who was seeking God like never before, but still I felt like a wicked spirit had latched on to me.

I can't fully explain what was happening. I do know that crack cocaine had such an insidious effect on the entire community that it seemed like it tapped into an evil power far beyond its physical properties. The substance, of course, was extremely addictive; I met folks who fell hard on their first hit.

I knew guys who robbed their mamas and grandmas for crack money, pawning every stick of furniture they could push out the front door. In the traps, addicts would find themselves subjected to abuse and humiliation—confronted by fourteen-year-old thugs waving 9mms, ordering grown men and women around. Women would sell their bodies for a hit or watch a best friend drop down to do it right in front of them. Addicts would get shot, stabbed, robbed, and beaten within a hairbreadth of their lives and then go back for more.

That, in fact, is what would happen to the survivors of the infamous Bathtub Massacre. I hunted them down years later for a major story. This is what I found:

- Kenneth Covington, who suffered brain damage and had an eye shot out in the 1990 attack, returned to selling crack. He was found dead, facedown in a wooded area, shot through the back of the head. His pants pockets were inside out, indicating he'd been robbed.
- LaTonya Williams, who had ten scars from bullet wounds, was HIV positive and awaiting release from her second stint in prison. After the shooting, she'd gone back to crack and supported her habit through prostitution.
- Daryl Oudems had been in and out of jail for drug dealing but had recently begun to turn his life around, thanks to the ministry of the most famous black Pentecostal preacher in the world, Bishop T. D. Jakes.

And I found the girl who'd survived by playing dead getting wasted outside her South Dallas apartment one searing afternoon. Her brain was completely fried. She couldn't put together a coherent sentence.

As Loony as Could Be

When Fredrick Lynn Eddington, known as Lynnie to his six siblings, or more cruelly and frequently, "Doofus," went to bed at night, he prayed what "every black kid in America learns how to pray":

Now I lay me down to sleep,
I pray thee, Lord, my soul to keep;
If I should die before I wake,
I pray thee, Lord, my soul to take.

Young Fredrick mouthed the words, but he found himself hoping for something altogether different. He wished he would never wake up. Or, failing that, he hoped that his father would not come home drunk. Or maybe that he wouldn't come home at all.

But his dad always came home, usually drunk and out of control.

Herthen Eddington Sr.'s disappointments and hatreds overwhelmed the Eddington household, drowning his wife's tender-heartedness. Brought up in a competitive clan of black and Native American ancestry in rural East Texas, Eddington Sr. knew his accomplishments didn't measure up to his brothers' and sisters'. Beyond that, his color—dark— landed him near the bottom of the hierarchy in the eyes of his color-obsessed kin. Some of them had college educations and successful businesses. Herthen, while possessed of a sharp mind, made a living as a house painter. He put sufficient food on the table for his five sons and two daughters, but being hardworking was his only readily discernible virtue.

Fredrick says that no meaningful communication existed between father and children. As far as he saw it, he and his siblings and their mother, Alice, were merely the outlet for his father's frustrations. Since

Eddington Sr. was so disgusted with what he'd achieved in his own life, he held his children to an unattainable standard. He might have been sloppy drunk and mumbling much of the time he was with his family, but he made sure they spoke proper English instead of South Dallas slang.

And in this environment, Fredrick, the fourth child, seemed doomed. He had a severe speech impediment. He couldn't help but stammer and mix up his syllables, horribly mangling longer words. From his earliest days, he sensed that he was an embarrassment to his family, the least of the Eddington children. His older sister and two older brothers were verbally nimble, always ready to argue a point. They "spoke proper." While the older siblings agreed on few things, they saw eye to eye on one point: Fredrick was stupid.

They ridiculed him for being ignorant, for talking like a poor black boy, for running like a spaz. He, in turn, derided himself for being slow, for stammering, and for struggling to master the simplest social graces.

Fredrick was headed for a damaging collision with his exacting father. While Fredrick adored his mother, she couldn't shield any of her children from her husband's bullying ways. And the boys got the worst of it. If Fredrick's father checked his spelling homework and found a mistake—which was inevitable, since Fredrick was a terrible speller—the young boy would get a "hard backhand across the eyeballs."

The most severe abuse followed Eddington Sr.'s drinking binges. He'd take his painting money, often earned by his sons while he dozed or drank, and park himself at a honky-tonk on Second Avenue. He would slam down beer after beer until his enormous eyes glassed over. Then he'd stumble home.

The boys knew exactly what to expect when Daddy arrived. They would listen for the creak of the screen door, knowing an evil giant was about to pounce. The boys would pretend to be asleep, or they would twist themselves in the sheets, curl into a fetal position, burrow into the pillow—anything to put up a buffer against what was to come.

The punishment would sometimes begin with a macabre serenade. Eddington Sr. would drag the boys out of bed and force them to listen while he banged out blues on an old guitar, blew his harmonica, and told stories. If the boys didn't show enough enthusiasm and laugh along with their drunken father, Daddy would extract it from them with beatings. His tools of choice were an extension cord, a switch, and a belt. "This hurts me more than it hurts you," Eddington Sr. would say while shedding big tears. In his drunken state, maybe he believed it.

To this day, Fredrick hates the blues.

Eddington Sr.'s most spectacular punishments displayed a creepy ingenuity. On a few occasions he tied ten-year-old Fredrick to the clothesline in the backyard, propping him up against the pole and winding rope around his arms, legs, and torso. Fredrick would stand there all night while the shadowy figures of drunks could be seen wandering home through the back alley, and he tried desperately to push away thoughts about the "Rabbit Man" that was reputed to roam South Dallas, cutting off children's hind parts.

Even when sober, Daddy was rarely a parent that a child could love. He would mete out harsh punishment for real and imagined infractions, such as not doing chores to his exact specifications or for venturing outside the yard. One time he accused the boys of stealing a handful of silver dollars from his dresser. He took two of his sons, hogtied them, and threw a rope over a rafter on the back porch. Then he pulled on the rope to suspend the boys in the air. While they dangled by their bound hands and ankles, Eddington Sr. beat them.

Fredrick can still recall his brothers' screams.

It's not surprising that Fredrick Eddington entered adulthood broken and mentally unstable, destined for drug addiction and multiple nervous breakdowns. He'd been ground to dust between his father's anger and his older siblings' contempt.

Fredrick grew up convinced that he possessed almost no positive qualities besides being generally a good kid. Even that trait was met with ridicule. In the pecking order of the Eddington family, he barely registered as a person. Yet the boy his family members hardly deemed worth knowing, the awkward, left-handed little brother who covered over his insecurities by acting like a goofball, hid within himself a vivid creative life. He dreamed of being a millionaire and a great architect. And though he could barely put a spoken sentence together, he could sing in a silky baritone voice, anything from classic hymns to P-Funk. Fredrick would release the deep emotions and dreams that he held inside every time he sang.

Still, the ability to speak properly was of paramount importance in his family, so Fredrick was sent to California when he was thirteen to live with his grandmother, Lucretia Ross. He assumed that in California people must be in the habit of speaking proper English. Fredrick could have taken the move as a form of rejection, but instead he was thrilled because now he could get out from under his father's tyranny. Well before his parents made the final decision to ship him off, he would dream about Pasadena, where his grandmother lived alone in a solid, lower-middle-class neighborhood. He imagined what the buildings and foliage looked like in the land of flowers and sunshine. In his dreams he saw a structure that resembled the Mediterranean architecture of Pasadena's City Hall, with its ornate circular tower.

California turned out to be everything he hoped it would be. Nanny Ross welcomed Fredrick into her modest home, one of the two she'd purchased with her earnings as a domestic. Small and wiry, fiercely protective of her grandson, Nanny dispensed love in her own way, but it was still love, a thing in scarce supply in the Eddington household. "Everybody loved Nanny," Fredrick says, but the little woman who would "starve herself so you could eat" also had a mean streak. When Nanny got mad, she'd grab any object within reach and start swinging. On a number of occasions, Fredrick had to run away from her to keep from getting hurt.

As Fredrick grew bigger, he came up with a way to restrain his tiny grandmother. He'd wrap his long arms around her and hug her tight, maybe kiss her on the cheek. Sometimes Nanny would start giggling.

But sometimes she wouldn't, and that's when Fredrick knew he had to tear off running before an iron skillet slammed into the back of his head.

Along with Nanny's temper came a stern probity that left an indelible impression on Fredrick. He recalls when, at age fifteen, he stole a pair of blue bell-bottom pants from a Pasadena department store and had the nerve to wear them home. Nanny, who kept track of every penny Fredrick earned, immediately began questioning him.

"Where did you get the money?" she asked.

"I cut someone's yard," Fredrick said, trying to sound nonchalant. But Nanny wasn't swayed.

"Whose yard?" she asked.

"The lady around the corner."

"All right," Nanny said, "let's go around the corner."

While they walked, Fredrick glanced around him, looking for a lawn that was freshly cut in front of a house where it seemed that no one was home. He picked out the perfect house and led his grandmother to the front door. Fredrick's heart thumped while they knocked.

The door swung open, and a lady stood there. Nanny dispensed with the niceties. "Did this boy cut your lawn?" she asked.

Fredrick, who towered over Nanny, stood behind her and desperately tried to motion to the lady at the door. But she refused to play along.

Not a word was spoken on the way home. Fredrick moved stiffly, as though he were approaching the pen of a wild beast, and he could feel Nanny's fire rising, passing from anger to fury to the white-hot beyond. Nanny, he says, was like a bomb—a little grenade that did a huge amount of damage. And she was fixing to detonate.

When the door of her home closed behind them, her rage had reached the boiling point—"It was *on* like a pot of neck bones," Fredrick recalls. Nanny took the pants and destroyed them. Then this one-hundred-pound woman tore up Fredrick's rear end with an extension cord or a clothes hanger, one or the other, he can't remember which.

"She got me real good," he says.

Away from his family's exacting standards, Fredrick's speech impediment improved. He performed decently at school and graduated with his high-school class. But even as his verbal agility increased and he became more confident in conversations, his grandma called him stupid. Not a day passed when he wasn't called stupid, stupid, stupid.

Finally Fredrick left Nanny's home because, he figured, he was too big to keep getting whupped. He entered the world poorly equipped for adulthood. On the positive side, he could speak more or less normally, sing exceptionally well, work hard, and get along with most people. He had tremendous deficits, however, in confidence and common sense.

He had also begun using drugs. First it was weed, then the hard drug in vogue at the time, angel dust, or PCP. Angel dust, the subject of sensational news stories decrying the drug's ability to make folks go bat-crazy, made Fredrick believe he had supernatural powers. Working at one of his first full-time jobs, picking up trash for the Pasadena sanitation department, he'd frequently upend the single-seat scooter used to shuttle trash from homes to the garbage truck because he was going too fast. He lost that job.

Drugs would come to define his life and the people he hung out with. He remembers spending the night at Nanny's house, where he washed her dishes as he watched leprechauns dart and dance around the sink, chirping and talking among themselves. Fredrick, riding an angel-dust high, scolded the leprechauns. "Shhhh. You're gonna wake up Nanny!"

Even Fredrick's spiritual awakening would be intertwined with drug-induced highs, lows, and hallucinations. As a child he didn't have much interest in spiritual matters. His family attended Mount Olive Lutheran Church, which was led by a white pastor who made an impression on South Dallas by knocking on doors and inviting people to church, something previously unheard of in black Dallas. The pastor later became prominent among Dallas civil-rights activists.

Eddington Sr., however, didn't choose Mount Olive for any of those reasons. He judged the Baptist faith, to which most of black Dallas belonged, undignified and overly emotional. Holy-roller churches, which were even *less* dignified than Baptists, were undoubtedly beneath him and his upward aspirations.

At Mount Olive, Fredrick and his siblings enjoyed playing games in the church's rec room and watching the white parishioners who casually indulged in alcohol after the services. This was a curiosity in black Dallas, where only two views on the substance existed: you were either a drunk or abstained entirely. Fredrick dutifully attended catechism and absorbed a catalog of Bible stories and hymns, but Lutheran spirituality had no impact on his soul. Folks attended church, listened to a sermon, then went about living their lives the same way they always had.

For Eddington Sr., that meant getting drunk and beating his wife and kids. The life of Mount Olive Lutheran Church and the life of his family—especially his abusive father—had little in common with the Jesus whom Fredrick learned about in Sunday school. He and his siblings drew their own conclusion: there was no connection between Christian piety and solutions to the problems they faced.

At age twenty-three, Fredrick was desperate for a fresh start. He had squandered his abilities and his education. His few possessions were piled in the bedroom of a small Pasadena apartment that he shared with a heroin dealer and the man's wife and two children. Junkies would pass out on the living-room floor, and in the morning Fredrick would step around the previous night's customers on his way out. At night he slept with one eye open as druggies traipsed through his room to shoot up in the bathroom.

Fredrick was lost, immersed in drugs and disappointments. His first serious girlfriend had become pregnant with twins, but she lost the babies after an auto accident. They were boys, weighing less than a pound each. Though they were stillborn at the hospital, neither parent was allowed to see their bodies. The experience pushed Fredrick into a tailspin—he wondered if, in reality, the twins had survived and the doctor was concealing their live births for his own nefarious purposes. The uncertainties tortured Fredrick, whose mental state was already fragile.

Today, Fredrick sees a connection between the deaths of the twins and a series of nervous breakdowns he suffered. Each year in February he'd hit bottom. He heard voices, "just a whole lot of noise going on in my head." He'd continually rehearse everything he'd messed up in life: the poor decisions, the dope, the busted relationships, the people who might have loved him and nurtured him if only he'd done better. Psychiatrists prescribed Thorazine and Prolixin, two psychotropic drugs used in treating the severely distorted thoughts and perceptions that accompany schizophrenia.

The symptoms were all there. Fredrick would see messages written on paper that no one else could decipher concerning the intricate science of gamma rays, a form of electromagnetic radiation produced by the sun. Fredrick would walk around by himself, having lengthy conversations with the wind and rain, the rocks and trees. As a child in Dallas, Fredrick had made a game of acting goofy and crazy. Now he really was.

"I don't deny that I was a mental case," Fredrick says today. "Everybody thought I was just as loony as could be—that I was gone. Nobody had any inkling of hope that I would be sane again."

Once more Fredrick's girlfriend got pregnant, and he married her a month after the birth of their son, Fredrick Jr. The couple stayed together only three months, while both of them battled drug addictions. But Fredrick knew he had to do better for his son, even if his own life was an irretrievable mess. When the boy was a few months old, Fredrick sent him to Dallas to live with his mother, Alice, who by then had divorced Eddington Sr. Fredrick hoped to wrap up his affairs in California, get a handle on his addictions and mental illness, and move back to Dallas to start over.

Fredrick had quit taking Thorazine and Prolixin, and the voices in his head were fading. But a series of strange spiritual experiences pushed him to despondency. He wasn't aware of the way his strange behaviors were perceived by other people. He would, in half-jest, assert that he was really an alien from the planet Tabalon. It sounded like a joke, but Fredrick knew at some level that he was losing his grip.

A few years earlier he had tossed a prayer up to heaven, hoping something would stick. "God, if you're real," Fredrick prayed on his twenty-first birthday, "I need some sign."

Nothing in particular happened that day. But soon afterward he began dreaming peculiar dreams. He wept a lot. He started noticing that some people, motivated simply by evil, despised him, and the realization was more than he could bear. If you were disliked because of mistakes you made, at least you could try to make things right. But if hatred grew out of pure evil, unrelated to what you had done or who you were, what hope was there to change things?

"The scales began to fall off my eyes," Fredrick says, and what he saw prodded him deeper into despair. He wanted to reclaim the days when he had at least been a good kid. But as a man, he knew he wasn't good; he was, in fact, nothing.

Having realized the fact of evil, Fredrick undertook a dream-state conquest to capture the devil. He would chase him from here to there, into houses and churches and hedges. One time he caught him, but he didn't have a clue what to do with him.

So he ate him.

At the airport in California, just before boarding a flight to Dallas, Fredrick needed a pack of cigarettes. For a moment he was clearheaded and optimistic. Moving back to Texas, where he would join his son, now two years old, was a step toward real change.

Fredrick walked up to a vending machine to get his cigarettes. *So expensive,* he thought. A strong sensation came over him to give up smoking. So he resolved to quit—as he'd done many times before.

Stuck in the smoking section of the plane, enveloped in other people's fumes, Fredrick realized for the first time how irritating cigarette smoke could be. But he also noticed something going on inside him: stirrings of conscience, a desire to preserve his body instead of destroy it. This time, his recognition of right and wrong didn't end with obsessive replays of his past failures. He didn't know it yet, but he had won this initial skirmish—he would never smoke another cigarette.

In Dallas, Fredrick moved in with his mother, took care of his son, and tried to pull his life together. He got a job at a psychiatric hospital, of all places. His mother, the only clear vision of good he'd ever seen, proved to be a strong support. After her divorce she had joined a tiny Holiness church led by an illiterate pastor named Elder M., and here they didn't just talk about the idea of God. At this church, God was present and hard at work. Alice had learned that faith was real and active, something that brought about lasting change. She continually told Fredrick that "something phenomenal is going to happen to you."

Fredrick wasn't ready to go quite that far. His immediate goal was much less lofty: he just wanted to keep a job and his sanity for more than a few days at a time.

He still smoked pot, even though he'd given up cigarettes, and one February day he got in his car to go and buy weed in South Dallas. Nothing about that day suggested that a drug-buying excursion would end up turning his life around. Fredrick was driving down Metropolitan Avenue, looking for the weed man, when an odd feeling overtook him. He looked at the trees, the cars, and the decaying wood-frame structures of the South Dallas ghetto. Everything seemed small and unreal, as though they were model-railroad props. He glanced up at the sun. He felt tall—immeasurably tall, shooting-up-into-the-sky tall—and believed he was close to the sun itself. He imagined he could get out of the car and reach up and touch it.

Around him was the broken-down inner city, the parched and dirty streets. Fredrick wheeled the car around and headed home. On the way he stopped at a corner store, a ghetto grocery with penny candy, bags of chips, and a few sorry meat selections. As soon as he stepped inside, he was overwhelmed by the repulsive smell of rotting meat.

"You ought to be ashamed," he told the clerk. Fredrick was a mild-mannered guy, but he found out later that he'd "told them off real good."

Everything was stinking. Fredrick saw his own faults, but whatever was happening to him magnified all the other things that weren't right. "Filth became filthy," was how he'd later describe it.

He got in the car again, where he started sobbing. He was sickened by the stench of his own life.

When he stepped into the house, his mother was alarmed. Fredrick was crying uncontrollably. *Surrender, surrender*—those were the words he heard in his heart. *Give up. Let go.*

Surrender to what? To whom?

Soon he found that interspersed with the sobs were strange sounds, gibbering utterances that matched no language he was aware of. It sounded like something his mother had become acquainted with in church, a holy-roller phenomenon known as speaking in tongues.

Alice called her youngest son, Anthony, who drove to the house. He didn't know what was happening to Fredrick, but he felt it was spiritual in origin. Anthony held his brother in his arms and rocked him and prayed. Fredrick stayed this way all night, alternating between sobs and tongues-speaking. When Anthony woke up the next morning, Fredrick was still in his arms.

That evening Alice summoned her pastor, Elder M., who came to the house and listened to an explanation of what had happened. The pastor reached a conclusion: Fredrick was demon-possessed. Fredrick wanted to cry out in protest.

Far from being possessed, he knew he had been "de-possessed." All the years of rejection, the pent-up hurt and pain, the feelings of worthlessness, were cut loose when he made the decision to let go.

To others, this episode could easily have looked like another of Fredrick's February breakdowns. But he knew he wasn't even remotely the same person he had been. From that day on, he would be a different man.

One of the Sanest People on the Planet

Fredrick Eddington felt clean and pure and purposeful for the first time in his life. He had found the Lord, something he had plenty of time to think about while he was on his way to the psychiatric ward at Parkland Memorial Hospital. The morning after his come-to-Jesus experience, Fredrick's mother sent him to Dallas's grim storage bin for nut cases.

Fredrick felt such clarity of mind that he refused to let his destination worry him. He spent a day or two at Parkland, then got shunted off to an inpatient facility called the Dallas Diagnostic Center. Here he interpreted inkblots, drew funny pictures, and talked to a battery of mental-health professionals. He'd spent some time in mental hospitals in California, but this was different. This time they didn't tell him he was crazy; they did something far more surprising. They listened.

Fredrick told his psychiatrist that his deepest desire was to be righteous, to live a godly life—the same impulse he'd felt for years. The difference now was that feeling this way no longer made him regard himself as hopelessly filthy. In his heart, Fredrick believed he had no option but to live a holy life. When he mentioned that to a psychiatrist in Dallas, the doctor told Fredrick: "There's nothing wrong with you. People just don't understand you. You have a desire to be perfect. The problem is, you live in an imperfect world." The psychiatrist told Alice the same thing. "Your son isn't mentally ill."

It wasn't until Fredrick got home and started delving into the Bible that he found a new way to interpret the chaos of his life. He read about Saint Paul, who earlier in his life stayed busy persecuting Christians with all the zeal he could muster. And then he met Jesus Christ in a searing flash of light. Paul, who at the time was known as Saul, fell to the ground and heard a voice from heaven: "Saul, Saul, why do you persecute me?"

"Who are you, Lord?" Saul asked.

"I am Jesus, whom you are persecuting," the voice replied.

For three days Paul lost his sight and was led by the hand to the city of Damascus. When he got there, God sent a man named Ananias to visit the famous persecutor of Christians. Ananias understandably was reluctant to confront Paul, but he sought him out and laid hands on him. Immediately Paul was filled with the Holy Spirit. "Something like scales fell from Saul's eyes," the book of Acts reports, "and he could see again. He got up and was baptized, and after taking some food, he regained his strength."

Fredrick absorbed those words and for the first time understood something that made his own life become clear. Paul had been blinded; then God directed him to Straight Street. After the supernatural encounter with Jesus and time in Damascus, Paul saw the world differently. Just like with Paul, Fredrick's conversion didn't happen in church; it happened in the street while he was on his way to do evil. But, he adds, "at the same time, my heart wanted something better. I was trying to get away from the pain and the reality of what I was living in."

God brought Fredrick into a new reality that finally made sense. From reading about Paul's experience, he extracted a revelation about himself: he'd been saved. His actions after the last nervous breakdown were, to him, abundant proof.

He stopped doing drugs.

He quit chasing women.

He tried to repair his broken marriage.

He worked up to three jobs at a time and took full responsibility for raising his son.

Were these the works of a crazy man? Far from being mentally ill, Fredrick says, he had become "one of the sanest people on the planet."

Fredrick started attending Elder M.'s church with his mother and younger sister, and when the pastor saw how much Fredrick had changed, he was forced to retract his earlier pronouncement. Elder M. had believed previously that a person could get filled with the Holy Ghost only if a Christian laid hands on him. But Fredrick was an exception to this rule. No one had prayed for him, and yet he was a deeply changed man.

It would have been impossible for Elder M.'s church to be any more different from the Lutheran parish Fredrick attended as a child. Elder M., a large, dark, exceptionally unattractive man, couldn't read, but he compensated for his deficiency with a prodigious memory. His sermons were filled with word-for-word recitations of Scripture. His messages revolved around a scant few themes: salvation, the baptism of the Holy Ghost with the evidence of speaking in tongues, and healing. The latter, in fact, is what persuaded Alice Eddington to become a holy roller. At Elder M.'s church, she was healed of stomach ulcers.

It wasn't unusual on a Sunday morning, Fredrick says, to find half the congregation fallen out on the floor under the power of the Holy Ghost. Often, there was outward evidence that parishioners had been purged of a particular sin, delivered from evil spirits, or healed from emotional traumas. In this church, the people expected God to intervene at any moment and touch them in their earthbound state.

During his time with Elder M., Fredrick immersed himself in studying the Bible. Though he'd been brought up in the erudition of Lutheranism, for the first time the Bible made sense. Elder M.'s preaching, accompanied by a demonstration of God's power, sank into his heart. Fredrick soaked up the teaching with the spiritual thirst of a new convert.

With no title, pay, or pulpit, Fredrick Eddington went out to preach the gospel. "When the Bible says to go out into the highways and hedges and compel them to come in, that's what I did," he says. "I was compelled by the Holy Spirit to go out and preach. I couldn't even imagine not doing it—it wasn't something I felt pressured to do. It felt natural."

Fredrick would position himself under a tree in South Dallas—across from Nanny's old frame house—and preach to people in the street. Sometimes he would go downtown and preach in front of a high-rise bank building. He was the sweaty guy in a tie and polyester sports coat, the guy you've seen preaching on street corners in every American city.

Fredrick held forth about hell and sin with the aid of a cheap

© Robert Conner, DFW Digital Photography

Fredrick Eddington went from street
preacher to pastoring a church

microphone and a small amplifier. He looked like all the other street preachers, but somehow he was different. He wasn't an angry dude who hollered at folks like a devil set loose in the streets. Fredrick would look people right in the eye, and he preached from his heart. Sometimes he would bring along a guitar and sing songs to Jesus. He preached on the streets and in parks for years, for nothing. Only a Texas rainstorm could stop him from preaching.

One time a well-dressed executive offered to buy him clothes, but Fredrick politely refused. He didn't want to risk clouding his motives by accepting money or gifts from anyone.

Over the years he'd cross paths with other street preachers, sketchy guys who, more often than not, would retreat after a hellfire-and-brimstone tirade to slurp down a bottle of fortified wine. There was one old white guy who wore diapers outside his clothing. While his mind wasn't sound, his preaching was, according to Fredrick. But most of the other street preachers were crazy or hateful or dissolute, which made Fredrick ask God why he put up with these freaks.

God's answer, he says, stunned him. God had tried to send the "proper" preachers to the street, but they wouldn't go.

Back at Elder M.'s church, Fredrick suspected all was not right. He started noticing things, like the heavy-handed tactics used to collect money from the congregants and the level of attention that was paid to relatively inconsequential matters. Elder M. adhered to a strict interpretation of the Holiness church tradition, which, over the years, was largely reduced to a code for proper dress. Women were prohibited from wearing pants, makeup, nail polish, and any jewelry besides a wedding band. In addition, they were urged to wear their hair long as a "head covering," indicating their subordinate position to men.

Ironically, none of the admonitions about modest attire seemed to apply to the few men in the church. They were free to bling with multiple pinkie rings and strut around in purple suits. It was obvious that women in Elder M.'s church were the focus of most of the pastor's attention. Fredrick didn't understand why so much teaching and ministering was directed toward the women. Were the men of this congregation so clean living that they had no need for biblical instruction? And then there were the women themselves, some of whom were stuck in awful marriages and seemed desperate for attention. In prayer lines, Elder M. would lay hands on the women and pray with great fervor, but men would be dismissed with a few gruff words. Despite all the impassioned prayers, it seemed obvious to Fredrick that church members continued to struggle with lust, envy, and bitterness.

He continued to preach the gospel on the streets, and men who stopped to listen were being converted. But when Fredrick took them to visit Elder M.'s church, they seemed to drown in the pastor's narrow, legalistic approach to religion. Apart from the intense focus on women parishioners, Elder M. had a distracting habit that well could scare off any visitor. He would sit in a chair behind the pulpit during worship services with his legs spread wide as he absent-mindedly fondled his genitals. Later, Fredrick would find out that Elder M. had engaged in numerous adulterous relationships with women in the congregation.

The church was not healthy, and Fredrick tried to understand how a man of God could deliberately victimize the people in his congregation. Much later, after Fredrick discovered that he had the spiritual gift of discerning evil spirits, he said of Elder M.: "There was something radiating out of him—you could just feel his spirit. It felt creepy. Now I associate that with a sex demon whenever I come across it."

Fredrick preached his first sermon from a pulpit in Elder M.'s church, but the pastor mocked him when he inquired about becoming a licensed minister. Fredrick couldn't deny that he'd witnessed miracles in this place, but there was an extraordinary disconnect among the spiritual fireworks and the immoral lifestyles of some of the members. For a young man who was determined to live a godly life, this was no place to be.

Years later, in the 1990s, Elder M.'s members confronted him about his immorality. The aging pastor responded by locking his own congregation out of the church.

Fredrick went on to join a Church of God in Christ congregation led by a renowned preacher who granted him his minister's license. But here he witnessed a more sophisticated version of what he had observed in Elder M. The pastor would flirt with women while he was speaking from the pulpit, crowing about how fine they looked, while his wife sat silently in a front pew. The pastor, who had a reputation as a playboy, appeared to be openly recruiting new girlfriends on Sunday morning.

During those years Fredrick attended a Church of God in Christ national meeting that drew church leaders and "missionaries," a title reserved for women evangelists, from all over the area. Fredrick ran into a middle-aged missionary who pulled him aside. The woman, reputed to be the mistress of a prominent bishop, listened to the young minister carry on about the privilege of living a godly life and preaching the gospel. Then she stopped him. "You don't belong here," she said. "Don't you get it?" She explained that these meetings were opportunities for leaders to hook up with their illicit lovers. Not everyone did it, of course, but this particular gathering was known for rampant immorality among the clergy. Fredrick was blown away.

For seven years Fredrick had lived a chaste life while waiting to see if his estranged wife would get saved. But during their separation, she dated other men and bore a child with one of them. Fredrick finally got a divorce. He was doing a good job of raising his son, he thought, and he wasn't in a rush to find a wife. But then he noticed a woman he'd never met before, and all he can say now is that she sure looked fine.

After the dark young woman with the hourglass figure took a seat at a wedding rehearsal dinner, Fredrick had to figure out how to get over there. He extricated himself from another conversation and hurried to her table. Diane Hines's best friend, Frederica, was the bride-to-be, and it just so happened that this tall, handsome preacher was the groom's best man.

When Diane first saw Fredrick, all she thought was, *Whoa.* Suddenly, this man was standing beside her, asking if he could eat the food off her plate. Fredrick was so nervous he didn't know what else to say. Frederica had told Diane before that Minister Eddington seemed nice, that all he did was talk about Jesus.

Why is this man asking me for my food? Diane wondered.

Fredrick reached over and took a bite of her turkey.

"How old are you?" he asked.

"Twenty-five," Diane said.

"Nah, you're not telling the truth," he said. To him, she looked about eighteen.

Diane stiffened. "I'm telling you the truth about my age," she said evenly. "I don't deal in lies."

"Can you cook?" Fredrick asked.

"Yes," Diane said.

"Will you marry me?"

Diane just laughed. *He don't even know my name,* she thought. But Fredrick had already made up his mind that this woman was going to be his wife. He knew somehow that she'd eventually get on board, because she hadn't flat-out said no. He decided to pop the question right up front because he figured he made a good first impression, and that's about it.

The two started spending time together—going to the park, eating out, talking for hours. And about all Fredrick talked about was Jesus. It struck Diane as a little strange, but the Holy Spirit told her one day, "Don't be no fool." She noticed a few other things: Fredrick talked about Jesus, but he didn't talk about church. So many young ministers were consumed with advancing in the pastoral hierarchy of the church, getting opportunities to preach in folks' pulpits and being appointed as assistants and adjutants to bishops. None of those concerns entered Fredrick's conversation. She also saw that her son, Christopher, took to him. Children, she says, are much more spiritually discerning than we realize, and even kids can be repelled by untrustworthy men or women without having the ability to explain why.

Diane had already figured that this man was serious about marrying her. But she wasn't at peace with his intentions until she heard a message given by Queen Esther Jones, a revered missionary in Dallas–Fort Worth Church of God in Christ circles.

"The way you can tell if a man is really saved," she said, "is if he chooses Jesus over you. If that man chooses you over Jesus, you in trouble. But if he chooses Jesus over you, you have nothing to worry about. If he loves Jesus, he'll take care of you."

Diane took those words to heart. Four months after meeting, the two eloped. They concealed their marriage and lived apart for a couple of weeks, waiting to have the church ceremony they'd planned, but then Fredrick confided in his mother.' "You better tell people right away," Alice said, "because if Diane gets pregnant, they're going to think it happened before you got married."

Sure enough, Diane was already pregnant.

Growing up in the Pentecostal church, Diane had witnessed plenty of sexual immorality and greed among the clergy. Congregation members seemed to wink at their leaders' indiscretions, offering up a short list of rationalizations, saying essentially that men will be men and that God would deal with a philandering pastor.

But Diane had been a sinner in her younger years, and now she was saved. She didn't see any nexus between darkness and light. You were one or the other, saved or unsaved, and she wanted no part of the purveyors of a gray area in between. Fredrick had already made clear to her that he wanted to be a pastor, but each of them harbored fears. Fredrick didn't want his heart broken by an unfaithful wife; Diane refused to cover up for a "player preacher," as she'd seen many pastors' wives do. She recalls warning him from the beginning, "If you don't live what you're preaching, I'm not holding you up in no lies. If you treat me one way in public and another way in private, I'm telling."

"He didn't have a problem with that," Diane says.

She, however, had a few problems with Fredrick. In their first year of marriage, Diane feared she had misinterpreted God's voice when she felt led to marry Fredrick. For one thing, Fredrick's family was cool toward her. Ever conscious of shades in color, they treated Diane like an outsider. "Don't bring that black girl to my house," one relative complained.

Fredrick also "had this thing about being older than me," Diane says, "and that I was gonna have to mind him. And I wasn't having any of that." Black Pentecostal churches held to a traditional concept of male and female roles in the home, despite the fluidity of gender roles in the church, where women were allowed to preach, teach, and lead others, though not always with a formal title. (In the Church of God in Christ, women can be licensed as missionaries, but they are not ordained as elders—a title equivalent to minister or pastor.) Diane hated to hear the word *submission,* so often directed at wives. All she could think of were the church ladies who got whupped by their husbands and treated like slaves, then fretted about whether that sorry man was cheating on them.

While Fredrick and Diane enjoyed a passionate relationship and shared the same commitment to Jesus, they differed in how their faith should be practiced. Fredrick, for instance, had picked up the obsessions of the Holiness churches concerning dress. After their daughter, Sherrel, was born, Diane bought her some colorful outfits with pants. Fredrick came home from work on a Saturday, saw the pants, and started muttering about Jezebel, the scheming wife of Israel's evil King Ahab. While they were arguing, Fredrick stepped into the backyard and lit up the Weber grill. Then he grabbed the pants, put them on the grate, and burned them.

While Fredrick barbecued the baby's clothes, Diane tossed her things into a suitcase, called her mother, scooped up Sherrel, and left.

The next morning, Fredrick was scheduled to be the guest preacher at the church of Bishop D. L. Smith. If Smith had known Fredrick was separated from his wife, he never would have allowed him to preach. But Fredrick got up anyway and launched into his message: "Living Too Close to Jezebel."

Diane, sitting right there in a pew, was not impressed.

For three days she stayed at her mother's house. Every day, Fredrick stopped by and asked her to come home, but he stopped short of apologizing.

Diane still wasn't moved. Finally, on the fourth day, he called, his voice gentle and contrite. He realized he'd gone overboard, Diane says, and that his daughter or any other female wearing pants didn't mean a thing about whether a person was right with God. He came to her mother's house with ninety-eight dollars in hand—the cost of the outfits he'd burned—plus several pantsuits for Sherrel that he'd picked out himself.

That night he prepared a candlelight dinner for Diane. While the dinner was a bit awkward, she recalled the wisdom of Queen Esther Jones. Clearly, this man's relationship with Jesus was more important than whether he got his way. (Fredrick had spent nights on his knees praying, asking God to heal his relationship with his wife.) That evening, the two of them decided they would make their marriage work, no matter what.

Diane knew she'd found something so much better than the wild life she used to lead. She had stayed high because she liked the feeling. She had resisted the influence of a Christian mother and the church they attended in Fort Worth. Now that she had a husband—a man who loved God above all else—she was determined not to repeat the mistakes of her earlier years.

One Last Joint, Then Jesus

In little Talco, certain lines were sharply drawn. Railroad tracks separated black from white in this rural East Texas town. And on the black side, you had a further division of darkness and light.

Darkness would be the men, plus a few sad-faced women, who gathered to drink cheap whiskey and home-brewed beer under what they called the Demon Tree.

Light was the folks who piled into the back of pickup trucks or hitched a ride with someone who had a car to travel to the holy-roller revival meetings in tiny White Oak, some fifteen miles away. A simple church house, part of the Church of God in Christ denomination, hosted a charismatic young evangelist named D. L. Smith. On Friday nights the sounds of washboard and guitar called to people through the summer heat. Inside, folks sang, stomped, and shouted—dancing, running, jumping—all under the influence of the Holy Ghost, the term for the Spirit of God in the King James Version of the Bible. Window fans circulated a rumor of cool, and on the wood-plank floors of this church house no butt shaking was allowed. They danced for God.

Every night saw a full house. Sweat hung thick in the humid air and mingled with the smells of working people—earth and salt and musty clothes. The revival meetings caused such a stir that people would gather outside the open windows, peering inside.

In the late forties, teenager Lola Mae Goldsmith would pull on a skirt—oftentimes home-crafted from a flour sack—and climb into the back of an open truck with her sister and cousins to attend revival meetings. She was invited by an older woman, Sister Shiny Savage, the appellation becoming a permanent part of the woman's name. (Holy rollers often call each other sister and brother.) Sister Savage had noticed that Lola had been hanging out at Talco's honky-tonk, "ruggin' it" (dancing) to the blues recordings of Howlin' Wolf and Muddy Waters on the jukebox while the young men slapped dominoes, played cards, and drank beer.

Sister Savage kindly but insistently told Lola that she was on her way to hell: "The ol' devil gon' get you if you don't get saved." These were hard words, but Sister Savage wasn't out to hurt anyone. The ladies who grew up in Talco invariably describe her as a loving person who treated everyone the same. She would deliver the same message to anybody she felt was straying down the wrong path. Her goal was to love you—and maybe scare you just a little bit—right out of hell.

For poor blacks living in Talco in the late forties, hell came from two directions. There was an earthly life of hardship and backbreaking work in the cotton fields, which embraced even the righteous. The other hell, of course, couldn't be seen from the city limits. It was the hell of everlasting fire, waiting for those who spurned God in favor of weekend pleasures on earth.

East Texas was cotton country back then, and the economy of black Talco kicked into gear in August when the four-lobed cotton bolls began to unfurl. As a toddler, Lola had been dragged between the rows, riding on a canvas sack as her mother picked cotton. When she got old enough to pull her weight—at seven or eight—she slung a flour sack over her shoulder and joined in.

Cotton-picking season was the richest time of the year. Lola's mother, Rosie Mae Boyd, hid her pay in a money belt that she wore under her skirt. The money she earned at harvest was parceled out through the rest of the year. It bought shoes for Lola and her sisters, Genetta and Dimple, plus a weekly quarter for each girl to spend at the general store. When the cotton harvest was finished, the girls left the fields to attend a segregated school. But Lola dropped out in eleventh grade to help Mama. There was no man in the house.

During the rest of the year, Rosie scratched out a living through domestic work. She grew vegetables in her yard and kept a few hogs and chickens. Nothing could be taken for granted.

No one talked about it much, but East Texas in the late forties was still in the waning days of lynchings and KKK violence. The civil rights movement was years away; segregation was still the law. Every black family knew of a male relative or acquaintance who'd been murdered in racially motivated incidents, or more commonly, a family member who had simply disappeared—having last been seen in the company of whites. One of Lola's uncles had gone on a camping trip with some white folks and never returned. He must have gotten lost in the woods, the white people later told his family. Lola's people didn't buy the explanation. They also knew they would never see their uncle again.

The black churches of East Texas were a safe and separate place, sanctuary and society all in one. Reflecting a class division that dated to slave days, when the house slaves held a higher status than the field workers, the churches came in two distinct flavors. The Baptist and Methodist churches were dignified, sober, and restrained, and their preachers often had formal theological training.

Then there were the Pentecostals, the so-called holy rollers. Use of the term would come across as derisive to some, matter-of-fact to others. Pentecostals got the nickname because of their penchant for ending up on the floor during church services in various states of agitation or ecstasy. The holy rollers' worship was exuberant and unchained; their preachers unschooled. Often there were no pianos in the churches, so the people made music with their feet and hands and the intricate rhythms of tambourines. In a black society that prized all the markers of upward mobility, the holy rollers were deemed unsophisticated and low class, and their prohibitions against dancing, short dresses, and makeup set them apart visibly from their peers.

Unsophisticated or not, the people who flocked to revival services in White Oak arrived full of a holy expectation. They would leave disappointed if God didn't break in and touch his children. He might bring a miraculous healing or provide comfort that a poor person would soon be able to pay an overdue bill. Or a soul might be convicted of sin.

White Oak, in fact, is where Lola first heard the gospel preached in a way that reached her heart.

"Come on over to Jesus while the blood is warm in your veins!" the preacher would intone to murmured amens and scattered hand claps. "Don't put off today for tomorrow—tomorrow may be too late!"

Sinners would rise quietly and walk to the front of the single-room sanctuary, kneeling at the altar, which consisted of a worn wooden bench. Some would find themselves rubbery and weak and weeping hot tears. The altar workers would hover nearby, poised like midwives to usher each soul into a new life in Jesus.

"Give up whatever in your life that's not like Christ," the altar workers would say, bending over a sinner, furiously fanning him or her on hot summer evenings. "Give it up now. Let go so you can be set free!"

As the sinner worked through the stations of repentance—acknowledging a sin, feeling its seductive pull on the soul, then cutting off that thought and releasing it forever—the sisters would push, "Let it go, let it go!"

If a sinner seemed to be repenting, the altar workers, usually mature women, would search for an outward sign that something real had taken place inside the person. If the sisters knelt beside a sinner and didn't discern that anything supernatural was going on, they'd be quick to say, "Hmm. That's not it." Then they'd move on to the next person in line.

The outward signs were familiar. Altar workers were looking for trembling, shaking, uncontrollable weeping—even retching and vomiting, when the Holy Ghost was cleaning house and expelling a demon or purging someone from a habitual sin. Or it might be something more subtle. The experienced saints could feel it, like a shift in barometric pressure. These women regularly fasted and prayed, which birthed a spiritual sensitivity. They knew it when something had popped loose in the spiritual realm. They were like wise and experienced clinicians who listen and observe and touch with their own hands, versus doctors who rely on textbooks, theory, and laboratory tests. It didn't take a lot of theological training; they just knew it when they knew it.

If that meant you cried at the altar night after night until you got your "change," then that's what you did. You waited, just like Jesus' followers waited in the Upper Room for the Father to send his Spirit.

Genetta Brown, Lola's older sister, was the first in the family to get saved, and it happened in White Oak when she was a teenager. She'd already made up her mind that she wanted to follow Jesus, but a couple of previous trips to the altar had proved fruitless. The holy rollers expected that you'd surrender all your sin to Jesus and then lead a changed life. This wasn't just a decision or an alteration of your beliefs. There had to be evidence of the changes. In the words of the New Testament, old things passed away; all things became new. Whoremongers stopped whoring. Liars stopped lying. Jickheads stopped drinking.

After the day of salvation, a holy roller never again called himself a sinner. Instead, he was a saint. At the same time he was saved, he asked for the Holy Ghost to fill the inside of him. This is the meaning of the storied "baptism of the Holy Spirit," the pivotal experience of the Pentecostal faith. Black Pentecostals would talk about salvation and the baptism of the Holy Ghost as though the two were interchangeable. You were saved for certain when you "got" the Holy Ghost, "and that with fire," as they'd say. The fire aspect is crucial. It is dual evidence of the presence of God's Spirit—speaking in tongues, accompanied by a burning away of sinful desires and deeds.

Genetta had spent several nights "tarrying" at the altar when she got her breakthrough. "A little bit of something came over me," she says. "I had my eyes closed and my hands up, and I saw Jesus on the cross in a white cloud. Then I went out on that floor." She toppled over and lay there, barely aware of her surroundings. "When I got up off that floor," she says, "I felt different—I got up speaking in tongues."

She had "got the Holy Ghost." Nothing else mattered. There were other men and women crying out at the altar, but Genetta was alone with Jesus.

There were times in White Oak when the Holy Ghost swooped in and a demon busted out. Genetta recalls seeing people jerking and writhing at the altar, even vomiting, as demons were chased out by the presence of the Holy Ghost. The preacher or an experienced altar worker would step in and rebuke the demon, ordering it to leave in Jesus' name, and at times the person who'd had a demon would have to be restrained.

Sometimes the demon screeched back: "I'm not coming out!" Since demons were known to fight back, only when a calm descended on the individual would the altar workers know that the unclean spirit had been cast out.

When a demon came out of a person, which Genetta saw many times, that person had a new look to go along with his or her new, sanctified life. To outsiders, this might sound like superstition, gullibility, or the overactive imagination of people who lead excessively hard lives and find their entertainment wherever they can. But to believers, this is New Testament Christianity being practiced in modern times. The things that occurred during the White Oak revivals were things with which Saint Peter and Saint Paul were familiar.

In East Texas in the late forties, Pentecostal beliefs brought solidity and order. Much more than a meeting place, a social gathering, or a religious club, the church enforced values and habits that were good for the community. If you were a "sorry" man, one who disdained work, you couldn't sit comfortably in a Church of God in Christ pew. Your kind was rebuked from the pulpit. If you were a "silly woman," meaning one who slept around, you would know that your lifestyle would become the subject of preaching and censure. The rules and expectations were clear: no more carousing at the honky-tonk, because each day belonged to God, and he had ordained work and family and

church—honest pursuits. Those who were guilty of laziness, carousing, or drunkenness were invited to the altar to repent of their sin and
start leading a new life.

You might wonder what gave church authorities the right to tell
people how to live. You can call it self-righteous, narrow-minded, or
sanctimonious if you want to. But these moral convictions gave order
to family life, improved the economic standing of desperately poor people, kept marriages together, gave children secure homes to live in, and
bettered the entire town.

Of course, there were those who spurned the altar. Hardheaded
sinners would end up sick and sorry, like the jickey folk loitering beneath the Demon Tree. Then one day God rendered his judgment on
them: a tornado spiraled down from the sky and ripped the tree out of
the ground. But a hardheaded sinner earns that designation honestly.
After the tornado struck, the drunks just moved to another tree.

The black holy rollers' congregational songs revolved around the
expectation of a clean life, the belief that through God's power and pro-
vision, a person already had victory over sin:

I'm saved and I know I am
Saved and I know I am
Saved and I know I am
I'm saved and I know I am

I don't have to sin no more
I don't have to sin no more…

As a teenager, Lola spent many evenings tarrying at the altar of the
little white church, with Sister Savage watching intently for signs of a
spiritual pulse. But unlike the usual pattern for sinners who visited the
church, Lola would end up getting the Holy Ghost in far more intimate
environs.

In those days the sisters would go on a circuit of homes through
the week, holding daily prayer meetings with their spiritual kin.
They'd read some Scripture, always in the otherworldly cadences of

the King James Bible, then sing and hum simple call-and-response verses:

> He sanctified me with the Holy Ghost
> What he done for me
> What he done for me
>
> He lifted me from the miry clay
> What he done for me
> What he done for me
>
> I shall never forget what he done for me…

Then the sisters would kneel for prayer, resting their arms on chairs or couches. Their voices would rise and fall, with one woman leading out, "Lord, bring salvation to the Davison home!" and the others would follow behind her, "Lord, make a way!"

There were no stabs at eloquence, just plain talk to a God who made himself available to common people. What mattered more than the precise words was the fervency—God, after all, knew their requests before the thoughts had even formed in their heads. What he desired was their love and the full commitment of their hearts.

Passionate prayer would usher in the palpable presence of the Holy Spirit, and a sister would sometimes break into "travailing," a mournful, tear-drenched prayer echoing the cries of a woman in labor. Her body would rock with each sob, and she would intercede with her heavenly Father in moans and cries, begging God to help someone who was ill or broke or weighed down by troubles. The sisters knew that such a prayer could only be prompted by the Holy Ghost, who "searches our hearts" and "intercedes for us with groans that words cannot express," in the words of Saint Paul.

It was in one of these prayer meetings that Lola got the Holy Ghost and began speaking in tongues. About a month later, her mother got it too. Whenever they could, Rosie Mae and her three daughters attended the 10 a.m. prayer meetings in people's homes. (Like many of the prayer ladies, Rosie Mae Boyd would do her cleaning work at a white family's house early in the morning, then bring the ironing home to do on her own time. This way she could break away for the daily balm of prayer.)

Long after Lola had married a Talco man and moved a hundred miles away to Fort Worth to find work and a better life for her family, her daughter Diane would experience the last days of the daily prayer meetings. They left a deep impression. Little Diane spent many of her summers with her grandma, running barefoot along black Talco's dirt streets. She loved to trail after Mama—that's what she called her grandmother—as she walked from home to home to pray for people. Sometimes Diane would sit on the porch and listen to the lowing sounds of prayers drifting out through the open windows. Other times Mama would let her come in and join the ladies.

Even at an early age, Diane sensed a warm, secure presence among the sisters who went about praying for people. The atmosphere of prayer inspired awe in her, yet it was comfortable and approachable at the same time. She identifies it now as the presence of the Holy Spirit. God was making himself known to Diane from an early age.

When Diane Delorse Hines hit her teen years in the seventies, she was nothing like her aunties, who had tarried at the church altar in tears, hoping for the Holy Ghost to come upon them. Diane, the youngest of Lola Mae's five daughters, was the wild girl who wore short shorts and low-cut blouses. Diane would run to the back of the house to get out of sight when Bishop D. L. Smith rolled up in his lime-green Cadillac. Like every Church of God in Christ preacher back then, the bishop didn't approve of a woman showing any cleavage, much less wearing pants. Diane respected the bishop—the same man who'd run revivals in White Oak decades earlier, then founded Lake Como Church of God in Christ in Fort Worth. She dutifully took her place in a pew at his church, but she had no illusions about whether she was saved. She wasn't.

Diane lived to party and smoke weed. She smoked pot just about every weeknight and stayed continually high through the weekends. In a single generation, the prospects of black Texans like her mother, father, and aunties had been radically transformed, and a semblance of prosperity had taken root. Surely such a dramatic social leap had never been seen in this country in the space of a mere two decades. Lola and Genetta knew the source of this change: nothing but the Lord. A favorite Church of God in Christ congregational song put it like this:

Jesus, I'll never forget, when away down in Egypt land
How you brought me out, with a mighty outstretched hand
Broke the bonds of sin, and set me free
Gave me joy, peace, and liberty

Jesus, I'll never forget what you done for me
Jesus, I'll never forget how you set me free
Jesus, I'll never forget how you brought me out
Jesus, I'll never forget, no, never…

But they had indeed forgotten, just like the generation of the Hebrews wandering in the desert after God freed them from slavery in Egypt. Diane didn't have to petition God for food on the table or shoes to wear or protection from the white man. Those days were gone, along with tarrying services and picking cotton.

Her father, Tony Hines, held down a good job at Mrs. Baird's, the popular regional bakery. Bishop Smith had summoned him from Talco to help out in his Fort Worth church. The Hines family lived in a comfortable home they owned in Highland Hills, a working-class black neighborhood in south Fort Worth. Diane's primary pursuit was having fun, and she saw little prospect of finding that in the church house.

Plus, by then, she'd seen too many of the saints leading double lives. Sisters slipping around, brothers cheating on their wives, preachers' illegitimate children popping up but, of course, never acknowledged as such. And lots of pettiness among women dressed modestly in long dresses. Like one missionary who falsely claimed that Diane had called her a "fat cow." The sister assumed (and hoped) Diane would get a whupping from her mother. (She didn't.)

Though Diane didn't show much interest in spiritual things, she did acquire a few hard-core convictions growing up. She learned that when you got saved, when you made a commitment to Jesus, you were a new person—a "new creation" as the New Testament terms it. There was an expectation in the Church of God in Christ that this radical change would be instantaneous. In preaching and teaching, if not always in practice, the church held a high standard for conduct. (This is common among all Holiness churches, not just the Church of God in Christ.) A decision to follow Jesus wasn't to be taken lightly, and everyone presumed that righteous works would immediately follow repentance. A young woman like Diane had to consider the cost of following Jesus. She found it too dear.

Unmarried and twenty-three, Diane got pregnant. Her mother reacted with disgust: "You little black heifer!" Though Diane adored her son, Christopher, whose father was a church musician and pastor's son, she wasn't ready to slow down. And the baby's father wasn't ready to be a husband.

One day near Christmas, in 1982, when Christopher was just a few months old, a friend of Diane's from the neighborhood invited her to a holiday party. Diane made the usual arrangement: she'd leave Christopher with his father, who refused to drink or party, two vestiges of his strict Holiness upbringing. Diane was at home getting dressed for the big night when her son toppled off the bed. Diane recalls that she dove and scooped him up just before he would have banged his head on the floor.

Later she would see this as a prophetic sign. God was dealing with her, and she found herself mouthing strange words without knowing why. "I can't do this anymore."

This time, she says, the Spirit of the Lord answered back, in questions spoken to her heart: "How many times did your mother leave you at home to go to a party? What kind of mother are you going to be?"

The words unsettled her, but Diane went to the party anyway. Once she got there, all she could think of was her son.

"I can't do this, I gotta go," she told her friend.

"Girl," the friend said, "you can't let no baby stop you from living. You got to keep going."

Her friend, after all, had left three children at home that night. But God's Spirit was talking to Diane. She couldn't get her mind off her infant son.

After the party, the same friend invited Diane to come by her house to smoke a joint. Diane usually stayed high on the weekends, but this joint didn't even give her a buzz. All she wanted to do was go home and see her baby.

The next morning, she found herself in a pew at Pentecostal Church of God in Christ, a Fort Worth congregation led by a strong, caring pastor named Elder R. L. Taylor. ("If you got sick," Diane says, "he would beat the ambulance to the hospital.") At the end of the service, she walked to the altar and gave her life to Jesus. Elder Taylor prayed for her, then the altar workers stepped in. Diane felt "such a peace."

For years, a devoted, sweet-singing young sister at this church named Frederica had been witnessing to Diane. She was one of the first to hear that Diane had gotten saved, and she was overjoyed. The same couldn't be said of Diane's party friends, who turned their backs on her. Frederica helped Diane get on her feet spiritually. Though Diane had been raised in the church, the dynamics of forging a personal relationship with God were entirely new to her. She wasn't even sure how to pray.

"The same way you're talking to me, talk to God," Frederica said.

Diane recalls that, just like she'd been taught in church, deliverance came instantly along with salvation. For years, she had been trying to quit smoking. Time and again she would flush the weed down the toilet, toss the cigarettes, only to start up again. But the day she got saved, she lost her desire to smoke.

She observed other changes: The recurring nightmares involving cats stopped immediately. The emptiness she'd felt was gone. She noticed it in the shower one day. "Oh my God, it's gone." When "I noticed that emptiness wasn't there," she says, "I knew I was really saved."

Diane still spent time with a sister who smoked, and she recalls being alone in the apartment and seeing a half-smoked cigarette in an ashtray. "The enemy said, *Smoke it*," Diane says. *"Ain't nobody here but me and you.*

"I just started laughing," she says. "I said, 'Devil, you such a liar.'"

Diane learned two unforgettable lessons early in her life as a Christian. One was to obey God, regardless of whether it made sense. The other was to rely on spiritual discernment rather than to always trust her natural faculties.

One morning less than a year after Diane got saved, she was going through her Sunday routine. She'd wake up, go downstairs, put a can of Dr Pepper in the freezer, then go back upstairs and get herself and her son ready for church. This time, though, with Dr Pepper in hand, she heard the word *fast*.

"Fast?" she said aloud.

Fast, the voice replied, communicating to her heart.

"Lord, is that you or is that me?"

She put the soda back in the fridge. Evidently, she thought, something big was going to happen in church that day. So she fasted.

But nothing remarkable happened. It was business as usual.

Afterward Diane went home, a little disappointed. Later that night she got a call from her ex-boyfriend. She'd broken up with him after she got saved, but they still saw each other occasionally. He wanted to come over and visit.

When he got there, he asked, "Can I kiss you?"

Diane hesitated. Sex was out of the question, but a kiss seemed harmless. She could kiss him and dismiss him. Her spirit, though, whispered to her: *Don't do it.*

She did it anyway. And within a few frenzied moments—all she remembers is wrestling with him and hollering for her sister Martha, who was upstairs—every stitch of her clothing was off.

"No!" Diane told him. "Please don't do this!" She started sobbing.

The man suddenly pulled away, startled by her tears. "I am so sorry," he said. He quickly got his things and left.

All this happened in the living room, and Martha never heard a thing.

Afterward, Diane says she "felt so dirty." She got in the shower and scrubbed and scrubbed, weeping and repenting to God. She called her friend Frederica and told her what happened. She didn't feel right until she had the chance to kneel at the altar in church and confess her sin. She had ignored the prompting in her spirit and had taken the easy road. And by compromising with a kiss, she had almost been raped.

After that, she says, when God said no, "I didn't."

The second lesson came with a physical affliction, one that would force her to rely on the Holy Spirit to an extraordinary degree. At age sixteen, Diane had noticed that her vision was deteriorating. Her friends would wave to her from down the street, and Diane couldn't recognize them.

© Robert Conner, DFW Digital Photography

Diane Eddington, pastor and fearless prophetess

Two years later, when she was a junior-college student, her vision diminished to the point where she knew she needed medical help. She stayed in the hospital for a week while doctors conducted tests, and they concluded she was faking it. Then an eye specialist in East Texas examined her, dilated her pupils, and made a diagnosis: she had a condition called Stargardt disease, a severe form of macular degeneration affecting juveniles. It drastically reduces central vision but often preserves peripheral vision. There was no way to treat it, and Diane was deemed legally blind at eighteen.

She recalls crying "for about five minutes." Then she rejected self-pity and accepted the circumstances of life. No driving; difficulty in reading; limited vocational options. Oh, well.

Looking back, she would see the evidence of God's mercy and care. Well before that point, she'd learned to perform some of the daily tasks of living without looking. She learned to press and curl her hair without a mirror. She could navigate the house in the dark.

She didn't know why she had done those things, but they helped prepare her for living without natural sight.

Gradually, and most remarkably, she began to develop a keen sense of spiritual discernment. Along with it came a spiritual gift that is mentioned often in the Bible: the ability to prophesy. God had chosen Diane to speak his word for a specific time and place, to be a supernaturally empowered messenger of his truth. In time Diane would be able to identify the presence of demons, even when no one else saw such evidence. While others relied on visible cues and personal knowledge that someone was oppressed by a spirit, Diane would pick up with spiritual antennae the nature of the unclean spirit. Sometimes she would literally smell a demon. What does it smell like? "Foul" is all she says.

What she lost in physical eyesight had been replaced by God with exceptional spiritual gifts. In the years to come, Diane would use those gifts to partner with her future husband, Fredrick Eddington, when they started a church in South Dallas. Fredrick's street preaching would reach desperate people, and Diane's discernment would root out the spiritual forces chaining them to sin.

Starting a Church on a Godless Street

Men and women were getting saved through Fredrick Eddington's street ministry. But how could he direct them after they were converted? The Holiness churches he knew were focused on outward appearance, not a person's heart, which was sure to push away the type of people who responded to his street preaching. In a Holiness church, a saved person was expected to dress a certain way, to testify according to an accepted format, and even to dance in a particular way—with stomping, shuffling feet, and minimal upper-body movement. When a new convert was confronted with the unwritten rules, his most likely response was to check out for good.

Just as disheartening, Fredrick often found that church people couldn't avoid looking down on the scruffy, unsophisticated folks he brought in off the street. Fredrick tried to explain that "you can't clean a fish before you catch it," but the veteran churchgoers kept trying to advance newcomers to a point of churchy acceptability.

It was obvious that Fredrick needed a place where his converts could learn over time what it meant to be a Christian, adopting the ways of a true follower of Jesus. Around that time, Bishop D. L. Smith, pastor of Lake Como Church of God in Christ, recognized that Fredrick had a calling from God to lead a church. Smith had founded numerous churches himself, and he encouraged gifted young ministers to strike out on their own and launch ministries—even if it meant they left the membership roll of Smith's own church, as Fredrick did.

Bishop Smith assigned Fredrick to a tiny, struggling church in Fort Worth. During the very first service, the proceedings were interrupted by an angry man who'd come to collect a debt the previous pastor owed. The lone bill collector outnumbered the congregation that day. With no one showing up for church, the project was abandoned, and Bishop Smith licensed Fredrick as a pastor to start a mission church.

If the word *mission* brings to mind adobe chapels built by friars on the uncivilized North American frontier, that's not far from what Fredrick set out to do. No one remembers much about the earliest days of The Body of Christ Assembly in South Dallas, because there isn't much to remember. Fredrick and Diane and their children—along with Fredrick's oldest sister, Dicloria Eddington, and her two daughters—were having a picnic one day in 1986 at the Fort Worth Zoo, and there the idea for a church in South Dallas was birthed.

"Why don't we use Nanny's old house?" Dicloria asked. Fredrick immediately saw the possibilities of his grandmother's former home. It was a nonthreatening place where he could minister to people who desperately needed help—the young guys who hung out on the corner selling drugs, or the men who congregated on ratty sofas underneath pecan trees, playing dominoes and sucking on paper-bagged 40s. He would follow the process used among the old-school black Pentecostals: through grit and sacrifice and hard work, he would start a church.

While the Church of God in Christ is a huge organization, with more members than any other Pentecostal denomination in the United States, it provides little if any financial support to fledgling pastors. There is no denominational church-planting department to assist with start-ups. You get a license to pastor and off you go. You learn on the job, with the Bible and the Holy Spirit as your guides. In exchange for doing it on your own, pastors are granted an unusual degree of autonomy.

Fredrick—now Pastor Eddington—took over his grandmother's house, a wood-frame structure built on a foundation of sections of tree stumps, and began gutting it to fashion a makeshift sanctuary. His mother, Alice, and her second husband, Freddie Hall, helped finance the renovations, along with Diane's oldest sister, Evon Dorn, and a couple of friends. But even with financial supporters, it was a hand-to-mouth existence. Inner-city Pentecostal pastors seldom drew a salary;

instead, tradition called for the members to give a love offering on the first Sunday of the month to the pastor and his wife. Some Pentecostal congregations at that time still carried on the rural tradition of "pounds," in which members would bring groceries—or, out in the country, chickens and collard greens—for their leaders in lieu of cash.

Pastor Eddington made ends meet by working full time at a state school for the mentally ill. Drawing the majority of his income from outside the church, as he still does, offered important advantages: he was free to follow the leading of the Holy Spirit without having to sell every point of his vision to a board of directors. He was at liberty to confront sin in the congregation without worrying about who'd discontinue their donations in retaliation. He would undertake ministry out of love instead of obligation or a need for career advancement.

Those were tough days, as Diane remembers it. Week after week they'd meet for church, using castoff pews and folding chairs in a rickety house with soiled yellow carpet and a window air conditioner that made a lot of noise but never worked properly. Church services involved doling out responsibilities to the five adult members and acting as though people were fixing to bust through the doors any day now. Dicloria, a gifted teacher, taught Sunday school, and she and the pastor led praise with their booming voices as though hundreds were gathered for worship. Fredrick would preach exuberantly—though briefly—hollering through a cheap PA system that periodically belched feedback. They started propping a speaker outside the church door so they could beam the message through the neighborhood.

But what do you do if you open a church and no one comes? For perhaps a year and a half, the congregation consisted solely of Fredrick and Diane and their three children, Dicloria and her two teenage daughters, and Alice Hall. But they didn't sit there wringing their hands in despair, wondering why the church wasn't growing. A visitor would sometimes wander in for a service, but no one stuck. The pastor responded by doing what he always did: he'd get out in the street and "compel them to come in," adopting Jesus' plan of action when his own people, the Jews, rejected him. The pastor would preach to druggies, winos, drifters, and others who needed hope and a word from someone who cared. He and Dicloria would walk up and down the streets around the church, praying for anyone they'd meet and singing and claiming territory for Jesus.

Pastor Eddington refused to get discouraged. No one who puts his hand to the gospel plow and looks back, he read in the Bible, is fit for service in the kingdom of God. So every week he'd set up a small PA system beneath the oak trees at T. C. Grocery, where folks bought booze, and he'd hold church outside.

"We are in despair," he'd call out, his words flowing through a crackly speaker. "We depend on drugs and alcohol and are heavy-laden with many burdens. How can we be delivered? Jesus is calling out to his people—'Come as you are! Come as you are! *Come as you are!*'"

Numerous city ordinances concerning noise and public disturbances were undoubtedly violated, but this was the 'hood, and a little noise was the least of anyone's worries. And here in the streets of South Dallas— the same place he got saved—Pastor Eddington would find his new congregation.

When he thinks about how it all came together, Fredrick sees God's peculiar symmetry. He got saved alone one day in his car, where God decided to meet him. No one preached to him. "That happened so I could completely depend on the Holy Spirit," Pastor Eddington says. He had plenty of opportunities to give up during the first year he started the church. Yet he held on to his unlikely dream of an interracial mission church in the middle of a desperate place, ground zero for broken hearts.

He recalls that one Sunday morning he arrived to preach, and the church was empty. Diane was at home in the final weeks of a difficult pregnancy, and the other regulars didn't show up that day. The pastor wasted no time feeling sorry for himself. He walked across the street to a vacant lot, rooted around among the broken glass and rubbish and empty crack baggies, and gathered a handful of stones. He carried them into the church and placed each one on the seat of a folding chair. Then he stepped behind the pulpit, opened his tattered King James Bible, and preached salvation to the rocks.

It was, he says, an act of faith.

He thought of Luke 19, where religious leaders in first-century Israel ordered Jesus to rebuke his disciples, who were praising him loudly in the streets as though he were the Son of God (which, of course, he was). "I tell you," [Jesus] replied, "if they keep quiet, the stones will cry out." That day in South Dallas, Fredrick dared the stones on the chairs to cry out.

"He came home and told me he'd preached to the rocks," Diane says. "And I said to myself, *Sounds like something Fredrick would do.*" She returned to church the next week to find her seat occupied by a gray pebble.

Not long afterward, during a week of sparsely attended evening revival meetings, Queen Victoria Curlin would walk through the church doors. She had been wandering the neighborhood, walking aimlessly down streets near her house, thinking about suicide. For seven years she'd been strung out on crack cocaine. As she tells it, "I'd lost self-respect, pride, and everything else. I was so out of it."

She says something told her to stop walking when she came to the church. She stood outside for a moment, listening to Pastor Eddington's words from the pulpit. His was a familiar voice, "so loud, so powerful." She had heard this man's voice resonating through the neighborhood many times, as she sat on her porch or lay on her bed. It seemed as though his words were echoing in the streets and in her mind: "Come as you are, come as you are, come as you are..."

Still, she hesitated at the church door. "Go in, go in," a voice told her. She braced herself and stepped inside.

When Victoria moved into the tiny sanctuary tinged with the musty scent of rotting wood, the handful of people inside were praying. All the adults immediately encircled the newcomer and put their arms around her. Then the pastor and Dicloria Eddington prayed. Victoria, Diane recalls, was dressed indifferently in T-shirt, jeans, and do rag and appeared to be drunk.

The visitor dropped to the floor after only a few words of prayer had been spoken. Lying on the carpet and only vaguely conscious of her surroundings, Victoria began "spitting stuff out," Diane says. The First Lady had seen this many times before. It was a phenomenon she associated with demonic spirits being expelled.

Victoria has no idea how long she lay on the floor. Her mind and senses were overwhelmed by "a feeling that I had never had in my entire life—a good feeling." Even today, twenty years later, she recalls it clearly. "It was like a miracle," she says. "God delivered me from crack cocaine that night. I'll always remember that feeling.

"When I walked in—I can't explain it—I had this feeling like I was going to leave everything there that night. That it'd never be the same."

By the time she walked back home, she had given her life to Jesus Christ. And she was completely sober.

Victoria started telling everyone she ran into that God had done something big in her life—something miraculous. Come to this tiny church and hear the preacher with the big voice, she would say. The people around her, many of them crackheads, noticed something different about Victoria, who was in her midthirties when she first visited the church. "My face, my expression, everything changed," she says. The pastor, in fact, had spoken words to her that presaged a physical transformation: "I know there's a beautiful lady up under there."

The revival services continued for several days, and one by one Victoria pulled in her relatives and friends. First, her husband ventured in. He had lost his job and blown his savings on crack cocaine. He even pawned his wedding ring. But after hearing the pastor preach one night, he got on his knees at home and begged God to heal him from his addiction. He never used drugs again.

Then Victoria drew in her older sister, Veronica Banks. For a year, she'd been able to speak only in a whisper, and just a few weeks earlier doctors had diagnosed her with throat cancer. When she walked into the church for the first time, she was in the midst of radiation treatments.

Veronica stepped in full of faith that she'd be healed of cancer. The pastor prayed, and at the end he pronounced, "It is gone. The devil is a liar, and you are going to be healed." Veronica simply believed. She says she took her healing and walked out the church doors. She didn't become a member till years later.

Within days of receiving prayer for healing, she returned to her doctor, who informed her that no trace of the cancer could be found.

Soon Victoria would pull in her youngest brother, Chris Edwards, who on his second visit to the church gave his life to Christ. "I started hearing about the love of God instead of this God that wanted to send everyone to hell that wasn't living right," Chris recalls. "Something kept drawing me closer and closer to God. I kept pursuing him to a point where Chris just died—he didn't exist anymore. I didn't remember my past."

Chris's longtime girlfriend, Yolanda, noticed immediate changes: He cleaned up his foul mouth. He began taking more responsibility for her son. And within weeks, he asked her to marry him. Yolanda was skeptical—she'd been married before—plus she hadn't grown up in a religious home. Chris asked her to visit his church, and she reluctantly agreed. "I'm coming with you," she told him, "but I'm sitting in the back pew, and I don't want nobody to talk to me."

She soon realized, of course, that one can't hide in a church with a half-dozen members. And to make matters worse, she felt throughout the Bible study she attended that Pastor Eddington was speaking directly to her, carrying on about how much Jesus loves every one of us, and how much we all need him. Toward the end, the pastor looked straight at her.

"Young lady, do you know Jesus?"

"I don't know," Yolanda said. Wrong answer.

"Come up here," he said. "Do you want to know Jesus?"

"I guess," she said. Yolanda desperately hoped he'd shift his attention elsewhere. But he didn't. He told her that when she accepted Jesus as her Lord, Jesus would forgive her of her sins. "Now do you want to know him?" he asked.

"Yes," Yolanda said, but at the time she didn't mean it. She continued going to church with Chris and privately made a decision to get saved shortly before they were married. "I made up my mind to accept the Lord and stop doing the things that would cause me to go to hell," she says. "I prayed on my own for God to help me."

Around the same time Chris and Yolanda visited the church, Victoria's brother Terry and his girlfriend, Monique Morgan, dropped in. They would also decide to follow Jesus—in fact, they would get married right alongside Chris and Yolanda within a few months of visiting the church.

Victoria invited many others, and the pastor prayed for them. Victoria says she can't think of a single addict she brought who wasn't delivered of his or her addiction. Many, however, melted back into the community and didn't make a habit of attending church. Like her sister Veronica, they took their miracle and walked away. She still sees some of those people in South Dallas, and they have remained free from crack cocaine.

Doris Spencer was a drunk—a woman who'd stand outside a liquor store at 7 a.m. waiting for the door to open. She despised herself for how low she'd sunk, because years earlier she had known better. At the age of twenty-nine, she had been saved and filled with the Holy Spirit at Full Gospel Holy Temple, a Holiness church led by Apostle Lobias Murray. When she got saved she experienced a turnaround: she got out of a sinful relationship, and God blessed her with comfortable places to live, nice furniture, and financial stability, even though she was a single mother raising seven children. Then she squandered every bit of it.

When Pastor Eddington ran into Doris outside T. C. Grocery in October 1988, a few months after Victoria joined the church, Doris was forty-five and a backslider. She'd lost her longtime job as a school-bus driver. "My life was in such a mess," she says. "I was miserable." She was too ashamed to show her face at church.

That day Doris was ducking into her car with a 40-ounce she had just bought. Pastor Eddington walked up and invited her to church.

"I set my beer down in the car, y'know, I was trying to hide it," Doris recalls. "When you see a preacher, you start moving. Especially when you know you're not living right. Then he says, 'Hey sister, can I speak to you?' And I said, 'Yes sir, you may.'

"He began to witness to me about the Lord, and I got saddened in my heart. I began to tell him my problems. I told him I was a drunkard and couldn't do nothing about it."

The pastor touched his hand to her forehead and prayed. "Tears started coming down," she says. "I got back in my car and took my bottle and threw it over yonder and smashed it.

"I went home and put on a nice dress. I brushed my teeth and tried to get the smell of drink off my breath. I headed back to the church that very night."

When she got there, the pastor was preaching about a backslider coming home. "I said to myself, 'Lord Jesus, I know you're talking to me,'" Doris says. "The pastor prayed for me again and the Spirit of the Lord came on me and I hit the floor. The power of God knocked me out. I don't remember anything else until I found myself sitting on a bench.

"I felt like a different person. I never took another drink. I never smoked another cigarette, I never smoked weed, I never said another cuss word."

It's easy to be religious around Christians, but what do you do when you return to the places where for years you've been practicing destructive habits? Praising God in church is one thing, but then going back to the neighborhood where you've been abusing drugs or alcohol or your spouse or yourself is something entirely different.

Victoria and Doris found out firsthand. Not only was South Dallas overrun with crack dealers, but users lit up inside Victoria's home, just like she used to do. Victoria admits that a couple of times after she got saved, she started to smoke a crack rock—but something kept her from giving in. She'd remember how she felt the night she got delivered, the most wonderful thing she'd ever experienced. The memory of the Holy Spirit freeing her from addiction outweighed the promise of a twenty-second high. And pretty soon she developed a revulsion for anything having to do with the drug. If crackheads insisted on hanging around her door, like they'd done in the past, she'd tell them she was gonna call the cops. It was no empty threat. She even called the police on her own family members.

She accomplished her goal: getting the users out of her face.

On the streets of South Dallas, Victoria would continually encounter reminders of her past—other folks who still got high, or the boys who'd peddle the drug, summoning one another by pager and walkie-talkie and strolling up to open car windows to deliver the product. While her relatives got saved and delivered one by one, Victoria found refuge among the few members at The Body of Christ Assembly. No one looked down on her. The pastor preached an uncompromising message about sin, but unlike many other Holiness preachers, he knew there was no hierarchy of evils in God's eyes.

Sin is a problem for everybody. If you keep returning to your sin again and again, the pastor would say, how are you any different from the crack addict? At least the crack addict knows he's messed up. Yet the pornography addict—and the liar and the hater and the backbiter—thinks he's better off than the crackhead. Now who among these is more deceived?

They were all in this together. They were desperate sinners in need of God's love and forgiveness. And the tiny, struggling Body of Christ Assembly was there to stay, letting the people of South Dallas know there was a better way to live.

The High Cost of Loving God

In the years when Fredrick Eddington was conversing with trees and rocks, trying to get a grip on sanity, I was dutifully attending church with my parents. The ritual already bored me, but one Sunday, when my family visited a new church, I sat with my eyes fixed on a woman singing all out in the back row of the choir stand. She wasn't paying attention to the congregation. She directed her song to an unseen audience, and I had never before seen such passion.

I had a meltdown right then and there. I broke into sobs, and pretty soon a couple of ushers rushed to my side with tissues. I had no idea what was going on, but at sixteen I knew that such a display of emotion was distinctly uncool.

This was only the second time in my life I'd been to a Pentecostal church, and the first visit had practically inoculated me against it. That first time I'd gone to a church in Fond du Lac, Wisconsin, known as Gospel Tab, short for Gospel Tabernacle. Within moments of taking a pew, my older sister, Jennie, and I found ourselves surrounded by keening women in long dresses, engaging in what I guess was a mass tongue-talking ritual. Their fanatical looks and bizarre dress—women with hair pinned in pioneer-era buns, men in misshapen polyester suits—freaked me out.

"Please don't ever take us back here," Jennie and I begged our parents. They didn't.

But when I was sixteen, my mother was casting about for a more authentic faith, and she took us once again to visit a Pentecostal church, Brookfield Assembly of God. Located in a bland middle-class suburb of Milwaukee, this was not at all our type of church. And sitting there while the choir sang a gospel song, I was crying uncontrollably. The woman in the choir, singing to God and oblivious to the crowd in front of her, undid me. My parents looked at me with puzzlement while my sister kind of sneered.

"Are you okay?" one of the ushers asked.

If I'd been my usual snotty self, I would have said well, duh, what do you think? But I couldn't get the words out. In that singer's face I saw something otherworldly, even holy. And at sixteen, believe me, I wasn't given to using words like *holy*.

With the benefit of hindsight, I'm better able to decode my experience: I went to that church expecting nothing, other than perhaps a weird repeat of my family's previous Pentecostal-church debacle. But while I sat in the pew and watched the singer in the choir, I came into contact with the presence of God's Spirit. Looking at that woman's face, I saw what I could only describe as the light of God—and it scorched me. I felt so dirty, like Saint Peter after his first close-up encounter with Jesus. "Go away from me, Lord," he implored, falling at Jesus' feet. "I am a sinful man!"

I don't recall doing anything official that day to confirm my encounter with God, but I realized something about the state of my soul—which was that I didn't know the state of my soul. I had all the proper church answers, like once saved, always saved; God will never leave you or forsake you. But I couldn't put away the feeling that I was slimy inside, that I desperately needed to get right with God or something dark was awaiting me. I was done with spiritual platitudes, I needed spiritual reality.

I was a teenager, and my family was disintegrating. I could try to explain it by pointing out the hurt between my parents that had built up over the years and was never resolved. I could point to my mom's years of putting my dad's career ahead of her own dreams. But I won't. After years of studying the Bible, I can tell you there is only one cause for the breakup of a marriage: sin.

That was the case with my parents. It's funny, because many of the high-school kids my mom taught in a Sunday-school class at the Dutch Reformed church we attended viewed my parents as role models. My

mother had a vibrant faith. She had met some nuns at a Catholic college who had experienced a direct encounter with the Holy Spirit. My mom followed suit and became kind of a closet Pentecostal. My father taught an adult Sunday-school class with his usual logic and precision. They were well versed in the Bible's teachings, generous with their time and money, and volunteered together in church ministries. Many Christians would tell you this is *the* recipe for success in marriage. How could they go wrong?

I know now that self-centeredness and unforgiveness can birth all kinds of devastating sins, and we all wrestle with these conditions of the heart. Sin is serious business, and it will wreck a marriage and your life. But I can't recall our Dutch Reformed church ever dealing with sin on a practical level. It was discussed in far more theoretical ways. If you'd been "saved," if you'd stepped up to the altar and asked Jesus to come into your heart, you were taken care of. It didn't matter if your life never changed after that moment of salvation; you and Jesus were on good terms forever. Tell him you're sorry for your "mistakes," shed a tear or two, and you're good to go. You've been equipped with a perpetual reset button for sin.

I realized later that God forgives us, but his mercy and our love for him should inspire us to obey him. And basing your life on the Bible's teachings makes your life different to the point that other people notice. There was a farmer in the church my family attended. At home he would beat his wife and son, then on Sunday he'd take a pew near the front. (The boy was a student in my mother's Sunday-school class, and he told her about his hellish home life.) The abusive man got a free pass. No one held him accountable or attempted to intervene to protect his family.

Likewise, my parents, whose marriage was falling apart, showed up at church every Sunday, but no one expressed the kind of love that dares to ask tough questions, to go below the surface and get at the truth of a person's struggles. No one tried to help them heal their broken marriage.

My sister became thoroughly disenchanted with this impotent

brand of Christianity. Disillusionment took root in me more slowly, but eventually I started searching for a Jesus who was real, who bore a closer approximation to the person I read about in the Bible.

My mom wasn't blind to the hypocrisy. She threatened to walk into our church, climb up on a pew in her high heels, and let out a high-pitched scream. Would the preacher stop his singsong sermonizing? Would the choir drop a stanza? My mother suspected they wouldn't, that they'd just amble on with their rituals of Sunday-morning piety—never mind the crazed woman in nylons in the center pew, screaming about something.

Mom wasn't just talking. Jennie and I knew she was just about unhinged enough to go through with it.

During high school I plotted my escape from Fond du Lac. The town was a place of unbearable unhappiness for me, and I planned to get as far away as I possibly could. I sent my SAT scores to schools on the West Coast and in the Deep South. I seriously thought about checking the box to American University in Tehran, but by the time I was a high-school junior, it had become a casualty of the ayatollah's revolution.

In high school I was different and apart from other students. I hung out with the smart kids, and on the surface I could appear to be sharp and funny and bold, but I had to muster every ounce of strength to engage in normal social interaction. I was much more comfortable withdrawing to my inner world where I would indulge my fascinations with New Wave and punk music—my best friend and I were two of only a handful of fans in Fond du Lac—and attempt to untangle the disparate strands of my sexual identity.

In adolescence, my lifelong lack of interest in girl things had taken a sharp left turn. I began feeling an almost overwhelming attraction to other girls. I was interested in boys too, but the interest was purely sexual, though never acted upon. The idea of having sex with boys fascinated me, but not boys themselves. I had another craving that seemed deeper, a desperate need for affection from girls. This duality of sexual desire was inward, powerful, and so frightening that I dared not put words to it. At the same time I began to experience bouts of depression, a darkness that seemed to envelop me for days at a time.

Once, when I was sixteen, I wrote a letter to my mom, telling her I was attracted to girls. I wrote it in tears, in smudgy blue ink. I pleaded for her help because I respected her Christian faith. I tucked the note inside an envelope, ran across the street, and stuck it in our curbside mailbox. A few minutes later, I ran across the street again and plucked it out. I was so ashamed that I tore the letter into tiny pieces. A few things from my fundamentalist Christian upbringing had been pounded into my head: I understood the fear of God, and I understood sin. All sex outside of marriage was sin to me; homosexuality, out of the question.

I don't recall what triggered my almost confession. I'm sure depression was wrapped up in it somehow. I'd earlier had a vision in which I was spinning in a vortex, being pulled up—yes, up—to hell. I never actually saw what it looked like, but I knew it was hell. I tried to call out the name *Jesus*—I'd been taught there was power in that name—but I couldn't get the word out. It was one of the most frightening experiences I'd ever had, and I understood enough about the supernatural realm to connect the experience to evil spirits. A battle was raging over my soul, and I knew it, but my childhood theology offered no solution except to "stand on the Word of God," that I had been saved and that everything was cool.

But clearly everything was not.

At college I searched for a deeper connection with God at the same time I was trying to figure out who I was and what my life was all about. In a certain group of Christian students that I was part of, I realized at least one of us was crazy. Maybe it was me, maybe not.

I looked around at the dozen or so well-scrubbed college kids seated on the beige carpet in Gary's nearly empty rental home. Gary was a friendly, well-dressed guy in his late twenties who acted as the Seattle-area recruiter for National Encounter with Christ, a mission organization that introduced nonbelieving college students to Christianity. Gary sat on a folding chair at the front of the room, chatting amiably with us about winning souls for Jesus. From time to time his harried-looking wife would dart into view in pursuit of their toddler. It always provoked a sharp rebuke.

"Jane!" Gary would hiss. "Would you get the kids out of here?"

Jane would hustle in, grab a chubby kid, and disappear into a side room, never speaking a word. She looked like a generic church lady, with her limp hair and floral-print sundress flecked with baby spit-up. It was disturbing and weird and kind of schizophrenic how Gary would pause in midsentence, yell at his wife, and then pick up the vein of biblical discourse without leaving a single space between thoughts.

My parents, of course, didn't always get along. (They would divorce when I was twenty-one.) But I'd never seen a man treat his wife this way, like a dog. Ever.

I had this impulse inside me to bolt out the door and run as fast as I could away from that suburb and that unhappy couple and those doughy children with chocolate-smeared faces and maybe let out a liberating scream or two as my feet put more distance between me and them.

I looked around the room again. Surely I wasn't the only one who was appalled. I checked out my friend Jillian, who'd roped me into attending this meeting. She sat there grinning, chuckling at Gary's jokes. I had to admit he was kind of funny when he wasn't screaming at his wife. And everyone else paid Gary rapt attention. Hey, we were gonna win the world for Jesus Christ. Who was I to criticize? If someone was crazy in this group, I concluded it was me, so I kept my mouth shut.

"You're just hypercritical," the National Encounter folks would later tell me, after I raised questions about some of their practices. I took their word about my hypercritical temperament, yet I couldn't stop myself from questioning their authoritarian view of husband-wife relationships, their disdain for Pentecostal Christians, and their cheesy financial practices.

I'd come to the Pacific Northwest to make Christian friends. This, I thought, would help me get my life on track. I'd never had a close Christian friend, so even though I'd been recruited by Ivy League schools, I enrolled at Seattle Pacific University (SPU), a small evangelical Christian college. It had the added bonus of being about as far away from Fond du Lac as I could get without crossing an ocean. Here I became buddies with Jillian, a fellow art student who shared my love for music and dancing and warped humor. Plus, we both wanted to save souls. It never struck us as an odd combination when we would carry on for hours about Jesus and the Bible and the curious proliferation of noodle dishes at bad church potlucks while we listened to the Ramones and Jillian sucked on forbidden cigarettes.

The summer after my freshman year, in 1982, Jillian and I traveled with a National Encounter with Christ (NEC) contingent of about one hundred to China, where I soaked up input from prominent Bible teachers and collected kitschy Mao souvenirs. After China, I continued on to the Philippines, where I'd been assigned to a team of junior evangelists. Jillian, meanwhile, journeyed to India with Gary as her team leader.

National Encounter styled themselves as sophisticated fundamentalists, distancing themselves from the backward, provincial, outmoded culture of closed-off evangelicals. They dressed in snazzy clothing, believing that evangelicals tended to turn people off with their denim skirts and their so-seventies (or whatever the previous decade was) suits.

The organization's leader was an intelligent man who cultivated relationships with skillful Bible teachers, and NEC devised a concise method for sharing the gospel based on a few simple premises: Jesus is the Son of God, the Bible is the Word of God, and every person has sinned and deserves the penalty of death. We carried around binders with that information inside as we walked randomly through the streets of Cebú City, attempting to lead men and women in the "sinner's prayer" so they could receive salvation.

I volunteered for this summer program; no one coerced me. And at the start I believed in NEC's mission. But the longer I was involved, the more I noticed there were fundamental problems. One was integrity. When the staffers ran low on funds, which happened all the time, they sent their clean-cut minions to "bucket" in front of grocery stores—collecting dollars, which they were allowed to pocket after the national organization skimmed off its share. Bucketing proved quite lucrative for some of the staffers, though not all of them participated.

And then there was our methodology for spreading the gospel. The material in our three-ring binders distilled a bare outline of the gospel message, but it touched only the intellect. The pitch was simple: assent to these few principles, and you'll be saved. Some people did assent, and at the end of the day we'd tally up how many people had prayed the required prayer. Like trappers gathering pelts, we'd notch them as names in God's Book of Life.

It made me wonder if we were really doing any good. Were we introducing people to God or simply getting people to accept our argument? I didn't feel any closer to Jesus, and I wondered if any of these excruciatingly polite Filipinos did either. I'd be out there on the streets reading words printed in my binder and praying cardboard prayers, while I heard people padding behind us whispering "Protestante," since the Philippines at the time was overwhelmingly Catholic. At night we returned exhausted to our compound at a Bible training center, where we fell asleep to the sounds of an outdoor disco that possessed all of five records, which were played continually till exactly 1 a.m. I'd depart six weeks later with Tom Tom Club's "Wordy Rappinghood" etched in my brain cells ("What are words worth? What are words worth?") alongside National Encounter's five-step salvation plan.

Words, I concluded, aren't worth a whole lot, especially when there are so many of them spewing from the mouths of junior missionaries. Our gospel presentation was logical and sequential, but something was missing. I didn't see people's lives getting changed, least of all our own. It didn't help that two or three of the NEC staff members took it as a personal project to disabuse me of my belief that speaking in tongues and other "charismatic gifts of the Holy Spirit" were valid for today. Their efforts were fruitless. I'd witnessed my mother's Spirit-filled faith, and while I didn't possess any of these spiritual gifts myself, I refused to dismiss something I'd judged to be authentic in her.

My one-year association with NEC ended when my mom called the leader and insisted that they pay me what they owed me, because I'd raised funds in my church and they'd used the money for something other than the stated purpose. My mom was a righteous dame, and she and my dad were two people you didn't want to tangle with. Right was right, wrong was wrong, and evangelical politesse got tossed out the window when they spotted an injustice. Without verbally abusing you or even raising their voices, my mom and dad could pluck you clean with sharp words and incisive logic.

At the end of the day, I got paid my share of the support I'd raised. Then I walked away, but not before I learned a lasting lesson at the hands of a hypocritical leader. While my friend Jillian was in India with Gary, she and the other team members started noticing bruises on his wife's face. He offered his own explanation for her black eye, some cockamamie story about how the two of them got up from the bed at precisely the same time and conked heads. When I found out, I was outraged. I had never heard of spousal abuse until I was in my late teens. It struck me then as so base that I was shaken beyond words when I discovered that it happened among Christians too.

I was disgusted with my cowardice that day. I should have spoken up. I should have run. I resolved never again to remain silent when I witnessed evil.

During my college years, the only thing that consistently incited passion in me was music. You could find me and Jillian at the punk and New Wave shows that swung through Seattle, at least the ones we were old enough to get into. I heard T.S.O.L. tell us how they wanna eff the dead, and back home in Wisconsin I watched Fear fans tear apart a Milwaukee club with sledgehammers. I sucked in pure exhilaration when Chrissie Hynde and the boys launched into the first few chords of "The Wait" at Milwaukee's Oriental Theatre, where we were watched over by a phalanx of gargoyles with glowing green eyes.

It amuses me now how fans of rock music mimic the choreography of Pentecostal worship—hands raised in the air, shouts and claps and ecstatic dancing, all manner of misplaced passion. I stood at the edge of the night scene, one foot in, one foot out. I wanted to inch up as close as I could without getting burned. Instead, after graduating from SPU with a degree in English, I just got depressed.

There was a particular moment when I looked around me, and all the people I'd admired the most had set aside the ideals they'd taught me. My parents had divorced, and the other Christians I knew well had gone AWOL from the faith, settling for a religious mediocrity marked by compromise—illicit sex, occasional drug use, general lukewarmness in their love for God.

Though I wasn't involved in the kind of big, juicy transgressions that pushed prominent television evangelists into the news, I was no prize. I couldn't shake the weight of my ordinary, everyday sin. I'd spend hours working my way through the writings of Christian thinkers such as Augustine, Calvin, and Luther, but I saw no compelling reason to fellowship with my Christian brothers and sisters. Nothing I did seemed to get me closer to God, and I had concluded that he selected just a choice few to be his friends, while the rest of us were consigned forever to a marginal, arm's-length relationship.

As a substitute for a real and satisfying relationship with God or man, I turned to depression—which struck me as a reasonable response. It looked to me like the dingy shadow of truth. In it I got a sense of my real condition, the filth of self.

At twenty-two, while looking for a copy of that week's *NME,* a British music magazine for cool people like me, I picked up a $4.95 paperback called *The Cost of Discipleship,* written by the great German pastor and theologian Dietrich Bonhoeffer. He wrote this masterpiece of Christian practice when he was in his early thirties, not much older than I was when I read his book. I sat on my futon and read it through in a couple of days, furiously underlining in blue pen.

I could never adequately describe what it was like to read those words. Imagine everything you'd ever believed ripped away from you at once, leaving a jagged-edged crater in your soul. I couldn't sleep; I feared for the souls of my family members. I sifted through my memory and asked myself if I'd ever known anyone who was *really* a follower of Jesus Christ—any Christian who loved God and people with the passion and desperation of Dietrich Bonhoeffer.

The little volume with the plain green cover would destroy my faith.

Today, both conservative and liberal Christians have appropriated Bonhoeffer's radical declarations, but no one should be so eager to cozy up to him. Faced with evil made flesh in the form of the Third Reich, Bonhoeffer, a Lutheran, set aside his pacifist beliefs and joined a conspiracy to kill Hitler. He saw Jesus' words, "All who draw the sword will die by the sword," as a matter-of-fact predictor of the outcome. Bonhoeffer's life would end in 1945 on a Nazi gallows, where he was executed for his role in the assassination conspiracy. The camp physician at Flossenbürg concentration camp, who observed the pastor kneel and pray before ascending the gallows, "so certain that God heard his prayer," marveled that "I have hardly ever seen a man die so entirely submissive to the will of God."

What confounds liberal Christians is that Bonhoeffer's faith was firmly orthodox, centered in the divinity of Jesus Christ and the teachings of the Bible. Theological liberals who would adopt him as their own gravitate toward his later works rather than *The Cost of Discipleship*, which emphasizes suffering, self-sacrifice, and instant obedience to God's commands. Bonhoeffer's grace is costly grace—one that exacts as its price your entire life, with all its ambitions, agendas, and lusts. His call is one of self-denial and sacrifice. His words cut me to the heart.

The Cost of Discipleship takes as its structure the Sermon on the Mount, in which Jesus pronounces blessings for the meek, the poor, and the persecuted. To Bonhoeffer, the Sermon on the Mount, commonly presented as an unattainable ideal—a list of noble aspirations—was in fact a realistic prescription for a life of following Jesus Christ. In a man or woman who'd been reborn in Christ, there should be found no untruth, none whatsoever. As well as no hatred, no envy, no worry, none of the afflictions of self-centeredness. Just as Jesus' words about sin demanded the unthinkable—"If your right eye causes you to sin, gouge it out and throw it away"—so sin should be unthinkable to a believer, Bonhoeffer wrote.

He decried the "cheap grace" I'd been taught in church, the sin license granted by my once-saved-always-saved brethren. "Cheap grace is the deadly enemy of our Church," Bonhoeffer wrote at a time when the Confessing Church—German Protestants who refused to cower before the Third Reich—was in mortal combat with the Nazi regime.

"Cheap grace means the justification of sin without the justification of the sinner.... Well, then, let the Christian live like the rest of the world, let him model himself on the world's standards in every sphere of life, and not presumptuously aspire to live a different life under grace from his old life under sin."

This is it, I thought. This is what I never understood, not since I was a child adrift in perilous family issues. To follow Jesus is to obey Jesus. Any other faith is a fraudulent faith.

Despondent, I drove at night along Puget Sound, playing over and over the New Wave songs that used to move me. I slept a lot; I woke up and immersed myself in sexual fantasies. I was caught in a cycle of feeling nothing and feeling too much. I grieved for my wasted life.

Then I got angry—first with Bonhoeffer, then with God. I saw their way as so uncompromising as to be impossible. (Two decades passed before I could summon the courage to open Bonhoeffer's book again.) Even worse than my anger toward Bonhoeffer, I felt as though God was refusing to speak to me. I tossed up prayers, and they bounced back. God had no use for me, I concluded, because of my pride and anger and lust.

I held out hope that someday I would know enough about what God wanted from me that I could obey him. So during a visit to Wisconsin, I embarked on a pilgrimage to the Brookfield Assembly of God church. The last time I'd been there I encountered something real, and I hoped that this time someone could explain it to me. I got directions from my mom and walked into the church office without an appointment. No sooner had I sat down in front of the pastor's desk than I began sobbing. I tried to explain my dilemma—that I didn't know if I was saved anymore. That my faith had been exposed as a fake.

The pastor looked at me uncomfortably, then slid a box of tissues across the desk.

"Have you ever invited Jesus into your heart?" he asked.

"Yesssss," I said, dripping tears and snot.

"Well, then," he said, in a sonorous voice, "you need to rest on the fact that you're saved."

"But…" I looked at him, silently begging for deeper counsel. I remembered the old evangelical saw: Facts, not feelings. Facts, not feelings. You can't trust your emotions, only God's unalterable Word—the Bible. I already knew all that, but it hadn't answered my innermost needs.

The pastor had nothing else to offer.

Somewhere in the space of a year or two, after graduate studies in journalism at Northwestern University and my first professional break, a job as a staff reporter at the *Seattle Times,* I came up with a plan. Really, it was the only thing I could think of: I would get baptized.

I had read in the Bible that baptism was the "pledge of a good conscience toward God." I wasn't sure I had a clear conscience, but I wanted to get one. For me, baptism was an act of desperation, my way of saying to God, "I've tried everything else and failed. Please accept this gesture, which I found in your B-I-B-L-E." I enrolled in a membership class at a Seattle church, and the class culminated in baptism. In 1988 I pulled on a white baptismal robe over my jeans and Batman

T-shirt and stepped into a basement pool still rippling after a pair of kindergarteners got immersed.

I'm not sure what I expected to happen, besides getting wet. The pastor spoke some words that didn't really register, and down I went. The water was cool as it swished around my head. When I came up, the wetness had exposed the outline of my bat wings, just as I'd planned. I had invited my three closest friends from the *Seattle Times*—Joe Haberstroh, Elizabeth Moore, and Alex Tizon—forcing myself to make public this small act. Now I waited to see if God had noticed too.

I was standing in a basement room, peeling off my wet clothes beneath an open window, hoping no one would walk by and see me naked, when a strange thing happened. I felt something totally new— what I now identify as *joy.* A brilliant substance that radiated in and around me. I had never experienced this before, and only later would I conclude that I had been baptized in the Holy Spirit, the defining event of the Pentecostal faith. Strange, but the church where I was baptized does not subscribe to Pentecostal teachings.

I was happier than I'd ever been before, and I felt like celebrating. I did what only a Wisconsin girl would do after her baptism. I partied. I went with my friends to my favorite restaurant, Campagne, where I dined on sautéed lamb and lots of fine red wine. When I stepped out onto the cobblestone streets of Pike Place Market, the wine buzz had worn off, but I still had the joy.

Naked Barbies and Intense Loneliness

I come from a long line of white people. And as anyone who's visited Wisconsin can tell you, they don't come any whiter than they do there. Set one in front of a snowbank, and you'll have trouble finding him.

My mother, Joanne, grew up in Wisconsin, but that didn't cloud her conscience or her strong moral compass. When she was exposed to a broader range of reality, she took it to heart.

As a teenager, she watched the images of Martin Luther King Jr. on her family's black-and-white television set and knew she had witnessed greatness. This man wasn't like anyone else, not even the most eloquent preachers she had heard. Something about those television images—the marches and King's speeches, the footage of teenagers like herself attempting to enter the halls of segregated high schools among jeering mobs—shook every pillar of her circumscribed world.

She lived in an all-white, working-class neighborhood on the south side of Milwaukee, and while the city had a sizable black population then and now, in her eighteen years her only contact with black people had been at high-school football games. The church she attended—full of conservative evangelical Christians—gave generously to foreign missions and occasionally hosted black musical groups, but Joanne had never in her life had a conversation with a black person, much less befriended one. She'd never been to the South, and what she saw of the civil rights movement unfolding on television astonished her. She had no idea that such hatred and injustice existed in her own country, that the tidy lessons in civics and American history she'd learned at Bay View High School had left out so much of the truth.

Watching Dr. King, Joanne had an epiphany—not unlike the day at age thirteen when she realized she was a sinner who needed to be saved and, as a gesture of penitence, threw out her entire collection of movie-star magazines. Right there in her parents' Milwaukee bungalow, with gray green fifties furnishings and tuna casserole in the fridge and a bright green Jell-O mold on the table, she concluded that Martin Luther King was right and that everything she'd been taught about race was wrong. A few years later, the portraits of activists murdered in Mississippi during the Freedom Summer of 1964—black and white young people—would etch the impression even deeper. Her life was forever upended; she'd been shaken up, caught up, moved by an idealistic notion of justice for all people.

Her first act was to shake a pale finger in her parents' faces and pronounce them racists. They didn't take it well.

She says now that if you didn't come of age in the fifties, you couldn't adequately understand how insular white America was, how an entire population of her countrymen could be victimized by racial hatred and an intelligent, inquisitive girl like herself would know nothing of it.

Joanne went off to college, and there she met other teens who were asking the same questions. "Young people were going to make the world a better place," she says. "We really believed it." Motherhood, however, would end her days as a budding university radical. Her newfound ideals were left to simmer inside. Married at nineteen to James Schuster, her high-school sweetheart and an aspiring engineer, she'd give birth to two daughters by the age of twenty-one. I was her second, Julie Brianne, born on Mother's Day in 1963. By then my mom had quit college to raise my sister, Jennie, and me while my father earned an engineering degree and went on to medical school at the University of Wisconsin.

The four of us prepared to settle in to what appeared to be a normal middle-class Midwestern life.

I grew up absorbing the paradoxes in my mother's life. She was extremely idealistic, with a righteous temper to match. While my father was more conservative politically, both of them felt so strongly that the war in Vietnam was wrong that they briefly considered moving to Canada, knowing that my father was in line to be drafted as soon as he finished medical school. We were involved in a series of strict evangelical and even fundamentalist churches, where the preachers railed against dancing, drinking, and immodest dress. From an early age I was immersed in flannel-board Bible stories, sword drills (a race in which children would try to prove they were the quickest in locating obscure Bible verses), and Vacation Bible School. I remember pulling on the same scratchy white tights all little girls wore, along with my black patent-leather shoes ("click-clicks," I called them) and the white Easter hat with the red ribbon. Our Sunday-school refrain was "The B-I-B-L-E, yes that's the book for me." We believed in good and evil, heaven and hell, and salvation through Jesus Christ alone. Living a good life wouldn't do it if heaven was your goal. You needed Jesus, plain and simple.

We were almost as strict as Pentecostal Christians—whom we viewed as our distant, decidedly kooky Christian kin—but without the speaking in tongues, the casting out of demons, and the dramatic visitations of the Holy Ghost. Still, my parents danced and drank in moderation—practically a given for Milwaukee families of German extraction—and my mother, a beautiful redhead, occasionally wore miniskirts, something that got her kicked out of one Baptist church we attended. (Mom would laugh hysterically when, years later, she came across a crudely illustrated Christian tract titled "The Miniskirt Speaks." Apparently the stern warning had failed to persuade her.)

A subversive streak ran in my mom's family, and the moral excesses of our fellow evangelicals were often the crux of the jokes we told. My Grandma Gray, whom my sister and I called Nerk, still laughs about spiking bowls of church punch with vodka. Her fellow church members would rave about her punch, then ask for the recipe; my grandmother provided it, of course, but without the crucial ingredient. When her friends would come back later complaining how it just wasn't the same when they made it, my grandma would play it cool.

I remember my mother's hauling me along to Vietnam War protests, where she stood off to the side, joining with the demonstrators in spirit. One time she hustled me away when a squad of gay activists walked past; she thoroughly disapproved. Ironically, my father ended up near the front lines in Vietnam anyway—but he reasoned that, as an army doctor, he had made the conscionable choice. In my bedroom, along with my blue-flowered canopy bed and collection of plastic horse models, my mother had pasted up a huge antiwar poster, which I never liked, though I was with her in sentiment—because she was my mom and I idolized her. Along the way, as I listened to my parents debate religion and politics, I acquired something I later found to be unusual among my theologically conservative brethren: a tendency always to examine, to reevaluate, to wonder if we really were living out our faith in the pattern set by Jesus.

As a young child, though, I simply believed. When a Sunday-school teacher at Middleton Baptist Church near Madison, Wisconsin, directed her four-year-old pupils to bow their heads and invite Jesus into their hearts, I did just that. Afterward I went tearing through the church basement with a toy vacuum cleaner. It is, in fact, one of my earliest memories (although I can't quite tell you what the connection is between vacuuming and becoming a Christian). Many years later, after I had been baptized in the Holy Spirit and reflected on that day when I was four, I sensed the Holy Spirit giving his approval to that small starting point of faith.

From an early age, my parents tell me, I had a strong interest in spiritual things—along with a very tender conscience. I guess you could say I was a good kid, but that wouldn't really capture it. I believed everything I'd been taught about Jesus; I abhorred sin. And I didn't feel then or now like I was being forced into an oppressive behavioral mold. If you loved Jesus, you did what he said. It was that simple. I took to heart my elders' exhortations that it was every believer's responsibility to spread the gospel of Jesus Christ to the world.

When I think about it now, I appreciate my parents' efforts to raise me with a conscience. They instilled in me an intellectual curiosity, an inclination to question the assumptions of religion and society, yet they practiced and taught a simple, heartfelt faith. I realize that my parents were the exception. I can't think now of many other conservative Christians from my parents' generation who shared their keen intellectual curiosity and eagerness to consider alternative views.

I recall my parents holding Sunday-night small-group meetings in our home when I was in grade school. They incited impassioned discussions on politics, history, and Christian doctrine—often extending well into the night. I loved to park myself in the hallway, around a corner and just beyond view, where I'd eavesdrop on the adults. I heard about war and race and poverty and a Jesus whose words and actions were applicable to every question in life.

There was also their biting humor, which I picked up and which would get me in trouble later in life. Lutherans in Wisconsin whose churches functioned more as social centers than places of worship were dismissed by my mother as "cocktail Christians." Celebrities whose personal morality was fluid and who flaunted a lavish lifestyle, but insisted on name-dropping Jesus when they picked up some big award on television, were disposed of with an acid "all this and Jesus too." At the core of the sarcasm was a conviction that Jesus should be the center of our lives and anything less than total devotion was suspect. Any faith that exacted no price—in commitment, in conduct—was at least intellectually dishonest and at worst a self-seeking, spoiled-rotten fraud.

Forty-five years on, I can't say I've departed much from what they taught me, though I doubt they envisioned me walking out their ideals as a ghetto-trained Pentecostal evangelist.

It is one of those things that has no cause or clear beginning; in a way it is liberating just to call it a mystery and leave it at that. But at some point in my childhood I began to show evidence of a deep emotional wound that expressed itself in extreme shyness and, later, a fear of rejection and abandonment that yielded life-altering consequences. What is the origin of this wound? I have no idea.

I do remember that, in kindergarten and first grade, when I lived in Wisconsin with my mother and sister while my father served in the army, all was well in my world. I had friends, and I excelled in school. At seven, when we moved to Ann Arbor, where my father did his residency in dermatology at the University of Michigan's University Hospital, everything changed—at least that is how my memory frames it. Now I had no friends, and I suffered from crippling self-consciousness. Around anyone besides my closest family, I would stay in the background and attempt to shrink away. If someone approached me, I would fold up within myself, physically and emotionally. I seldom spoke.

I can point to a few factors that made the shyness worse. I was born with a skin disease that, in the cold climates where we lived, caused extreme scaling and permanently wrinkled hands and feet. The condition is most severe in childhood, and my classmates noticed, asked embarrassing questions, and occasionally made fun of me. I remember my sister calling me "elephant skin." It didn't help that my father was a dermatologist; rather, it seemed like a cruel joke, because little could be done about my skin except to slather on gobs of smelly, greasy lotion. I responded by always wearing long sleeves and pants, even in warm weather.

My parents' marriage had also hit troubled times. When my father returned from two years in the army, my mother didn't know if she wanted him anymore. She'd endured too many hurts by that time, and she had set aside every dream of her own to raise a family. She was creative and highly intelligent herself, and she did well as a graduate student in English literature at the University of Michigan, a hotbed of political activity in the late sixties and early seventies. I had little understanding of what was going on when I was a child, but I did pick up my father's sadness. (If I'd been older, I would have caught a clue from the fact that my parents weren't sleeping in the same bed.) They managed to work things out for a time, but damage had been done from which they'd never recover.

When I was seven there was another change that seemed to spring from nowhere with frightening intensity: I had my first crush on a girl. Her name was Stephanie, and she represented everything I was not. She was cute, with long, dark hair and stylish clothes. She was athletic, at least more so than a skinny, awkward girl like me. Most of all she was popular. In a few years, these crushes—never reciprocated—would take on a different form; I struggled with something I can put words to now: same-sex attraction.

You could say that the first revelation I had about Jesus was that he was a friend to an emotionally wounded girl with no friends. I can still see, feel, and smell what it was like to stand outside the back door of Lawton Elementary during recess, shivering in the cold. I had no one to play with, and I'd wait there for someone to open the door so a blast of air could momentarily warm me. You'd see me hunched, hands shoved in pockets, right beside the school's other outcast: an Indian girl named Abha Sangal. We never spoke. Funny how I remember her name and the pink chiffon dress she wore, so pale against her dark skin.

I dealt with the loneliness any way I could, constructing my own world through drawing, reading, and writing. My parents recall that I had twenty imaginary playmates, complete with names and distinct personalities, compared to my sister's two. I clung to my mother as well, and she was always protective of me. My mom represented everything that was good, from her compassion—I saw her literally give the clothes off her back to a needy woman one winter—to her spirituality. My father made an effort to teach me about the Bible too, and I remember one time when he sat me down on the basement couch, pulled out a medical diagram of the tongue, and proceeded to instruct me, physiologically and spiritually, about what the book of James calls "a world of evil among the parts of the body." He must have known something I didn't, because I would inherit my mother's sharp tongue.

As I got older, I did make friends. And I noticed that certain things changed with my female classmates, but not with me. They obsessed over their hair, their dresses, their dolls. I couldn't have cared less. I much preferred to play with my menagerie of tiny plastic animals, for which I built cities, minted currency, and waged wars. Hoping to spark some interest in normal girlish amusements, I think, my mother bought me Barbie dolls. I recall their names: Christie and Julia. Oddly, they were both black. Christie, introduced in 1968 by toymaker Mattel, was the first black Barbie doll, equipped with an ultramod wardrobe of lurid pinks and purples.

My mother tells me now that she was trying to instill tolerance. (If tolerance were the principal aim, though, I'd have to question why my sister's Barbie collection remained strictly segregated.) My mom would stay up all night before Christmas, painstakingly sewing outfits for our dolls. I'd open my gift, feign interest, put the outfit on my doll one time and pull it off. My Barbies were always naked. Since all I could do was change their clothes—so dull—I made plastic parachutes for them and hurled them high into trees. Naked.

My mother taught me that God loved everyone, and I should too. This precept grew deep roots—it became my firm intellectual conviction throughout childhood. But I would discover that good intentions go only so far. There was a time when my dad invited a black family to our Ann Arbor home for dinner. Dad had served in Vietnam with Dr. Brown, who that afternoon brought along his wife and daughters. I remember sitting in green lawn chairs in our backyard, eating grilled something-or-other, trying not to stare at our guests' dark skin and alien features.

We shared ice cream with the Browns, and in the summer heat it melted into little pink pools. The girls ate with silver teaspoons, and I recall the soft pinkness of their tongues, the residue of pink on the utensils. I felt revulsion for their physicality, their otherness; I wanted them to go away.

I would never eat with those teaspoons again. Despite all my mother's best efforts, I was prejudiced. Why had her careful teaching on tolerance failed to sink in? For many years this memory would make me wince. Like so many white people of my generation, I acted surprised to find the plaque of hatred in my heart.

I view things simply today, in black and white, if you will. Only Jesus Christ can dissolve prejudice. Education and legislation against racial and ethnic discrimination play their part, but you cannot legislate a change of heart. Talk of tolerance and casual contact with people of other races won't erase innate prejudice and the way many of us are conditioned to view anyone who is unlike us.

In America, virtually every white person older than thirty has grown up prejudiced against blacks to some degree. Only repentance can treat this spiritual disease. For those who've never explicitly repented of the sin of prejudice, it is only a matter of time and of contact with people who are different from them before the stain is exposed.

That happened to me, and God would pull me deeper and deeper in concentric rings of repentance.

Every afternoon in Ann Arbor, where we lived for three years, a cardinal would perch in a tree outside my bedroom window. I'd hear its call—always the same—and look outside so I could catch its dark, glassy eye. I imagined it saw me.

"Look, there he is," I told my mom. Brushing past, going about the household chores, she gave me the sort of half-tuned-in answer moms give. "It must be an angel," she said. The answer satisfied me. I couldn't see God, but I accepted without reservation that he was there. Now I had a token of his realness, this red bird. A word made flesh.

The cardinal was with me for a season. When my mother developed ovarian cancer and was hospitalized for weeks and I came home from school each day to an empty house, he was my grace, a sign to point me through. One day the cardinal must have stopped coming. Or maybe we just moved. But by then my mother had recovered, and my world had snapped back to predictability.

As I grew up, I held to the religion of certitude I'd been taught,

fundamental principles that hinged on "facts, not feelings," as any traditional evangelical Bible teacher will tell you. "Jesus loves me this I know,
for the Bible tells me so." Like every child brought up in an evangelical
or fundamentalist church, I learned this simple chorus. But by my teen
years, when my family made its last move, to Fond du Lac, Wisconsin,
where my father would launch what became a hugely successful private
dermatology practice, I would grapple with depression, same-sex attraction, and the beginning of the end of my parents' marriage.

When the hardness of life intrudes, the evangelical mantra of "facts,
not feelings" offers little comfort. In those times, you need real-world
faith, and preferably something with flesh on it.

The Belfast Terrorist

The Irish Republican Army (IRA) was hard at work again. This was the second time I'd been jolted awake by a thundering *whoomp*—the sound of a bomb exploding on the edge of a residential area in West Belfast. I sat up in bed and held my palms in front of my face. When I saw the dim outline of ten pale fingers, I concluded I was unharmed. The next morning I read that the IRA had blown up the railroad tracks near the working-class housing estate where I was staying.

A few weeks later I was sitting on a fence outside a grocery store when a car roared by with a dude leaning out the window, firing a handgun at the Royal Ulster Constabulary (Northern Ireland police) station a block away. My flat was a few hundred yards from a place where Catholic and Protestant housing estates butted up against each other, so stuff was always happening there. Despite my sleep being interrupted a few times, I kind of liked the excitement.

I ended up in Belfast because I'd been invited by a former terrorist to write his life story. But I ended up writing my own.

After I was baptized, my life took a radical turn. Something inside was pushing me to leave behind my self-centeredness and destructive habits and live a godly life. I knew I wasn't completely on my own to bring about these changes—I now had spiritual help. I had found that I could refrain from certain sins, such as impure sexual thoughts and masturbation, habits that had weighed me down for years. I didn't know this at the time, but the baptism of the Holy Spirit had given me a direct channel to God's power that was helping me resist sin. I couldn't articulate this; I simply recognized it was there.

Water baptism has a rich history in Christianity, serving as a sacrament in many Christian traditions—an act that conveys God's grace in a special way to an individual believer. And in Pentecostal circles, the baptism of the Holy Spirit imparts an anointing of God's power and spiritual gifts to a believer. But I have found that even the act of water baptism has been drained of much of its power in Protestant churches, including evangelical ones. As a child, I had been taught it was the outward symbol of an inward act, a mere sign that one had made a public commitment to Jesus Christ. Now I know there is so much more significance—and actual spiritual power—in plunging under the water to identify yourself with the death of Jesus Christ. Just as he rose from the grave with power, we do too—if we have faith.

By 1989 I was living in West Belfast, in a city that still was in the throes of the Troubles. I was there, essentially, because I was impulsive. One day I bought a classified ad asking for pen pals in *NME,* the English music weekly for exceptionally hip people. I was hoping I'd make some friends with whom I could stay when I visited England and sampled its music scene. I listed some of the bands I liked, calculated for maximum coolness, such as the Cocteau Twins and the Waterboys, and noted that I was a Christian. I netted some fascinating correspondents, but none more intriguing than the former terrorist. Keith used to be a member of a banned paramilitary group responsible for carrying out retaliatory attacks against other terror organizations. He was eventually sent to prison. (Like many other young working-class men caught up on either side of the religious and ethnic conflict in Northern Ireland, he was sentenced in the juryless Diplock courts, which achieved ridiculously high conviction rates.) Along the way, Keith became a believer in Jesus Christ.

When we started writing each other, Keith was engaged to a lovely Catholic woman named Emer. She shared his strong faith, and, of course, she was really hot.

It didn't take much persuading when Keith asked me to write the story of his life. I quit a good job at the *Seattle Times,* took three months to finish my master's degree at Northwestern University, and flew to Belfast with a suitcase containing a Bible, a tape recorder, and my prized Sleeping Bag Records letter jacket. (I loved Jamaican dancehall reggae before it became irredeemably crude.) I boarded a TWA 747 wearing the same Batman T-shirt I was baptized in.

I was planning to spend enough time in Northern Ireland to write a book and become famous, but my agenda quickly fell apart. Not long after I arrived and moved in with Emer, certain events indicated Keith was in danger from people who knew about his past. My new friends backed out of the book project, and for a while I was devastated.

I let go of a dream, but I gained a new understanding of God. In West Belfast, Emer taught me everything she knew about being baptized in the Holy Spirit. She had been filled with God's Spirit just like a Pentecostal, but she attended Mass and belonged to a nondenominational church. It was clear that she had a real relationship with Jesus. She had something that so many Protestants lacked—an intimate friendship with the Lord. Emer was full of joy and laughter, and she spent many hours telling me how she spoke in tongues and listened in her heart for little twinges of Holy Ghost presence and power.

Through my friendship with Emer, I was introduced for the first time in my adult life to a God who actually seemed to like me. I had been convinced that God just barely tolerated me, that he was itching to slap me for some misdeed, even the things I did without knowing they bothered him. If you're twenty-five years old and you finally learn without question that God really does like you, it's revolutionary. You're never the same after that.

I loved Emer and her contagious spirit, but I was turned off by the supreme dorkiness of this habit that some Christians practiced, known as speaking or praying in unknown tongues. The thought of suppressing my intellect and babbling unintelligibly made me extremely uncomfortable. Emer eventually pried open my prison of self-consciousness and pride and helped me become receptive to whatever God wanted for my life. It still took another year for me to get over my tongues phobia, but what the hey—lots of Christians *never* do. Evangelical theology is dominated by left-brained, linear-thinking white dudes who believe they can explain just about everything concerning God and the Bible. The thought of yielding one's tongue to the Holy Spirit—horror of horrors, *losing control*—can be terrifying to someone who grew up in that tradition.

Early in my six-month stay in Belfast, Emer was talking to me about Jesus when she saw the Holy Spirit resting on me. She had this ability, sometimes, to see a sort of light or cloud indicating God's presence. I was shocked and almost moved to tears. I could hardly believe that Jesus wanted to hang out with someone like me. You might say that Emer walked me through the steps of forging a relationship with Jesus, enjoying his presence—which I soon learned to detect—and opening the Bible not just to read a good story but to hear something from God that applied directly to my life right then and there. Many times I would pop open my Bible at random, select a passage, and begin to read. I always found comfort and direction in the words. Though "Bible roulette," as my parents called it derisively, could be deemed a rather primitive Bible-study technique, I found that it worked to the extent I had faith it would work. Numerous times I opened my Bible, felt the palpable presence of the Holy Spirit, and landed on a "word" that unlocked God's will for my immediate circumstances. Truth is, I still sometimes do Bible roulette, and I still trust God to speak to me.

My stay in Belfast was one of the best times I'd had in my life. Through Emer and Keith, I got to know a group of Spirit-filled Christians. I loved the slow pace of life in Northern Ireland, the closeness of families, and the gatherings for tea that would last till midnight in front of a coal fire. They called this warm-hearted socializing the *craic,* from a Gaelic word meaning "the best fun ever." We enjoyed many a night of good craic, and some of my hard edges got filed down as I rested in the love and companionship of those like-minded Christians.

I'd never experienced anything like this before, and I didn't want to leave.

We were watching a ceilidh—a community party—in County Donegal when the darkness dropped on me. While husbands, wives, and children did the Irish version of square dancing to the sounds of an accordion, I sat in a chair and watched them as sadness choked me. Suddenly I was overcome with regret for my broken family, for the years I'd wasted in sin, for the loneliness I'd felt just about everywhere but here. By the end of the evening I had slid into deep depression. It felt as though an incubus were crushing my shoulders.

Emer noticed what was happening. The Holy Spirit, in fact, often would give her glimpses of my heart. One time I'd gotten depressed and discouraged and had begun to walk home, planning to pack my bags and leave Belfast. Emer drove up in her car, got out, grabbed me by the shoulders, and physically stuffed me into the front seat. I wasn't offended; on the contrary, I felt loved. She loved me fiercely and wouldn't allow me to sink.

After the ceilidh, I folded into a chair at the cabin that Keith, Emer, another friend, and I had rented for a holiday in the countryside. I put my head in my hands and sat motionless. This kind of depression could be triggered by random things, like hearing an old song or smelling a certain smell—like the warm scent of my mother's clothes when I'd lay my head in her lap as a little girl. It seemed as though I had no control over the darkness. It could grip me for days at a time.

On my job at the *Seattle Times,* these precipitous mood swings had earned me a reputation as a talented head case. My performance was wildly inconsistent. I could write a page-one story that garnered praise from seasoned colleagues, then struggle mightily over a stupid ten-inch story about a meeting of a suburban sewer board. Here in Belfast and Donegal, the attacks of depression were particularly severe, even though most of the time I was as happy as I'd ever been.

On the night after the ceilidh, as I sat frozen in a chair, my friends did something no one had offered to do before: they prayed. Keith and Emer laid hands on me and called on the Holy Spirit to break a curse of hereditary depression on my life. Within moments I was filled with joy. I thought I saw a vision of wispy figures with dimly colored faces scurrying away. I didn't show much of an outward reaction, but I knew something had snapped inside me.

I would never suffer from that kind of depression—independent of circumstances—again. The only thing that came close was the brief bout of postpartum depression I experienced when my son was born. That, I believe, was purely chemical, and it quickly disappeared as my hormones stabilized.

Delving into my family tree, I found there was a history of despondency in my family. My maternal grandfather, whom I've never met, was a Congregational minister with a dark side. His two sons committed suicide in separate incidents. One of his daughters tried to take her life in an attempt that was serious enough to land her in a coma. I had watched my mother fight depression while I was growing up.

The truth is, without Jesus' love and care, I would be mentally ill today. I exhibited many of the traits of bipolar disorder in my early twenties. As I developed a closer relationship with Jesus, all those harmful characteristics gradually faded. I did retain my generally introspective disposition; Jesus, after all, isn't in the lobotomy business. Today, I believe depression is primarily a spiritual condition, though it undoubtedly has physiological and emotional components as well. The curse on my life was broken as though a twig had been snapped, but I still had to make a decision to put an end to the many behaviors I'd added on over the years, such as withdrawing from people, sleeping too much, and indulging excessively in sexual fantasies. All of these were things I had used in an attempt to blunt my inner pain.

None of them, by the way, ever worked.

Belfast is not exactly the vacation capital of the world. That was certainly true in 1989, when bombings, shootings, shakedowns, and the murders of innocents were still regular occurrences. (Americans have an obnoxious habit of romanticizing the conflict. What many don't realize is that the IRA and its Protestant counterparts obtained a significant part of their revenue through running protection rackets, much like the Mafia.) So it was a little surprising when an old friend, Larry Lyons, wrote and asked if he could come there to visit.

Keith and Emer immediately began to tease me about what they presumed were his romantic intentions, but I said no way. Larry and I had met the day after we graduated from college, and he was a rugged kind of guy, a navy veteran from a blue-collar family, who'd never shown any kind of emotion or sentiment toward me. I did respect his Christian faith. After college, when I was wrestling with depression and questions about my faith, he and I would talk for hours about religion and politics. In my jaundiced view, our fellow SPU students landed in two categories: those who accepted the religion they'd been taught without question, and those who were in the process of discarding their faith. I didn't want to go either route. Larry had a fervent devotion to the teachings of the Bible, yet his life hadn't allowed him the luxury of leaving his faith unexamined. For that, I admired him. At the time, he was working for a caterer and studying at Alliance Theological Seminary, north of New York City. What I didn't know yet was that he'd been baptized in the Holy Spirit, like me.

While Larry was getting ready to travel to Belfast, his boss had a dream. She'd seen Larry standing in a calm blue sea with many other people our age, and off to the side and different from the others in manner and dress was a young woman with brown hair and blue eyes. Larry stood near the woman, and they were "with the crowd but apart from it." They understood that the woman was me, which I've always found kind of funny, because God evidently deposits me in dreams with my natural hair color. (Me? I'm not even sure what my natural hair color is anymore.)

So Larry arrived late one night, dropped his duffel bag, and promptly fell asleep on Emer's living-room floor, snoring loudly. Emer looked at me from her overstuffed chair with a silly grin. "Hmm," she said. "I wonder about that Larry..."

I shook my head. "Nah," I said.

Two months later we were engaged. But not before I staged a temper tantrum with God. One afternoon I was alone in Emer's flat reading the Bible, when I landed on some obscure psalm—probably one of those where David is calling down curses on every man and beast that had ever raised hand or paw against him—and I thought I heard the Holy Spirit telling me that I would never marry.

I squinted and read the verses again. Indeed, I concluded, God was saying that I, who struggled mightily with strong desires and sexual temptations, would live a celibate life as some sick test of my devotion to God.

I was ticked off big-time, and I got a little dramatic. I tossed my Bible across the floor in protest. It skidded to a halt, undamaged, and then I started to cry. I can laugh at it now, but at the time I was shattered. I was committed to taking God at his word, and I believed he'd given me a clear message. I dried my tears after a while, facing what I figured to be a bleak, sex-starved future of sacrificial service to the Lord. I apologized to God and said in a weak voice, "I'll obey you...but I don't like it."

Looking back, I see how God graciously accepted my imperfect gesture of obedience. It was really about the best I could manage. Obviously I misinterpreted that psalm, whichever one it was. Anyone can tell I would have made a lousy celibate.

If this was a test, though, and I believe it was, God in his grace had judged me as being willing to sacrifice for him and to obey him. At least I had been real about it, though perhaps a bit whiny.

I got a ticket to fly home to Milwaukee just before Thanksgiving, a few days before my visa ran out. I cried. Emer cried. As soon as I got on the plane, one of its wing tips fell off. So I got to sit on the plane for an extra hour and cry some more.

I had left everything behind to go to Belfast. Now I returned with no money, no job, and a boyfriend who couldn't afford an engagement ring. (He ended up proposing to me over the phone.) None of this bothered me too much; I was full of faith and expectation. I pulled together a résumé and started applying for newspaper jobs all over the country. The first place to bite was Dallas, a city I'd never even visited. They flew me down in January 1990, and I remember standing on the hotel balcony, looking at the neon-lit skyline from the city's oil-boom days and marveling that it was 70 degrees in the middle of winter. Back then, if you were relatively inexperienced like I was and got offered a metro-desk job at a big-city daily, you took it. Even if it meant going to a place like Detroit or Dallas. So I signed on as a crime and general-assignment reporter for the *Dallas Times Herald,* the smaller of Dallas's two dailies. The plan was I'd work there until our August wedding, Larry would join me in Dallas, then we'd stick around for about a year so we could pay off our debts.

It didn't work out anything like that, of course.

I was in my Dallas apartment in 1990 when I listened to a cassette tape in which a Bible teacher was explaining the baptism of the Holy Spirit. The teacher was Francis MacNutt, a former Catholic priest and pioneer in a major spiritual renewal movement in the Roman Catholic Church. He taught about speaking in tongues, and at the end, after praying for the intervention of the Holy Spirit, he invited listeners to give it a whirl. I did, and I spoke in tongues for the first time.

At work I sat near a talented reporter named Scott Baradell, and he ended up doing some groundbreaking investigative stories on Dallas-based Pentecostal televangelist Robert Tilton, whose ministry would soon become infamous for plucking the donations out of donor envelopes and throwing the prayer requests in the trash. Tilton was a theatrical guy in the pulpit, and Baradell insisted that when he spoke in tongues during a television broadcast, it sounded like "pepsicola-pepsicola-pepsicola-pepsicola…"

For all I know, my initial attempts at tongue-talking sounded like "pepsicola" too. It would be years before I could freely exercise that gift.

I passed another spiritual milestone shortly before I got married, when a Christian counselor in upstate New York administered the one and only premarital counseling session Larry and I received. During our meeting, Arline Westmeier calmly prayed to break a curse of sexual perversion on my family. I don't recall how it came up; I might have mentioned that a disproportionate number of extended family members had been involved in aberrant sexual behaviors, including several gays and lesbians from an era in which such a lifestyle would have been dangerously taboo. I didn't reveal that I'd struggled with same-sex attraction myself. I was so ashamed of my fantasy life that I hadn't told a soul, including Larry. I'd never acted on this attraction by getting involved in a romantic or sexual relationship with a woman, but it was still there, a frightening force that consumed my thoughts.

I don't know if I can point to an obvious aftereffect of Dr. Westmeier's prayer, but I believe I was just healthy enough in soul and spirit to get married and stay that way—just enough. As I write this, eighteen years after our wedding, Larry and I are still together and enjoying our marriage more than ever before. But a big part of our success came from our decision to become an integral part of a church family. At The Body of Christ Assembly, there are people who love us enough to tell us the truth about ourselves.

Working the Word of God

"You gotta hear the Word, girl," Sister Diane Eddington told me, loudly, as we faced each other on the front lawn of The Body of Christ Assembly.

Larry and I hadn't been attending church as regularly as we could. Part of it was the length of the services; not a few of them clocked in at five hours, Sunday school included. I could only cross and recross my legs, drum my fingers, and wiggle my feet so many times. But the bigger part was just plain laziness and lack of discipline. At home, I could lie around with my husband or watch a football game or eat a leisurely bowl of Cocoa Puffs. It was so much easier when you didn't go to church. At least until your spiritual life started falling apart.

"You need the Word so you can stand on the Word," Diane continued, drawing out the *o* in Word.

I guess it was a sign that I was accepted, the day Sister Diane chewed me out. It was such a vivid contrast to the traditional churches I grew up in. There, you never confronted anyone.

I was a headstrong person, to say the least, and a bit of a know-it-all—an unfortunate family trait. I didn't see my pastors, Fredrick and Diane Eddington, as inferiors, but I was blissfully unaware of my sense of cultural superiority. I figured God had sent Larry and me to help spruce up this backwater congregation, to instill some theological correctness. After all, I had years of advanced flannel-board studies behind me, and Larry had two years of seminary. I remember a Bible study led by Pastor Eddington in which Larry spent the entire eighty minutes rustling through his New American Standard Bible, the tone-deaf but achingly literal translation favored by many conservative seminarians, looking for proof texts that refuted what the pastor was teaching. From time to time Larry's hand would dart up, and he'd offer some argument. Finally the pastor gently reproved him. "Maybe you should listen," he said, "instead of flipping through your Bible."

The two of us must have been a frustrating mix of unrealized potential and in-your-face obnoxiousness. Sister Diane assures me it really wasn't that bad, but I kept a journal in those early years, and I can only read tiny snatches before I get disgusted with myself.

More than anything, I was a spectator. I didn't muddy myself with the mess of people's individual lives. I looked at Larry, who had an extensive knowledge of Scripture, including all the minutiae so favored by evangelical Christians—like the names of Father Jacob's concubines—and saw him as the guy who was going places. People in the church joked that he had black ancestors. When I ask them why today, they just smile. But it probably had something to do with his curly hair—it grows out in a 'fro—full lips, and…well, let's just say he didn't have any difficulty adjusting to the decibel level at The Body of Christ Assembly. He fit right in.

Me? They said I had no black ancestors. None.

I also committed a few dreadful faux pas that further cemented my excruciating whiteness. Once I referred to a church member's sister as "the one with the nappy hair." I'm lucky I didn't get a backhand across the face, though the man's eyes did get real big. I didn't know that to refer to a black woman's hair as nappy was extremely insulting and, in many people's childhood experiences, a racial epithet as well. Where I grew up, in the land of white people, it carried a completely different meaning—a certain type of wavy hair texture that also is found among Anglos.

Then there is the word *funky,* which many white people—as well as younger blacks who've spent a lot of time around white people—use as an adjective for something offbeat and unconventional. Hey, James Brown used it, didn't he? (What I didn't know was that he probably had in mind the original meaning: the odor of sex.) Larry and I, in our ignorance, misused that word more than a few times; we even applied it to the church building. Once I became attuned to the word's less-savory associations, I banished it from my vocabulary forever.

Male-female relationships were another area in which my dazzling whiteness shone through. I was convinced back then that a man and a woman could be friends and nothing else, in a completely platonic relationship. But in South Dallas, there was a nonnegotiable belief that there is no innocent context whatsoever for a close friendship between a man and a woman, unless they are married to each other. Ghetto rules—and black Pentecostal rules, for that matter—always assume that something is going on.

I decided that people who held this view were being unreasonable. I sniffed indignantly when I heard that one of Diane's relatives thought I sat close to my husband because I was afraid other women would steal him. (I actually sat close because I was shy, and Larry was my social surrogate.) Well, two decades of experience later, I totally agree with the ghetto rules. Ninety-nine percent of the time, something *is* going on. It's just that white church folks act surprised when the truth comes out. Black Christians already figured it out.

Through our many missteps we were treated with kindness at The Body of Christ Assembly. People tried to understand us, and we tried to understand them. All of us realized at some level that the bond of the Holy Spirit was stronger than the bond of color, but becoming a spiritual family takes time and trials. There are no shortcuts, and a footwashing ceremony here and there plus a statement of public repentance for the accumulated sins of white people won't do it.

Sometimes I wonder why Diane put up with me. She persisted in being friendly, even when I was not, and even when the differences in our backgrounds, educations, and spiritual traditions were laid bare. She would call me, leave Scripture verses on my answering machine, pull me aside at church and encourage me—or rebuke me. Now I know that this is real love—sisterly love—and I recognize that it is exceedingly rare, even in the church world. Diane was giving me a gift that no one else had ever offered me.

I recently asked her what she saw in me. She took me back to that first time I came to her house to interview Pastor Eddington, when she walked across the carpeted room once and hardly said a word. I thought she was suspicious of me. Instead, she was sitting in her bedroom, and the Holy Spirit told her, *She's here for you.* Diane would recall those words when people whispered behind my back or secretly opposed Larry and me. Instead of being swayed by the few people who found me annoying and distasteful and of suspect motives, she made her own decision: "I had to get to know you for myself."

Pentecostalism is the religion for basket cases. I've known for most of my life that I fit in that category, and I have gradually developed an appreciation for how God brought me to a place where the diseases of my soul could be healed. I'd been brought up in a faith tradition that emphasized Bible knowledge, superficial piety, and paying a few religious professionals (badly) to do the work of the Lord in our stead. At The Body of Christ Assembly, I was confronted with a crucial reality: the sin in my life put me in exactly the same place as the men and women sitting in the pews with me. Many of them had gone through catastrophic failures, such as drug addiction or lives of crime, but we'd now given our lives to a God who commanded that we "be holy, because I [God] am holy." My little exaggerations and deceptions were just as disgusting in God's eyes as the violence of a sexual predator. And all the biblical trivia I'd acquired over the years meant nothing if I didn't believe it and work it just like Jesus did.

Worshiping alongside black Pentecostals, I realized that for them the Bible wasn't words, it was *the Word.* The Bible was not a collection of interesting stories and rules and statements. It was the way to *live*—wisdom and direction and comfort and help. It was God speaking directly to them. They had little interest in debating the finer points of theology since they had real needs and burdens and questions to be answered. Their faith was real, and the Bible spoke to them personally. I learned to love the bracing simplicity of black Pentecostal spirituality.

White evangelicals fight over things like the inspiration of Scripture. They contend that if we doubt that every single word of the Bible came straight from the mouth of God, we also will be slack in submitting to the authority of the Bible's rules. They have coined words to clarify their stance on just how strongly they believe in the full inspiration and authority of the Bible. Black Pentecostals don't weary themselves with such bickering, yet you will not find a group of Christians with greater confidence in the authority of Scripture. They rarely even use the word *Bible;* that would diminish the status of this living, breathing substance known as the Word of God. It's not a book, it's God speaking. Today. They don't split hairs, they listen for God's voice in the Word and then they let it change their lives.

This Word of God in writing is wound inextricably in Jesus himself; you couldn't say where one begins and the other ends. "In the beginning was the Word, and the Word was with God, and the Word was God," according to the first verse of the gospel of John. Black Pentecostals take from this an understanding that is both elementary and profound. God, they tell you, created the earth with a Word; Jesus cast out demons and healed the sick with a Word. The Word is not a body of information that is typeset and printed and bound into a book, to be passed on through lectures and methodical teaching. It is the essence of Jesus himself. And it's some powerful stuff.

One Sunday morning I was sitting in my usual pew, in a dark corner where few people sat. (There were two sets of pews facing a small stage made of thin plywood that bounced and bowed as the choir did its thing. One set of pews was on the north side of the sanctuary, where Larry and I usually sat, and the other set was on the west side.) I happened to glance at the other side of the room and saw a large rat sitting under the second row of pews. It just sat there contented and calm, watching through rodent eyes as the pastor preached. Me? I kind of freaked. I made big eyes at the pastor and pointed frantically at the rat.

Pastor Eddington seemed a little annoyed. He didn't stop the flow of preaching but looked at me and looked at the rat, like, *And?* Then he abruptly stopped. "In the name of the Lord Jesus Christ, I curse that rat!" he said sharply.

Now, of course, all eyes were on the rodent, and a few of the ladies gasped and scrunched their legs together, which sent the rat scurrying off into the curtained back room. There it no doubt found refuge in the array of junk that the church stashed there, including piles of used clothing that even the poor did not want and an old organ that was always broken.

I managed to make it through the service with just the occasional glance at my feet to ensure that a rat wasn't chewing on them.

When we came back to the church on Tuesday night for Bible study, we opened the doors and there was the rat, in exactly the same place under the second row of pews. Except it was belly up. Dead. There wasn't a visible mark on its body, and we hadn't gotten around to buying rat poison yet. Though we would later.

I don't doubt for a moment that the pastor's curse killed the rat. "Whatever you bind on earth will be bound in heaven," Pastor Eddington often would say, repeating Jesus' words. "Whatever you loose on earth will be loosed in heaven." Pentecostals use this statement of Jesus to bind up evil forces. In other words, to call down the power of God to protect a person from the attacks of Satan's spirits. I grew up in churches that would consider such a thing overly simplistic, naive, or presumptuous. But what if Jesus meant exactly what he said? What if we started taking him at his word instead of discounting his teachings as admirable ideals or metaphorical speech?

This gets to the core of Christian faith. In a black Pentecostal church, faith is an obvious and powerful thing. You believe the Word of God in its naked simplicity, and then you act on it. That is faith. "If you hold to my teaching, you are really my disciples," Jesus said. "Then you will know the truth, and the truth will set you free." Pentecostals believe that Scripture is more than inspired words straight from God. They believe it is *a living entity,* the Word with a capital *W,* and when the words on a page or scroll are mixed with Holy Spirit–derived insight, we can obtain something called revelation—a Word from God that applies precisely to the *here and now.*

That's why you won't find black Pentecostal preachers spending hours in the church study, typing up that Sunday's sermon, and that's why they prefer to call a sermon the "message," and that's why they often eschew notes in the pulpit. The aim is that they impart a revelation from God, not a learned discourse on, say, the motif of new wine in Scripture. Not that there's anything wrong with that. But in a church where you've got people addicted to drugs, people who've made an utter wreck of their lives through sin, tidy lessons and general exhortations to do good and read your Bibles daily just aren't gonna cut it. You need to hear straight from God, because a timely Word could deliver someone "from death to life."

These revelations cannot violate or supersede the written Word of God, which holy rollers accept as the perfect revelation. But hearing from God today is the basis for the Pentecostal understanding of prophecy, one of the most important supernatural gifts of the Holy Spirit. Prophecy is intertwined with other revelatory gifts mentioned in the Scriptures, such as the ability to discern evil spirits and exercise words of knowledge and wisdom. The distinctions among the various spiritual gifts tend to blur, and you might see several of them in operation at the same time. What they all share is a basis in divine insight, or revelation.

Black Pentecostals also believe that you tap into real, robust spiritual power through the practice of "testifying about the goodness of God." Now some of these testimonies track a rote formula, which anyone familiar with the Church of God in Christ can tell you: "I give all honor and glory to God, and to his Son, Jesus Christ, and to the pastor and First Lady, and to all the elders and missionaries on the roster. I thank God for waking me up this morning and clothing me in my right mind. I thank God for saving me and filling me with the Holy Ghost, and that with fire. Pray that I grow stronger in the Lord."

Pastor Eddington didn't see much value in testimonies such as these. But he understood, with a literal application, what is said in the book of Revelation: "They overcame him by the blood of the Lamb and by the word of their testimony." Especially for people who were new converts, or folks coming out of particularly devastating sins that involved entire lifestyles, the act of testifying in church wagged a finger in the devil's face and boosted the faith of the person giving the testimony. "Faith cometh by hearing, and hearing by the word of God," black holy rollers always say, quoting Saint Paul in his letter to the Romans.

Diane used to have this little message on her answering machine: "The Word of God works," she said, "as long as you work it." And one of the very first things the pastor told me when I visited the church as a worshiper was that it was of utmost importance that I "continue in the Word." Quite a few people got delivered from something that had been plaguing them, and then they walked away from the church. Only a handful stayed "under the Word," thereby experiencing all the benefits of belonging to Jesus Christ. That Word tended to cut both ways, building you up one week and exposing a slippery spot in your character the next. Not everyone welcomes that second part of divine revelation.

Throughout the nineties, we would often troop to other Pentecostal churches for special evening services or choir events, and one night we went to a Church of God in Christ south of Fort Worth. As was usually the case, my husband and I were the only white people there. At the end, Elder Floyd G. Taylor, a respected pastor who led Heavenly Gospel, a large Church of God in Christ congregation, was laying hands on people and praying for them. I'd never met Elder Taylor and at the time didn't even know who he was, though he was a prominent figure on the black church scene.

He put his hand on my forehead, closed his eyes, and proclaimed in a raspy voice, "Your ways please him." I'll never forget what Elder Taylor said next. I would encounter many trials, he prophesied, but the answer to every one of them was readily available to me. "It's in the Word," Elder Taylor said. "It's all in the Word."

When I bowed my will to that simple word of prophecy, trying to tap into the living meaning in every Scripture passage, I found that Elder Taylor's words were absolutely true. The Bible offers help and guidance, not just history or information. Hearing from God doesn't depend on how much you read or whether you've learned a good explanation for what exactly happened to that big pile of foreskins at Gilgal. There was only one pertinent question: did I believe what I knew? Would I take Jesus at his word and run with it, or would I spend another decade sitting on a pew absorbing gobs of information?

I wanted to take Jesus at his word, and I wanted to experience all the power that his Spirit makes available to us.

The Holy Ghost and Fire

When you set foot in a holy-roller church, you enter a supernatural world. Even if you don't believe in such things, take my word for it. When you are among Pentecostal Christians, you're in a different realm.

For starters, there's God. When Pentecostal Christians gather for worship, they don't doubt that God is there. And he isn't there in some spectator role. He's front and center, the star of the show. And he has a speaking part.

I mention this because God is a supernatural God. He's on the move, he's active and involved, he's doing things. In many corners of Christianity, including the ones I grew up in, Christians prefer to keep God safely contained in their rituals and dogma and confessions of faith. They like to say and believe all the right things, but they prefer to keep God himself on the sidelines. They feel more comfortable when he remains an idea or theory. And on the rare occasion when God shows up at one of their meetings and shakes things, it makes everybody ill at ease.

The Christians who influenced my faith when I was coming up didn't seem to be all that interested in a supernatural Jesus, the guy who cast out demons—lots and lots of them—raised the dead, healed the sick, and made a fig tree shrivel up by cursing it. That might have been acceptable back in the first century, but we were modern people. We knew better than to expect such goings-on in our day.

Demons, for instance, were easily relegated to the superstitions of benighted brown peoples living in developing nations who, theologically speaking, supposedly couldn't find their backsides using both hands. They were "a mile wide and an inch deep" in doctrinal thinking, or so the stereotype goes. We "enlightened" Christians understood that biblical references to demons were the way premodern people explained things like epilepsy, mental illness, neurological disorders, and the like. But today, looking back at the biases of my childhood Sunday-school teachers, it doesn't take a genius to see that some of this thinking is rooted in Eurocentric bias and racial prejudice. I'll throw in another factor: a need to discount the spiritual experiences of other Christians who had something going that we weren't experiencing in our own church circles.

Pentecostal Christians see things differently, literally. Every part of a holy-roller service is designed to move people into the supernatural realm. You praise Jesus not to adhere to a religious ritual or because it's expected, but because, as the Bible says, God inhabits the praises of his people. If you are a congregation of believers who really do expect God to show up for church, you do the thing that invites him to participate. You praise him.

Likewise, among Pentecostals, prayer is not rote recitation or obligatory lip service. It's highly personal, even intimate. You pray to get yourself right with God and to present your requests to him, fully believing that God will listen. He will care deeply about your needs and struggles, and he will answer you with the kind of friendly intimacy conveyed in the old black congregational song, "Jesus on the main line, tell him what you want..."

And then there is the preaching, which is lengthy, passionate, energetic, and convicting. Pentecostal preachers don't preach to entertain or to impress the audience with their knowledge. They preach because it literally imparts faith to those who are listening, because the Spirit of God takes the words of Scripture from the preacher's mouth straight to the hearts of those in the congregation.

There are also acts that might seem ceremonial or ritualistic, such as laying on hands, but which are in truth acts of passing on the power of God to another person. You lay hands on people and invoke the power of God not only because Jesus' apostles did it, but because you're operating in an invisible spiritual dimension that is just as real as what you see with your physical eyes. No one has to talk a Pentecostal Christian into believing in God's power. If God is God, and he is, then his power is assumed. And if God shows up for church, which he does, then he brings power with him.

When Larry and I joined The Body of Christ Assembly, we had to confront a lifetime of our own religious biases and move past our limited spiritual vision. You don't realize how tightly you are tied to prescribed ways of doing things until you join a church that isn't. And people who believe in "the Holy Ghost and fire," who operate in the power of God's Spirit, can intimidate those who don't.

In 1990, when I decided to write a feature story about a church where crack addicts were supernaturally healed, I expected to find a church that prayed for such healings. But I didn't anticipate that helping addicts escape their dependence on drugs would involve confronting demons. Pastor Fredrick Eddington approached most addictions as though they were the work of evil spirits. He would cast out crack demons and alcohol demons, commanding them to leave "in the name of the Lord Jesus Christ and by the power of his blood." He also discerned sex demons, meaning that he supernaturally detected their presence, though not many people sought prayer for those.

The act of discerning through the Holy Spirit, he says, is difficult to describe in words. "Usually at the time I'm praying for a person," he says, "it just pops into my mind"—meaning an impression about the specific nature of the spirit. "Sex demons are a little different. There is usually an odor I pick up—a real foul odor. There is nothing I can liken it to. I used to have to fight back vomiting, and I tried to cover it up, because nobody knew what I was going through." Many years later in Africa, Pastor Eddington would come across demons of witchcraft. "When I approach someone to pray, there is often something visual that I'm not sure other people notice, like with the witchcraft spirits I encountered," he says. "The mouth would shut tight and the chin would curve to the side. It happened each time."

Pastor Eddington's experiences reminded me of something unusual I came across when I was working as a crime reporter: quite a few crack users told me how the drug would talk to them, enticing them, bringing to mind the delicious anticipation of every step of getting high, from fingering the cash to buying the rock to lighting it. Their descriptions were sensual, almost sexual. They were lured by the elaborate seduction of a demon whore.

Pastor Eddington doesn't dismiss the value of traditional drug-treatment programs. But interestingly enough, none of the people I know who got freed from drug addictions through his prayers had ever gone through a program.

If you're tempted to think Pastor Eddington overspiritualizes the problem of drug addiction and that he overlooks the physiological explanation for the problem, let me tell you about demons introducing themselves. I have been present when the pastor has prayed and laid hands on someone, and a demon would manifest, or become exposed. I saw a dude flop like a fish on the floor—up and down, up and down, up and down. More typically the person would begin jerking and twitching, often physically pulling away from the Christians who were praying. The reason behind this was obvious, from a black Pentecostal perspective: the demon didn't want to be cast out of the person. If the spirit could get the person to run out of the church, that was one way to forestall being cast out. More than once we saw a person who was being prayed for streak from the altar to the exit. It was common for a person to begin walking backward, jerking and twisting the entire time. Sometimes we just got behind them and blocked their progress toward the door.

Then there were demons that *didn't* try to escape because the person wasn't ready to let the unclean spirit go. If a demon-oppressed person wasn't willing to give up the sin attached to the evil power, such as drinking to excess or indulging in illicit sexual relationships, then the demon might fake it. The demon would manifest in some way, usually during prayer, and the person's agitated movements would calm down after a while. But there was no resolution to the casting-out process, no sense of peace in the individual—something an experienced altar worker would notice. When a demon did leave—often with a shout, a scream, or vomiting—we would always pray over the person, "pleading the blood of Jesus," because the blood of Jesus cleanses, purifies, and protects. We would ask the Holy Spirit to bring restoration and peace to the person's soul, and we would strongly encourage the individual to confess the name of Jesus out loud, indicating he had made Jesus the Lord of his life, above any evil spirit.

In movies, demon possession and exorcism are dramatized to create a maximum impact of horror. Often, a priest is called in to cast out the demon—using a centuries-old formula or rite dating back to the ancient church. But among Pentecostal Christians, casting out demons is not a ceremony; it's God's power going to war against the spirits that serve Satan's purposes. When Pastor Eddington rebukes a demon in the name of Jesus Christ, he isn't employing some primitive exorcism rite. He uses the name of Jesus Christ because there is power in that name when a follower of Jesus wields it against evil.

After I got involved in The Body of Christ Assembly, I learned that Diane Eddington has a special ability to detect spirits. Like her husband, she, too, can often smell an evil spirit. Pentecostals call this the gift of discernment, and it's a necessary weapon in spiritual warfare. The person who has this ability can identify the specific demonic spirit, though sometimes the spirits identify themselves when they are asked. (At The Body of Christ Assembly, however, we're not in the habit of asking spirits to do this. We don't believe in carrying on conversations with demons, which are, after all, agents of Satan, the Father of Lies. We don't trust them or the information they supply.)

Demons are like predators. They circle like cowardly hyenas and pick off the sick and the weak. Then they devour their prey from the inside out. One time I saw an older female pastor—a visiting evangelist—cast out a spirit of seduction from a woman. The woman spoke in a growling, guttural man's voice—really, very much like the voices used in horror-movie portrayals of demons. The woman contorted her body into extreme backbends and was thrashing so powerfully that several men were needed to restrain her.

It's important to make a distinction between demonic *possession,* which isn't all that common in our experience in the United States, and demonic *oppression.* The latter is a demonic force that essentially sits on its victim, tormenting her by attacking her mind with destructive thoughts and delusions. Depression is a vivid example of this. The delusions are built on lies, such as no one loves or cares about you, your life is bleak and hopeless, and so on. It's a spirit that weighs a person down, steals her hope, and directs the person toward darkness, doubt, and destruction.

I know about this firsthand, because at one time I was oppressed by demons of depression and suicide. But because I belonged to Jesus Christ, there were limits to what the spirits could do to me. Their influence did not outweigh the work of the Holy Spirit, who lives inside me. I would feel the flirtations of these evil spirits as they brushed against my soul, inviting me to touch them, to crack open the door for them. They were so real, their suggestions and insinuations so familiar, so reasonable, that I often allowed them to linger there. But when I was "under" darkness, a hug from a friend could dispel the depression instantly. Then through prayer, as well as through expressions of love by friends, the forces could be held at bay until their power was permanently broken.

I know that many will conclude that I'm in denial or naive to think that depression is something that comes from Satan and can be cured through prayer and the kindness of a loving friend. I'm not suggesting that all depression is the result of demonic oppression, nor am I opposed to professional counseling. But in my personal experience and the experiences of many people I know, spiritual oppression is the cause of deep despondency and debilitating depression. So many times through prayer, I've seen people experience instant relief from this spirit—it feels exactly like a weight is lifted from their bodies.

Demonic *possession,* by contrast, involves a hostile takeover of an individual. You see this in the Gerasenes demoniac described in the gospel of Luke, a man who was so crazed and violent that he had to be chained so he wouldn't hurt himself or others. When Jesus asked him his name, the demon replied—not the man—indicating total possession by spirits.

You don't have to believe in demons, or even entertain thoughts about them, to be possessed by one. You can be an atheist, a skeptic, a neo-pagan, an intellectual, or even a nominal Christian and have a demon. People acquire demons through repeated, willful wrongdoing, including such "mild" forms of sin as a lack of forgiveness toward others that is allowed to fester for years. Then there are more direct ways of entertaining evil spirits, such as through practicing voodoo, witchcraft, divination, and the black arts.

And then there is the tragic experience of many who were afflicted by a spirit after being sexually violated by a person who had some type of sex demon. Often, the victimizer is a person who should have been protecting the victim, such as a parent or a pastor. Satan sometimes uses an adult to victimize a child, and the child can then fall victim to Satan.

How do those with the gift of discerning spirits know these things? The Holy Spirit impresses the knowledge on the hearts of those with this spiritual gift during prayer or while listening to a person talk about his problems. I once saw the word *abuse* written in my mind's eye while praying for a woman, and she later confided to me that she'd been sexually violated by a church leader.

In the nineties, and even today, South Dallas had a high concentration of drug users and the mentally ill, and we encountered demons fairly often. There are reasons why people are stuck in these conditions. And the problems can't be fixed by spending more money on social programs or by white middle-class churches sending a ministry team to the ghetto every few months, then crossing the tracks back to their own side of town. These are spiritual problems that require the power of God to break spiritual bondages that keep people addicted, mentally unstable, and in poverty.

Pastor Eddington didn't cast out evil spirits every week or even every month, and he wanted nothing to do with ministries that treated every problem as though it were caused by a demon. There are conditions that are caused by laziness, injustice, and lack of education. But we recognized that in instances where evil spirits were at the root of the problem, spiritual diseases required spiritual solutions.

The most important spiritual truth I have learned at The Body of Christ Assembly is that I can live a victorious life—meaning that with the aid of Holy Ghost power, I can gain the upper hand over sin. "It should be easier for a believer not to sin," Pastor Eddington preached many times, "than to sin."

This simple statement posed a razor-edged contrast to what I was taught growing up, which was that I was caught in a pathetic state between not wanting to sin but sinning anyway. The Christian teaching from my childhood was based, I believe, on a misreading of Saint Paul—that there is always grace from God to cover over our sinful acts, thoughts, attitudes, motives, and words. To an evangelical Christian, grace is God's unmerited favor, similar to mercy and forgiveness. We don't deserve it, but he gives it to us anyway when we mess up and then ask his forgiveness.

But to black Pentecostals, grace is that and much more. It is power over sin. "For the grace of God that brings salvation has appeared to all men," Paul wrote. "It teaches us to say 'No' to ungodliness and worldly passions, and to live self-controlled, upright and godly lives in this present age."

This insight hit me hard, knocking out my theological underpinnings. I'd been living as though there were an acceptable level of sin, and as long as I abstained from the really nasty stuff and regularly confessed my failings to God, I was doing all right. As the pastor's teaching sank in, I had to completely revise my understanding of the New Testament. Now as I read, I saw everywhere that God's expectation is that we live lives that are free from sin. It isn't an option. Holiness is, in fact, the natural and necessary outcome of a relationship with Jesus Christ. "No one who lives in him [Jesus] keeps on sinning," wrote Saint John. "No one who continues to sin has either seen him or known him." These words resounded and echoed like the heavenly creatures in the book of Revelation. The creatures could do only one thing—cry "Holy! Holy! Holy!"—when they saw God on his throne.

What does it mean to be saved anyway? I asked myself. Is it merely a handy plan to escape hell? If so, why is it that most of the Bible concerns itself with living a godly life here on earth?

Jesus, who never sinned, set the standard for our lives: we were to become his followers, people who are being "transformed into his likeness." That means we are not to sin. Dating to the beginnings of Pentecostal practice, growing out of the Holiness movement of the nineteenth century, the goal has been perfection in this life, while we still live on earth.

Diane Eddington believes that The Body of Christ Assembly witnessed an atmosphere of miracles and spiritual phenomena because its leaders and members "held up a standard of holiness." Folks couldn't "come in the church and be comfortable in their sin," she says. She and Pastor Eddington had made up their minds that they were going to "upset the devil's peace" by dealing with sin head-on. She recalls a time when a certain guest preacher took the pulpit and became deathly ill before he could give his message. The preacher left hastily to go to a hospital emergency room, where he recovered from his illness.

Diane and the pastor found out later that the woman who had accompanied the guest speaker to their church that day was actually his mistress. "God wouldn't allow him to stand up there and preach," Diane says.

The Holy Spirit, she says, will expose hidden sin in the church if the pastors and other leaders live pure lives and teach their congregation to do the same. This has been demonstrated so many ways during my time at The Body of Christ Assembly. In the early nineties there was a woman named Mica who attended the services with her young sons. Diane noticed something about Mica right away: She'd never look you straight in the eye. She'd bow her head and peep upward. After she'd been coming to the church for a while, she started bringing a man, and Diane discerned in the Spirit that they had some kind of relationship, even though they'd never sit together.

One Sunday, two women showed up for church and took seats in the back row. None of the regulars could remember having seen them before. Diane recalls, "Immediately when they walked in that building, I got an uneasy spirit. 'Oh, Lord, what is going to happen here?'" She discerned, in fact, that one of the women had a gun. The women sat very quietly through Sunday school; at some point, Mica wandered in late. She was alone. For the first Sunday in weeks, the man who had been coming to church with her didn't show up.

As the service shifted to praise and worship, the pastor asked if someone wanted to lead testimonies. Just then Mica raised her arms. Pastor Eddington said, "God wants you to lead testimony service today—come on up."

Mica walked to the front of the stage, taking the mike to officially open the service for testimonies.

In her spirit, Diane felt "Oh no."

Another church member got up and offered a few words of testimony. When she sat down, one of the unfamiliar women rose from the back row.

"I just wanted to come and see what y'all are teaching over here," she said with a note of agitation.

The whole church got quiet. Everybody knew something was up.

Diane, seated in the front row, was prompted by God's Spirit to begin praying in tongues under her breath. Something was gonna blow.

"Because y'all got a woman in this church," the lady said, her voice rising, "that's fooling with my husband, and she told my husband to leave me because I was a witch. And I had to come and see where my husband was going and what y'all are teaching, because that's not right. She's got him thinking she's so spiritual."

The precise moment she stopped talking, Mica, still standing in the front, meekly raised her hand.

"It's me, pastor," she said.

Things got deathly quiet.

The pastor seemed flustered, but only for an instant. He told Mica to sit down. "I'll talk to you after church," he said. Then, addressing the woman in the back, he said, "but you're not going to interrupt the service like that."

Then the pastor got up and preached. Diane says now, "I don't know what he preached, and I don't know that anyone could tell you what he preached. But I do know it wasn't long."

Mica slipped out immediately after the service ended, and the pastor talked to the man's wife who had stood and spoken. Turns out she and her friend had parked their car out of view of the church, which suggested sinister intentions. Pastor Eddington assured the woman that he didn't in any way condone adultery, and Mica disappeared a few weeks afterward, never to be seen by us again.

Pentecostal and charismatic Christians have spent a good deal of time debating whether speaking in tongues is the required sign of baptism in the Holy Spirit. The oldest Pentecostal denominations, such as the Church of God in Christ and the Assemblies of God, point to tongues as the initial evidence of being filled with God's Spirit. But in my experience at The Body of Christ Assembly, the sign of the baptism of the Spirit is *power*—power to heal, power to cast out demons, power to discern and speak in tongues, and power to prophesy. It is what the black Pentecostals mean when they speak of being "filled with the Holy Ghost, and that with fire." This fire burns outward and it burns inward: it is supernatural, God-given power, and it is a fire that refines a person's character and produces something pure.

Holy rollers point to a couple of pivotal verses of Scripture: John the Baptist prophesied about Jesus, "I baptize you with water.... But after me will come one who is more powerful than I, whose sandals I am not fit to carry. He will baptize you with the Holy Spirit and with fire." And just before Jesus returned to heaven, he told his disciples, "You will receive power when the Holy Spirit comes on you."

I found that the more I allowed that refining fire to burn in me, consuming my lusts and selfishness, the more I experienced Holy Ghost power. At times this was an excruciatingly painful process. Diane told me at one point, "You pity black people." She was too kind to complete the statement, so I did it myself: "But I don't love them." I was so shaken by her words that I was left with two choices: either give up on this strange enterprise of trying to be part of a black Pentecostal church or submit myself to God's refining process in my life. It was hard to try to become part of a spiritual family that looked and thought so differently from the one I was born into.

But I made my choice. I decided to burn and burn and burn.

Fakin' and Shakin'

I arrived at church for Saturday prayer to find two long legs with worn black shoes stretched out across the stage. A murmuring voice slipped back and forth between intelligible words and the slightly jagged cadence of tongue-speaking. It was Pastor Fredrick Eddington, lying prostrate, having a conversation with God. He prayed for the unsaved, for the sick and the shut-ins, for people on drugs, and for families in poverty. He waged war in the Spirit against "principalities, against powers, against the rulers of the darkness of this world," meaning the princes among the demons that deploy to places such as South Dallas.

The pastor prayed that God would draw in the damned and save them—and after he prayed, visitors would pop in out of nowhere saying a voice sent them to the church. One guy strolled in on a Sunday morning and announced that he'd been sitting in his house smoking crack, and the crack told him to kill his wife. He got up to do as commanded, but instead of murdering his spouse, he ran outside. Something drew him to the tiny white church, he said, and he decided to stop in on his way to break into a place and steal something to sell for drug money. Pastor Eddington prayed for him, and "the Holy Spirit ministered to the man," as Diane tells the story.

After the prayer, the man informed the pastor that while he wasn't going to kill his wife after all, he still needed to leave as soon as possible so he could rob that place. Well, whatever.

Then there was a tall, wiry, disheveled man named Jackson who used to wander up to the church at odd moments, but he seldom came inside. Jackson had a huge dent on the left side of his head from an apparent injury, and his attitude corresponded with the smashed-in look. One night, when he walked into a church service, it was obvious he'd been drinking. He told the pastor, "I want to confess—I got to confess."

Pastor Eddington took him aside to listen, never losing hope that God would make a change in the man. But Jackson wasn't done talking.

"I murdered someone," he said in a gruff voice.

The pastor and Jackson stepped outside the church and talked for a while, man to man, and the conversation culminated in the pastor's summoning Dallas police so Jackson could give himself up to the authorities.

An officer approached him warily. "Who did you kill?" he asked.

"Peter, James, and John," Jackson replied, naming three of Jesus' disciples and releasing a blast of boozy breath.

So much for the big confession. The officers told the pastor they'd book Jackson and let him sleep it off in jail.

"Girl, that was so funny," Diane told me. "Everyone bust out laughing."

There is something about The Body of Christ Assembly and Pastor Eddington that pulls in lost souls. A lot of wayward folk—from backsliders to lapsed ministers to the totally bizarre—sense that the pastor is somehow their brother. He doesn't try to control the members of the church, empty their pockets, or pimp their wives. He is a man of God without the unsavory overtones and baggage often associated with men of God in South Dallas.

When I joined the staff of the *Dallas Times Herald,* I worked on crime stories with a black photojournalist who'd grown up attending Baptist churches. He held a low view of the clergy. "To me," he said, "the preacher is the dude who gets the most girls." When I spoke glowingly about Pastor Eddington, my colleague would just smile and shake his head. I'm sure he thought I was a naive white girl, ignorant of what was *really* going on in the church.

It took Larry and me years to recognize how unusual the pastor and Diane really were. Not once was there even a rumor of sexual impropriety involving the pastor. Sure, there were women who hit on him, a dynamic I believe to be more common in black churches, where preachers hold a higher status in the community. (No one I grew up with in white-folks' land ever aspired to be a preacher.) One woman, whom I'll call C., must've weighed three hundred fifty pounds or more, yet after the pastor visited her in jail to try to motivate her toward a better life, she fantasized that he wanted her. All she had to do was figure out how to get Diane out of the way. She engineered various crises in an attempt to orchestrate time alone with the pastor. Diane saw right through C. and realized that the woman hated her.

Situations like this happened with distressing regularity. Diane gave hours of her time to troubled women, counseling them on the phone and in person, using scarce church and personal resources to pay their rent and utility bills and buy school clothes for their kids. I couldn't imagine a more difficult job than that of a pastor's wife, and I watched Diane perform this thankless job with grace. But she did know where to draw the line. The telephone calls in the wee hours, from women who had married men that Diane had warned against, got old. Finally she told the entire congregation, "When you go on and marry that unsaved boyfriend and he start beating your tail, don't call me up crying in the middle of the night."

Later, her admonition got more to the point: "I don't counsel sin." In other words, if you're doing wrong and suffering the inevitable consequences, make a decision to stop sinning. Then we can talk.

The Holy Spirit warned Diane that C., the woman who had a crush on the pastor, dabbled in witchcraft and intended to kill her. Diane let C. know that she was welcome to come to The Body of Christ Assembly as long as she kept her distance from Diane. That was the last time we saw C.

God had a way of weeding out folks with evil motives, though I noticed that he first gave this ragtag stream of troubled souls a chance to repent. The pastor and Diane continually confronted sin, and many,

many people weren't ready to change their ways. They couldn't take the heat and drifted away.

C., however, was in a class of her own. Back when she was attending the church, she had somehow injured her hand. During a visit by C. to the pastor's house, Diane had to accompany C. to the toilet and even yank her underwear down and back up. She did all this selflessly, and if she complained, I never heard it.

Diane told me later: "How do you think I felt with all that up in my face, and then she turn around and hate me?" One time when Diane and I delivered groceries to C.'s house when she was ill, the woman said to Diane's face: "The pastor is a kind and giving person, and you get in the way."

C. desperately needed spiritual help, but she wanted the pastor more than she wanted Jesus.

Holy rollers have a term—fakin' and shakin'—for folks who ease into church and try to impress you with their superspirituality, yelping hallelujahs at inappropriate moments, jerking and jiving and babbling in tongues for all to see. As Larry and I worked with the church, we realized people would fake their religious devotion to keep church leaders from dealing with the deep issues of hidden sin in their lives.

I never saw any of the regular members at The Body of Christ Assembly fall into spiritual phoniness. It's hard to think you're "all that" when you walk into the church on a Saturday morning and the first thing you see is a dead rat floating in a water bucket used to catch rainwater from the leaky ceiling. Or when you try to figure out why the air conditioner isn't working on a sweltering summer day, and one of your legs falls through the rotted wood floor. Or you have a guy up in the attic after Tuesday-night Bible study, trying to fix the wiring, and you hear a muffled scream from above as he crosses two live wires and nearly electrocutes himself.

You don't think of yourself more highly than you ought when you take up a collection for the building fund and net five dollars. Or when for the first time—after more than five years of service—the church establishes a salary for the pastor, at five hundred fifty dollars a month. Or when you repeatedly need to send someone to retrieve the pastor and his family from the shoulder of the highway between East Fort Worth and Dallas, because his hooptie has broken down yet again.

There is nothing ennobling or quaint about being poor. It doesn't make a person righteous or even humble. But being poor does give you a certain perspective on life, a way of confronting reality with eyes open, since you don't have a lot available to you to cushion the blow. And at The Body of Christ Assembly, reality led us to develop a deep respect for our leaders. No one could say that our pastors had become ministers of the gospel to make a buck or to manipulate people for their own prestige and selfish purposes.

One church member, Queen Victoria Curlin, recalls an episode that illustrates how Fredrick's and Diane's characters shone. One of her South Dallas childhood friends had become extremely ill with AIDS back in the late eighties when there was still much paranoia and misinformation concerning the disease. The woman was on her deathbed in the hospital, and her own pastor refused to visit her, fearing he'd be exposed to the virus. Many of her family members shunned her as well.

Victoria asked Pastor Eddington if he'd visit her friend, and without a moment's hesitation he said yes. The pastor and Diane saw the lady and prayed with her, making sure she was at peace with Jesus Christ, and she was "so happy and so grateful," Victoria says, that she wept for a long time. She died a few weeks later.

Jesus taught what the Eddingtons practice: the last shall be the first, and the person who is greatest is the one who serves. But among Christians, these words of Jesus commonly fall in the category of routinely ignored teachings. Other pastors looked down on The Body of Christ Assembly because we met in a rickety building. That would markedly change in a few years—even though we were the same men and women of God that we were back when we preached from a homemade pulpit with the occasional nail sticking out and snagging the speaker's Sunday clothes.

There is an oft-heard saying in black Pentecostal churches, appropriating the words of a fragment of Scripture that I'd never noticed before: "The gifts and callings come without repentance." It's from chapter 11 in the book of Romans, and while its context has to do with the Jews' irrevocable status as God's chosen people, holy rollers use the verse to explain why you encounter men and women in the church who appear to possess genuine spiritual gifts but have zero character. There are ministers who will dazzle you with their speaking ability and singers who can quiet a restless crowd or bring people to their feet. But when it comes to ethics and morals, honesty and integrity, these ministry leaders come up empty.

This interpretation of Romans 11:29 suggests that God gives special gifts to certain people, and the gifts are effective when practiced even though the people who possess the gifts are no longer faithful to God. God's gifts can't be denied, since he is the one who chooses who receives which gift. And even if the person who receives a spiritual gift lives in a manner that denies God's commanded way of living, the gift God gave is still valid.

From the earliest days at The Body of Christ Assembly, we observed a procession of flashy, impressive fakes—maverick ministers who couldn't stick at any other church. They saw our church as an easy mark, thinking we presented a prime candidate for a ministry takeover. They took advantage of our pastor's willingness to open his heart and his church doors to any brother, and they tried to bend his generosity to their own benefit.

Sometimes they thought they were more advanced in the Christian faith than they were, and when their deficiencies were exposed, they couldn't handle it. There was the guy who called himself Apostle. Many a Sunday-morning church service was punctuated with the *skronk-skronk* of a saxophone as he blew his rendition of "Amazing Grace." He was a man with endearing qualities; I remember the joy on his face when Larry and I took him to play miniature golf. There was a boyish sweetness that peered through at times, but something had happened along the way that made him hard and judgmental. He had been in prison, where he'd had a conversion experience and somehow acquired the title Apostle. Larry and I tried to help him out, offering encouragement and getting his saxophone out of hock at the pawnshop.

One day a friend of ours, a former pastor, came by the church, observed Apostle's judgmental attitude, and said, "That young man needs to be discipled."

Pastor Eddington tried to bring the man under the guidance and instruction of the church. The problem: how do you disciple a man who calls himself Apostle? The answer: you don't.

Apostle was adept at seeing all the flaws in others, yet his fatal character flaw—the inability to receive correction—became obvious. One time he stormed out in the middle of the message because he thought the pastor was picking on him. Larry ran after him and persuaded him to come back inside. Apostle eventually wandered away from the church, disappointed that we lacked the spiritual discernment necessary to embrace his calling.

Among Pentecostal Christians, I have seen the very best and the very worst Christianity has to offer. For just about every person I know who was delivered of drug addiction, alcoholism, or serious illness by the power of the Holy Spirit, there are the freaks and flakes who gain pulpit time to showcase their dubious messages. The more charismatic and talented among these preachers amass a considerable following. And then there are the shakers and fakers who come not to take over the pulpit but simply to make a public display of themselves—including a woman who tried to throw a punch at another person during church—under the guise of being moved by the Spirit.

There was the skinny, high-strung guy with the prodigious intellect, who, at his best, could hold you spellbound with his preaching for two hours straight as he wove strands of intricate theology and down-home storytelling. He strolled in off the street, looking for a place that would invite him to speak. He found us to be a welcoming group that was willing to help him as God worked to shape his character and his gift for speaking.

The man was estranged from his wife and kids, and once he got settled in the church and received a dose of the pastor's strong teaching on the sanctity of marriage, he decided to try to patch things up. Nothing wrong with that. I remember well when his wife came down from Oklahoma to join him for a weekend rendezvous and an attempt at reconciliation. She was a lovely woman, but you could tell she was weary of his game. Over dinner at a Mexican restaurant, she said to me, "I don't know—I just don't know."

She told me about her husband's fiery temper, saying that in the past he had abused her. Still, she harbored just a little hope that he had really allowed Jesus to work a change in his life.

Two days later, she hopped the Greyhound bus back home. I guess he hadn't changed.

He, too, would fade away from the church. The discipline of following Jesus Christ, of dying daily to one's selfish desires, was too much of a grind for him. He'd rather just preach.

And we'll never forget the "prophet" and his toothless "fiancée"— who appeared to be a neighborhood street walker. His eyes rolled in the back of his head while he delivered a "word" to Fredrick and Diane on a Sunday morning. The really creepy thing? Much of this man's prophecy came true. He said that God would prosper Pastor Eddington in the midst of an obscure and impoverished place. Some years later, it happened.

That verse in Romans 11 goes much deeper than being about successful preachers who get an oversized ego. A pastor isn't a business manager shuffling papers in a big office—he's a leader on the front lines of spiritual warfare.

When you're messing with evil spirits, who are bent on nothing other than destruction, you've got to watch your step. The spirits will search for any crack in your character, any area of unconfessed sin, looking for an avenue to mess with you. Ministers who fail to live righteously kick open the door for the agents of Satan to victimize them. By living without morals, they invite spirits to come in and wreak destruction.

This is no horror movie, it's real life. Satan is not your friend. And until the time when Jesus returns to earth, demonic forces will do what they can to drag as many people as possible with them to damnation. In the Pentecostal church world, you are continually tapping into a supernatural realm of holy and evil forces. It isn't an equal contest. God is the Almighty, and Satan will be doomed in eternity. But in the meantime it's open warfare, and those who are careless about righteousness and morality might as well stencil a big red bull's-eye on their backsides. Untold misery awaits them.

12

The Humble Voice of God

Sister Johnson had a way of cutting through the mess. I found this out after I started teaching a Sunday-school class, replacing the previous teacher who quit unexpectedly. Standing in front of a roomful of adults, I asked a question: "Why do we sin?"

Sister Johnson, who was in her sixties, piped up as soon as the last word left my mouth.

"Because we want to."

At that moment, a thousand volumes of Christian theology were rendered redundant. Innumerable sermons were exposed as hopelessly trivial. Arguments were shredded, excuses eliminated, hidden motives revealed.

Sister Johnson had spoken, and I found out she was an expert on the subject of sin, specifically "lying, cheating, cussing, stealing, back-biting, all that stuff." She volunteered that she had done it all, adding, "I didn't see no reason to stop until I had to."

Back in the days of segregation, there was a community southeast of Dallas called Joppy, spelled in various ways. If you enjoyed a long walk, you could hike from Joppy to downtown Dallas, but Joppy was another world entirely. It was cut off from the larger city by a railroad yard, the Trinity River, and surrounding forestlands. Even today it can't be seen from major Dallas streets. Joppy was a former freedman's town whose population was all black, and with its dirt roads and outdoor plumbing and paucity of city services, it resembled a village in rural East Texas.

This is where Catherine Mornes—Sister Johnson—grew up, along with her nine brothers and sisters, including Doris Jean, whom I came to know as Sister Spencer. Catherine's father, Fred Mornes, did field work and dug cesspools, then drank away much of his pay. Ruby Lee, his wife, was a domestic and the only constant in her children's lives. She married Fred when she was sixteen.

Fred Mornes abused his wife and many of his children, bequeathing as his legacy hatred and bitterness. He did his best to keep his wife away from the only place of refuge she had, the Pentecostal church, bellowing at her that she wasn't "gonna give no money to a preacher." Ruby Lee would get on her knees and pray in desperation whenever Fred abandoned his family. She loved her husband and kept taking him back. Catherine grew up watching all this, and she concluded that her father hated her.

During one of Fred Mornes's frequent absences from his family, Ruby Lee was given a three-room house by a white landlord who recognized her upstanding character and took pity on her. In this home, the finest living quarters the Morneses had ever had, the children slept on pallets in one bedroom and Mama slept in another, waiting for her husband to return. The third room was the kitchen.

When Fred Mornes heard about the new house, he grew insanely jealous. He crept inside late one night while everyone was asleep, stuffed rags and wads of cotton in the cracks under doors and windows, poured gasoline on the wood floors and struck several matches. Then he climbed a nearby hill where he could sit and watch the house burn.

A neighbor smelled smoke and promptly rounded up some men who kicked down Ruby Lee's door and helped pull her children to safety. Fred Mornes could easily have murdered his wife and children in the fire. At the time, black-on-black crimes, particularly acts of domestic violence, weren't taken too seriously by Dallas police. Mornes was sentenced to a few years in prison, and the people of Joppy felt so bad for Ruby Lee and her kids that they gave her another house, complete with furnishings.

Catherine experienced the only brightness in her life at a one-room, wood-frame Church of God in Christ. On Wednesday and Thursday nights and Sunday mornings and evenings, the sounds of electric guitar and tambourines would seep out of the building, crossing the dirt road and filling the space between the live oak trees that ringed Joppy. Catherine remembers dancing in the open fields to those joyous sounds.

Whenever she could, Catherine went to church. "At church everyone was happy," she says, "and there was nobody fussing all the time. They'd sing and shout, with all the women beating tambourines." These were holy-roller tambourines, pounded in intricate, syncopated rhythms rather than shaken, the higher-pitched counterpoint to foot stomping. The percussive rhythms and sounds arose when the saints began the "shouting," or holy dancing, on the church's rough wooden floor. A couple of times Catherine visited a Baptist church in Joppy, but "it was like being in a graveyard," she says. "Those people sit and they just talked. I couldn't even figure out why they called it a church."

On a Sunday morning in 1945, ten-year-old Catherine went to the holy-roller church by herself, and she giggled as she watched a missionary named Sister Jefferson "shouting" with all her might, jumping and jigging in front of the altar.

Today, Sister Johnson, as we all know Catherine, describes what happened next: "I was laughing because the woman was shouting so hard. Then it seems like the roof of the church just opened up, and there was a light shining on her—and there was like dust pouring down on the lady. I was sitting in a corner on a wooden pew. The next thing I knew, I was on the front pew, and Sister Jefferson was saying, 'Say thank you, Jesus.' I don't know what happened or how I got there."

Sister Jefferson knew that Catherine had an encounter with the Holy Ghost, a whirlwind force that whooshed the girl from the back of the church to the front, then knocked her out under the power of God. Like any seasoned altar worker, Sister Jefferson urged Catherine to thank and praise Jesus for touching her with the Holy Ghost.

"I was looking around—everything looked so strange," Sister

Johnson recalls. "I don't remember anything—I don't know how I got up there. I think God got me for laughing at Sister Jefferson."

Back home later that day, Catherine was scared to tell her mother about what had happened, but she eventually blurted it out.

"Do you believe you're saved?" Mama asked.

"Yes," Catherine said.

"Well, you're saved."

Just a week later, Catherine was getting ready to go crawfishing in the Trinity River with her brother Roosevelt, and she pulled on a pair of pants so she could wade into the mud and water. Sister Jefferson happened to walk by and saw little Catherine wearing trousers.

"You done backslid," Sister Jefferson said in a stern voice. "You know you ain't saved no more."

Catherine felt like she'd been slapped. The good feeling she'd had since the previous Sunday drained out of her in an instant. When she told Mama about it, her mother backed up Sister Jefferson. "You know you don't have no business wearing pants," Mama told her, and Catherine pondered how, in a matter of days, she had gone from redeemed to condemned.

"Something just fell over me like a black cloud—like something dumped on me," she says.

Confused and in pain, she went on crawfishing. She didn't catch a thing.

Much later in life, after Catherine had become a drinker, the pain was so intense, the feeling of loss so excruciating, that she searched desperately for a way to snuff it out. Her mother had passed away when she was only fifty-six, in 1966, after years of backbreaking work. She'd been the sole caretaker most of the time for ten children, working every day in white people's homes, bringing home bacon grease, jelly, and two dollars. Her husband continually mistreated her, even brought another woman into the house while she was sick in the hospital, announcing to the children that "this is your mother now." Yet she was happiest during the few occasions when Fred Mornes was happy with her—and when she was able to provide food and shoes for her children.

With her mother dead, Catherine lost the person who loved her the most. Completely sober but in deep grief, Catherine walked slowly into the middle of Grand Avenue in South Dallas one midnight, lay down in the street, drew her arms to her side, looked up at the sky, and waited for a car to run over her.

"And no one hit me," Sister Johnson says. "They just drove around me."

Catherine had failed again—this time at dying. So she returned to a life of drinking, fighting, and misery.

Looking back, Sister Johnson sees a steady downward slide after her short-lived salvation experience, rendered null and void by the common belief among black Holiness churches that wearing pants, for girls and women, was serious sin and that any willful misdeed could disqualify you from the ranks of the saved. At the age of ten, Catherine wasn't able to muster any arguments to the contrary. (Though many of the smaller and more traditional Church of God in Christ congregations still frown on women wearing pants, makeup, or nail polish, Pastor Eddington teaches that "wearing pants don't send you to hell.")

Tragedy had always seemed to stalk Catherine's family. Her brother Fred Jr., an intelligent, handsome, eighteen-year-old, showed up at home one day in 1949 with an attractive older white lady. She brought the family a gift of a crate of eggs, which she gave to Ruby Lee, and asked permission to bring Fred Jr. to live and work at her chicken farm in Wilmer, a rural town south of Dallas. Ruby Lee gave her consent, and the white woman drove off with Fred Jr.

Fred Jr. was never seen again, and the address the woman provided turned out to be fake. Ruby Lee lived the rest of her days tormented by her son's disappearance. It's quite possible, Sister Spencer says, that the woman was dating Fred Jr., an extremely dicey venture in 1940s Texas. He could have easily been the victim of a hate killing. Whatever the case, he joins the rolls of the missing among many black families with deep Texas roots. So many tell in family lore of a male relative who vanished after passing through an all-white town or mixing socially with white people.

"No one ever heard tell of him," Sister Johnson says of her brother. "Back then, a white man would hang a black man for looking at a white woman."

Catherine had found trouble of her own, growing up. She snuck her first cigarette at eight and started drinking at age eleven. She dropped out of school and careened between honky-tonks and bad relationships. The day of her mother's funeral, while she was walking down a street in South Dallas, three black men pulled up in a car, shoved her in, and drove away. "If you holler, you know I can kill you," one of the men said.

As the car picked up speed, Catherine tried to prepare herself for what was about to happen. At the very least, she'd be raped and robbed and abandoned somewhere. But she suspected much worse. "I was begging them to let me out," she says. "They said, 'Oh, we're gonna let you out.' That scared me—I knew they was gonna kill me."

One man stuffed a rag in her mouth to shut her up.

While hurtling down Highway 75 south of Dallas, the car they were in collided with another car and spun out. After the impact, the driver hit the gas to leave the scene, and at that moment Catherine threw herself out the open passenger window. Her head slammed into a curb as the car sped away. One of the men had been hanging onto her clothes, and she ended up lying in the street in her undergarments.

"God let me out of that car," Sister Johnson says. "I jumped out 'cause I figured I was gonna die anyway. That was the scariest situation in my life."

A police officer gave her a jacket to wrap around herself, and she walked away without injury.

Sister Johnson reels off the other tragedies in her family: One sister was stabbed to death by a male stalker while Fred Mornes Sr., sick and bedridden, listened to her cries—unable to help. After being stabbed, Lillie Mae left a trail of bloody handprints along the wall to her father's bed, where she collapsed and died. Their oldest surviving brother, Roosevelt, a drug addict, was found murdered in Oklahoma.

Catherine took to heavy drinking. When she drank, she raged and fought. Her ex-husband told her, "Cat, you change into a different person when you drink." Catherine believes she was influenced by an evil spirit. "I would fight anybody—with my fists, if that's all I had. I'm so glad God got a hold of me before I got killed or killed somebody."

On a Sunday morning in 1991, a tall man walked up to Catherine's door, and she saw that her sister Doris Jean was with him. She instinctively hid her cigarette as she looked out the screen door.

"Are you Catherine, Doris's sister?"

"Yes."

"You know you have to go to church today—the Lord sent me to come and get you."

"Well, I'll come next Sunday," Catherine said. "I don't have no dress to wear."

"No, you have to come today," Pastor Eddington said, smiling.

Catherine ducked into her closet. She had recently bought two new dresses, she says, but they were both too small. Now she tried one on, and it was too big. "Ain't that something," she said to herself. Before she left the house that day, the pastor prayed with her. "God reclaimed me right there," Sister Johnson says.

"I knew I needed to go to church," she explains. "I was having such a hard time. Me and my husband separated. I'd been with him thirty-some years, and he just walked out and didn't leave no explanation. Everything I did just turned to mud. I was drinking a lot. I thought I was gonna lose my mind."

Catherine walked into the church while Diane was up with the choir, singing lead.

Weeping may endure for a night,
but joy cometh in the morning.

Catherine took a seat across the church from Larry and me. She was dressed stylishly and had her hair pulled neatly into a ponytail. Tears streamed down her face.

"I remember I was sitting there in church," she says, "and I said, 'Lord, help me.' I was just so messed up in my head. And it was like something poured down on me. Everybody was up clapping and going on. I tell you, that was a wonderful day in my life. God just got me while I was there. He took away everything—my desire for cigarettes and alcohol. I smoked like two packs a day. I never had any desire for drinking, smoking, any of that again.

"I gave it to God. He took it."

As she relinquished her soul to Jesus, she heard a voice in her heart. "I could hear this voice—sound like it was coming out of me—I know it was God's voice," she says. "It was the sweetest, humble voice—ain't no voice like that voice—telling me everything was gonna be all right."

When Sister Johnson told me her story years later, she was sitting at a kitchen table in her apartment with full china place settings, every utensil precisely arrayed. A black velvet painting of a praying Jesus hung above us, a fitting image. I came to know Sister Johnson for her kindness and her prayers. She gives a hug to anyone who walks through the church doors, from the white visitors who live across town to the smelliest drunk.

Sister Johnson has transformed her loneliness into fervent prayer. She travails in the Spirit like the old saints did, rocking and wailing and crying out to God to help the troubled and the lost. The Sister Johnson I know bears no resemblance to the fighter and drinker she described to me. "When I say God brought me from a mighty long ways," she said, "the truth is he did."

At the age of seventy-three, Sister Johnson still prays on her knees, getting down in front of a couch or chair. She prays first thing in the morning, calling down blessings on the pastor and every family in the church by name. What, I asked her, had she learned through all these years of prayer? "You can't do nothing without putting God first," she said. "You think you can, but you really can't. You can get in a place in life where you can't depend on anybody else.

"And prayer," she said, "is always the answer."

13

Facing Your Own Evil

"Come out of the bushes! Come out from behind those trees!"

With giant speakers propped up in the grass and an extension cord snaking out the church's front door, we gathered on a makeshift wooden platform. Larry and I, plus about a dozen other members of The Body of Christ Assembly, were singing and preaching from the stage just a few feet from the street. It was Saturday afternoon, and my husband was calling out to men and women who ducked behind the overgrown bushes in vacant lots to drink or do drugs. While we were there, we threw some charcoal on a grill and roasted hot dogs and links while Larry and Pastor Eddington shouted the gospel message to the neighborhood. God's Word and charred hot dogs: we figured one or the other would smoke the people out.

Larry parked his boat-sized Chevy Caprice in the middle of Brigham Lane, and we lined up the pastor's hooptie a half block away, closing off the opening to the street. Then the brothers dragged our heavy church pews onto the asphalt. People who weren't ready to enter the church building came by to take a seat or to ask for prayer. (In black Dallas, regardless of how many times the pastor says "come as you are," it's considered irreverent to show up for church in grungy street clothes.)

While we had church outdoors, Diane prayed several times for a woman named Betty. The alcohol was so thick on her breath, Diane says, you could actually taste it when Betty spoke. Though Betty said all the right things—the things you'd expect from someone who sincerely desired to break loose from substance abuse—she never got free. I saw the same thing in other people who came to church for prayer, and it bothered me deeply. It hurt so bad to see people suffer like this, and I didn't understand why some got free and some didn't. Diane had to set me straight.

"When a person loves something, it's hard to let go," she said. "A lot of people getting drunk and high, they enjoy it. They love the drugs more than they love God. They can't make a decision to let it go.

"It's a sad scenario when they're crying out to God to deliver them. But after you've done all the screaming and hollering, you still have to make a decision to obey God. And a lot of people choose to obey the flesh."

Pastor Eddington's preaching that day was so loud that people in the neighborhood couldn't escape it if they tried. The sound system carried for nearly a mile. The Body of Christ Assembly had a building that desperately needed repairs, but our speakers were bigger and badder than any church in the neighborhood. On the days we held outdoor services, we would go through the area, knocking on doors and talking to everyone we passed on the street. "Jesus can save you and set you free from the sins you feel powerless to fight," we would tell them.

Many people heard the pastor's testimony about how he'd been hooked on PCP, and how he'd been put in a straitjacket and tossed into a padded cell. As his words blasted up and down the streets over the PA system, he invited people to break out of their prisons through the power and sacrifice of Jesus Christ.

People stopped and thanked us for what we were doing. Many considered Pastor Eddington their shepherd, even if they didn't attend his church. Of the dozens of small churches in that neighborhood, ours seemed to be the only one ministering to the people who were stuck in South Dallas. Most of the churches drew their membership from other areas—people who drove in on Sunday mornings because they had ties to the neighborhood from childhood.

But it was tough building a congregation this way, and there were many times we had to fight off discouragement.

Larry and I arrived at church one Sunday morning and found only seven people there, and that included Pastor Eddington and Diane. With so few people present, the meager surroundings were magnified. The soiled yellow carpet looked even more soiled and yellow, the battered air conditioner continued to make a big noise with precious little cooling going on. Two key members had just left the church (they would later come back); others were flagging in faith and not showing up for services. With so few people active in the church, I felt my heart sinking.

Then Sister Monique, whose entire life is an illustration of overcoming extreme hardship, looked at the sorry few of us gathered in the sanctuary and started laughing. "Well," she said, "whether it's a lot or a little, we've still got to know that we serve a big God. All things are possible." We went on and had church that morning, as the black Pentecostals say, praising God as though we were many, clapping our hands in lieu of musical accompaniment.

There were days when nothing seemed to be going right, but I experienced joy anyway. I had never felt that in the churches of my youth—never. A dry exposition of Christian doctrine delivered from the pulpit does not elicit joy. Neither do greeters with brittle smiles or preachers with clever aphorisms and the requisite fake anecdote cribbed from the book of fake anecdotes. I have mentioned my extreme shyness before, but there have been times when a woman would come into The Body of Christ Assembly straight off the street, and my shyness would be overwhelmed by a feeling of compassion. This wave of love was so powerful that it pushed me out of silence into a welcoming embrace. The feeling was so strong that I realized it was an embodiment of God's compassion for hurting people. It's as though my heartbeat were synchronized with Jesus' for a few moments, and my love was his love.

One time during the Sunday service, Pastor Eddington told everyone to run out of the church on the count of three. We were to fan out into the neighborhood, praising God. We felt like kids playing Simon Says, and people at The Body of Christ Assembly still laugh about the events of that day. I'm sure we weren't like any holy rollers the neighborhood had ever seen before. Pastor Eddington isn't bound by tradition, custom, ritual, or habit. He is guided by the Holy Spirit. So if God directs him to do things differently, even if the methodology seems odd or unorthodox, he goes ahead with it. On this particular morning we shouted hallelujahs and ran, walked, or waddled down sidewalks and streets, accepting by faith that our very footsteps were claiming territory for the kingdom of God. We laid hands on buildings, including a drug house disguised as a fried-chicken joint, and we prayed over the patch of scorched earth across the street from the church—where the winos used to hang out. We spoke imprecations in Jesus' name against the neighborhood honky-tonks, all but one of which would be closed within a couple of years.

Not long after the day when only seven adults showed up for church, Evangelist Dicloria Eddington, the pastor's sister, had a vision. She saw a line of scraggly looking sheep gathering at the church door, and we were ushering them in. Some of the sheep had patches of wool missing; others were dirty or feeble. They hobbled inside, and Pastor Eddington received them as their shepherd.

I thought of the broken people who gravitated toward The Body of Christ Assembly, folks who lived underneath layers of disappointment and pain. For these people even to set foot in the church was an extraordinary act of faith, because their hopes for a better life had just about been extinguished. So many times I'd see a visitor enter in the middle of the service and sit on the margins, waiting to see if there was anything they could grasp onto—an encouraging word, a gesture of love, an offer of prayer. In many instances they found the strength they needed.

But needy people come in every color, shape, size, sex, religion, and class. I realize now that those of us who felt a calling to ministry, including Larry and me, were just about the scraggliest sheep of all. We might not have been crack addicts, but we had deeper issues—selfishness, pride, rebellion. It was one thing to cast a crack demon out of an addict who came for prayer. It was another thing altogether to take under your wing a hardheaded woman like me and love her throughout a process of becoming more like Jesus. Diane traveled that entire tortuous path with me, as God convicted me of stubbornness and selfishness. She mentored me, loved me, and stood by my side as God broke me down and then restored and refined me.

Reading my personal journal from those days is an excruciating exercise. I want to smack that girl who wrote it—smack her good. Evidently I thought I was an expert in spiritual matters, considering how irked I got at the small imperfections in the church and among my brothers and sisters. I recorded my impatience with the fact that church services seldom started on time and the pastor was partial to the nonword *irregardless.* How could I have been so hung-up on nonissues? Yet it was clear that God was revealing things to me, dreams and words of prophecy, and that he was using me at the same time I was being an insufferable twit. Still, the pastor and Diane chose to nurture the potential they saw in Larry and me.

Within a couple of years of our joining The Body of Christ Assembly, the pastor appointed Larry as youth minister. Larry was a grown man with the energy of a big kid. Boisterous and goofy, he dove into the assignment with everything he had. He acted out Bible stories on the church lawn, where the children's Sunday school was held, and he took all the kids on their first-ever camping trip, where they were deluged with Texas rain. And he taught just about every kid who attended The Body of Christ Assembly in those years how to swim.

I would realize only later that the pastor and Diane put a remarkable degree of trust in Larry by allowing him to work with the children. For *any* church to entrust their children to an adult leader, especially one who is not a parent of one of the kids in the group, is a big deal. At that time, it wasn't uncommon for kids to get molested in churches in black Dallas. And at any given time in the 'hood, there were more shifty characters than you could keep track of. The parents at the church were justifiably cautious about whom they allowed to associate with their kids, but they warmed to Brother Larry. When he was ordained as an elder in the Church of God in Christ, the pastor's daughter, Sherrel, asked him, "Do I need to call you Elder Brother Larry now?" He assured her that no, he was still just Brother Larry.

But after some years, Larry's enthusiasm took a beating. Disappointments and offenses piled up. I didn't support him the way I should have, because I was selfish and wanted him to spend his time with me on my terms. And Larry, orderly guy that he is, with a strong tendency to control, bucked against the constant changes in schedules, the lateness, the disorganization, the fact that some things at the church were done in a haphazard way with the guiding ethos of "it's good enough." He didn't think people respected him the way they should after his years of devoted, mostly unpaid service. I, in turn, got offended when people didn't treat my husband with the regard I thought he deserved.

Diane responded by turning up the heat on me, pointing out some areas where I needed to mature as a Christian. She would call and tell me things I didn't want to hear. My home was unbalanced, she said, because I was the main breadwinner. My husband and I had anger and control issues; we pouted when we didn't get our way. People saw me as stuck-up, a perception rooted in a misunderstanding of my shyness, but a common perception nonetheless. I'm sure, in response to Diane, that I sputtered about cultural differences, and what a good marriage we had, and how we were just trying to do things right. But I knew in my heart that my attitude was lacking. Something in me was amiss.

There were times when I would sit in church fuming to the point where I couldn't hear the pastor's message. I'd be obsessing over something inconsequential, like the sloppy way the carpet had been laid on the stage. Larry became known for occasional temper tantrums. The kids from those years still remember how Brother Larry blew up one Saturday morning and hopped in his Chevy, screeching away from the church because he thought the kids weren't listening to him.

The children stood there with wide eyes in their drill-team uniforms, waiting and hoping he'd come back. He didn't. He stayed away until just a few minutes before the special service that evening when they were scheduled to perform. In our self-absorption I'm sure we never picked up on their sadness—that someone they loved had given up on them, if only for a moment.

In those years at The Body of Christ Assembly, the miracles were few, and people came and left with unsettling frequency. I realized that the members were getting discouraged by the squabbles and petty jealousies within the congregation. I knew that down times were to be expected. Pastor Eddington would remind us, you can't spend all your time on the mountaintop. Still, our congregation was about to spend extended time in the valley, and I was learning that I tended to see everyone else's faults as worse than my own.

The sexual and financial improprieties committed by high-profile pastors and evangelists are what get in the news. But I now know that personal offenses knock far more people out of effective ministry.

Some of the people in The Body of Christ Assembly assumed that because Larry and I were white, we wanted to take over the pastor's ministry, but that was never the case. It was disturbing to us that people from the neighborhood would sometimes approach Larry as though he were the leader, simply because he was white. When we became a common sight in the neighborhood, that perception pretty much ceased. The truth was that we had seen enough of Pastor Eddington's and Diane's struggles and hardships that we had no interest in being senior pastors.

But we still wanted to exert a degree of control, although we would have denied it at the time; our own inclinations were mostly invisible to us. It's so easy to deceive yourself—to be blind to your motives—that it's frightening. At some level, Larry and I assumed that our sacrifices of time, money, and even status had *earned* us a degree of influence in the church.

Disappointments, insecurities, and real or imagined slights devour people who start out with a sincere desire to serve and please God. The first thing that disappears is your joy. It becomes nothing but a distant memory, and replacing it is the knot in your stomach that grows when things don't go your way. The knot becomes so familiar that it starts to feel normal, and that's a problem.

Then you find that you no longer experience the presence of the Holy Spirit, one of God's most exquisite gifts, the force that guides and comforts you and stills your heart when you pray. Ministers who attempt to preach or teach or pray or even give an encouraging word without what we call the anointing—simply put, the power and presence of the Holy Spirit—sound like jagged noise. The words themselves may seem appropriate and well aimed, but they're like a football glancing off the uprights. They have no effect.

It took me a while to realize that God could use me to do things like prophesy, even though I remained an achingly immature person. In The Body of Christ Assembly, what counted was character and whether one had an anointing and walked in love. Those attributes were available to anyone who was willing to submit to God's cleansing, his maturing process, and his guidance. "God is no respecter of persons," Diane would always say. Yet the price for obtaining the anointing of God's Spirit is steep. God demands your entire life. You can't hold anything back. "Offer your bodies as living sacrifices," Saint Paul wrote, "holy and pleasing to God—this is your spiritual act of worship."

At The Body of Christ Assembly, no one was overly impressed that I had become editor-in-chief of the *Dallas Observer,* the influential weekly newspaper that during my tenure brought down a corrupt Dallas Public Schools chief and produced a mayor (Laura Miller, the *Observer*'s former news columnist, who successfully ran for city council and mayor), or that Larry would earn a master of theology degree with high honors from one of the most academically demanding seminaries in the country, or that he could translate the Bible into English from ancient Greek and Hebrew. We were simply Brother Larry and Sister Julie at the church, and it was the best thing that could have happened to us.

While the pastor and Diane took joy in our worldly accomplishments, cheering us on if we got a raise or a promotion, they also confronted and gently corrected us when they noticed a serious character deficiency, such as the need to control. Pastor Eddington's profound understanding of the Scriptures still astonishes me, yet he never had a lick of formal theological training. Larry spent four years in seminary, and what he learned from his professors often tracked with uncanny precision what the pastor was preaching in church, as though God were saying, *Hey, the Holy Spirit is your teacher, and he will "guide you into all truth"*—as Jesus told his disciples.

The pastor and Diane weren't concerned with the quantity of a person's biblical knowledge. The question was, Do you *believe* what you know? As Diane put it, "Why are we so concerned about learning the Scriptures in Greek and Hebrew when we don't even obey them in English?"

Somewhere along the way God convicted me of my pride. I realized I needed to humble myself in a way I'd never thought necessary before. I found myself getting jealous and resentful when other people didn't make the financial sacrifices Larry and I made for the church, and I began to notice that subtly pointing out others' flaws gave me a sickening injection of pleasure.

Pastor Eddington could listen to even the weakest preachers and extract something of value, because he looked beyond the person and connected with the living Word of God. I wanted to have a similar humility, to stop picking apart every little mistake. When I listened to the pastor teach Bible study, I might hear a small error, such as substituting David for Daniel, or scrambling a few pieces of the Old Testament historical chronology. I wanted to ditch my critical spirit and instead listen for God to speak through the pastor's teaching. I had to make a moment-by-moment decision to humble myself, to seek and destroy my ungodly thought patterns.

The wisdom of one of my favorite preachers, John Bevere, resounded in my ears: it isn't so much what you do, it's how you do it. If we organize a neighborhood food giveaway but do it with a rotten attitude toward our brothers and sisters in the church, our work is nothing but noise. If we disrespect our spiritual leaders and are always jockeying for position, seeing who we can push down to advance our own interests, our service is worthless.

I got an object lesson in humility when a couple of people in the church took it upon themselves to criticize my every move, sometimes to my face, sometimes not. I was talking to Diane and her daughter-in-law, Rashanda, and I started agonizing aloud about a member who frequently seemed to oppose me. Diane listened patiently. "I just don't get it," I said, close to tears but more perplexed than anything. "What did I do? What is it about me that's so offensive?"

Rashanda, who'd been silent through the whole conversation, spoke up.

"Duh," she said.

Diane laughed. She hadn't bothered to point out the obvious. I was white—that's why I was so offensive to some people. Bullies and bigots will push until you push back, she told me. But we've got to do it with love and patience.

She and the pastor were the ones who showed me what it meant to "walk in love." Pastor Eddington was laid-back, slow to take offense, and he laughed or shrugged off most of the reproaches and snubs that came his way. Because he never allowed himself to become bitter, he was always ready to minister with a clear conscience, even to a former enemy. Diane wrestled within herself, because there were many times she hadn't felt accepted by the pastor's own relatives, and it hurt her deeply. She taught me that love goes hand in hand with truth, and if you truly love someone, you will confront that person about his or her sin. Love isn't some fuzzy sentiment—it's a fierce thing that cares more about the well-being of another person's soul than their feelings.

Later I'd preach something that encapsulated what Diane demonstrated to me: Love without truth is powerless. Truth without love is just cruel. I saw with dismay that a weak and phony facsimile of love had made cowards of many men and women in ministry. They refused to deal with sin in their congregations, fearing the backlash.

Diane always told the truth, and she suffered the consequences: lost friends and lost church members.

My husband and I found a way to face the hardships, and it had a lot to do with not taking ourselves too seriously. One thing that set The Body of Christ Assembly apart from many other Pentecostal congregations was its ability to laugh and have fun. Few of the core members had been brought up in holy-roller churches, so they hadn't developed the outward religiosity that often is seen in lifelong church members. That had very little of the spiritual smugness that looks askance at any irreverence or simple lightheartedness. At The Body of Christ Assembly, there were times we laughed until we nearly peed our pants. Like the Sunday morning one of the kids suddenly leaped out of his seat during praise service, and some of us thought he'd "got the Holy Ghost" and had begun to "shout," or dance under the influence of the Holy Spirit. But a couple of the other kids saw what really happened and broke out in giggles. A giant cockroach had dropped in his lap.

There were relaxed afternoons at the pastor's house, eating barbecued brisket and iridescent yellow soda cake, playing spades and watching the Dallas Cowboys get whupped. (Well, that's my story, and I'm sticking with it. I'll admit I'm a lifelong Green Bay Packers fan.)

The joyful attitude came from the top, because the pastor and Diane never took themselves too seriously. I had to learn to lighten up myself.

One time I was so angry with someone who was giving the pastor problems that I grabbed the arm of Sister Monique, a dear friend, and pulled her into a back room just before a service started. "Pray for me, Monique," I said. I'm sure my eyes were bugging out. "I swear I'm gonna punch her."

I guess I missed the irony—that I was in church and wanted to pop my sister.

"Do you understand?" I asked Monique. I held her wrist in a white-knuckle grip. I was sure I was gonna lose it.

She just smiled. She knew exactly how I felt. "Oh, you just trippin'."

"Have you ever felt this way?" I asked.

She laughed and squeezed my hand tight, and we prayed right there. I didn't walk into the sanctuary shouting hallelujahs, but I did manage to pull it together enough to mumble through a few praise songs and maybe even raise my arms once or twice.

In 1999, when I gave birth to our son, Conor, my time spent studying the Bible and praying gave way, and I found myself struggling with resentments and mood swings. These struggles reminded me all too much of the days before I recommitted my life to Jesus Christ and was filled with the Holy Spirit. It took Diane to set me straight, to give me some perspective, because she struggled with the same things. "Look at Paul," she said. "He was one of the greatest apostles, and at the end of his life he said, 'I die daily,' and he wrote that he had to 'press toward the mark for the prize of the high calling of God in Christ Jesus.' Why did he say that? Because he hadn't arrived. We fool ourselves if we think we've arrived and no longer have to die to our selfish desires.

"It's a pressing way. If Paul had to press, if Jesus had to struggle right up until the cross, then how much more will we have to press? But the good news is the press can be fun. If we have nothing to fight against, it's boring.

"Salvation is free, but it's expensive to maintain, babe."

Diane knew about pressing for something better. And the proof was her life. God had transformed her from party girl to fearless prophetess.

14

Hell Is Real, and Somebody's Going There

By the midnineties, The Body of Christ Assembly had outgrown Nanny's house, the small structure propped up on sections of tree stumps. We had our eyes on a vacant commercial building sitting kitty-corner from Nanny's house, a combination fried-chicken joint/crackhouse, which we suspected sold more drugs than chicken. One day I sat myself defiantly on the front lawn of the church and stared at the people going in and out of the Chicken Shack. I did not see one box of chicken leave that place.

By 1996, the two-room brick structure was empty, and we purchased it from the out-of-town owner and moved in. The pastor, Larry, and several of the brothers refurbished it, and in its recesses Larry found a few shorn chicken bones but a whole lot more syringes and crack baggies.

This building also came equipped with hot and cold running rats, and we never saw it as a permanent location. In the early 2000s we started to make plans to build from scratch a church with enough room to accommodate more than the forty or so people who fit comfortably in the former chicken joint. We knew one thing for sure: our interim building didn't reflect well on the God we served.

Over the years, we had acquired vacant lots in the neighborhood, hoping to build there some day. In the meantime, a community center run by some well-connected local women was built a block from the church, funded by the city and federal grants. We were holding an outdoor service one Saturday in 2003, and one of the community-center

© Lyons family collection

Fredrick Eddington, Chris Edwards, and Larry Lyons remodeled
this suspected crackhouse for use by the church

ladies got in a conversation with Pastor Eddington. She pointed to a
vacant lot across the street. "That's our land right there," she said.

What she didn't know was that our church already owned that
property free and clear. Evidently the community center had designs of
its own for the site.

The pastor was shocked to walk into a community meeting later
that year and see a lovely watercolor rendering of the community center's development plans for the area. Residential housing was pictured
right where Nanny's house stood on a piece of land we still owned and
would need for the church's expansion. It became clear that we were
being shoved aside for someone else's big project. Since we didn't have
a fancy building or a large membership roll, we were nobodies in the
eyes of local politicos and community leader wannabes.

Still, we forged ahead with our building plans, despite some strange,
muted opposition from our city-council representative, who was friendly
with the community-center ladies. The pastor and a church member,

Vincent Spurling, met with the councilman to try to get his support for the rezoning we needed. During the meeting, they realized they had stumbled into a mystifying web of back-scratching neighborhood alliances. The pastor brought along our site plan and architectural drawings to show the councilman, who supposedly was a champion of development in depressed South Dallas. But he wouldn't even look at them.

"I'll support your project if the community supports it," the councilman said.

That should be easy, Pastor Eddington thought. Our church already enjoyed support from just about all the residents in the area. But the councilman wasn't finished. "Now let me define community," he said. "By 'community,' I mean the community center." He strongly suggested our church seek and obtain the blessing of the community-center leadership before we tried to move ahead with our building project.

From my work as a news reporter, I knew a thing or two about petty neighborhood politics, and I figured the fix was in. Sure enough, no one from the community center would return the pastor's calls to schedule a meeting.

We ended up going before the City Plan Commission without the support of our councilman and his appointee on the commission, which we had been told was necessary if we hoped to get our measure passed. Clueless about South Dallas politics, which we'd always avoided, we turned to the only heavy we knew: the Holy Spirit. The pastor organized prayer shifts every hour, and we took turns getting up in the wee hours and petitioning the one Judge we could trust to be fair and impartial.

Then strange things started happening. We showed up en masse at a Plan Commission meeting, even though it was scheduled during the day. All forty or so of us—both adults and children—sat quietly through hours of droning discourse about plats, rezones, and other minutiae.

When our request came up on the agenda, Larry and the pastor spoke about the church's vision, its work in the community, how we reached out to Dallas's forgotten residents instead of opting for a big barn in the suburbs. My son, Conor, and his friend Diamond, the pastor's oldest granddaughter, sat next to me, and the two of them were scrunched into a single seat, paging through a picture book. Sister Monique's seven children sat at attention in a row behind us.

We kept waiting for our South Dallas Plan Commission member to show up. Larry and the pastor had approached him at an earlier meeting, attempting to court his vote, but he just shook his head and walked away. Still, since he had the power to single-handedly block our rezone application, we held out hope that he would change his mind. (The other Plan Commission members would not go against the wishes of a fellow member concerning a project in his own district.) But the man never showed up. We found out he had resigned from the commission the night before, and no one had taken his place.

At one point we noticed that a couple of Plan Commission members had tears in their eyes. Then one of the members addressed us publicly. She was so moved by the courteous behavior of our children through hours of boring proceedings that she knew we represented values and a vision they needed to support.

The commission unanimously approved our project.

We thought it was over. But seven months after the Plan Commission meeting, while our application for a building permit was pending with the city, we got a letter from the city's real-estate division announcing its intent to exercise eminent domain on the vacant lots we owned across the street from the church. It was the property where we planned to build our new building. We were flabbergasted—didn't one city department have any idea what the other departments were doing?

This time I decided to wade in myself. I called a well-known city activist, Sharon Boyd, who had dedicated herself to exposing corruption in Dallas city politics. The *Dallas Observer* sometimes had a contentious relationship with Boyd, but to her credit, she listened patiently and focused on the issues instead of her past run-ins with the paper.

None of what she said reassured me; in her mind the fix was indeed in. She directed me to a lawyer she knew.

The lawyer did a little checking around with his South Dallas contacts to figure out what was really going on, and he came back to us with a hint: go after the community center's financial records, which were supposed to be available for public inspection. I came up with a blitz offense to shock and awe the community center and our councilman, who evidently figured we were nonentities with no support that mattered.

On a single day—April 8, 2004—a church couple, Martin and Ingra Johnson, descended on the community center armed with a copy of the applicable IRS rules and politely asked to view the financial records. Their request elicited a shouting, arm-flailing response from the older of the two women who ran the center.

Martin and Ingra took that as a no.

Finally, the younger of the two community-center leaders grabbed the older woman's arm and said, "I'm aneed you to go back to your station where you belong."

At the same time, Diane, Monique, Valoria Spurling, and I, plus several of the brothers, fanned out in the community, distributing colorful flyers that said UNFAIR! IT COULD HAPPEN TO YOU! Dodging stray pit bulls as we went door to door, we singled out our city-council member and the community center for attempting to seize the property that the church had owned for years. At one point we were stalked by a particularly nasty looking South Dallas hound, and we could only walk so fast with a blind lady (Diane) trailing us. "You need to go on now," Monique told the dog through clenched teeth. "I don't have time to play with you today." The instant she spoke, the dog pivoted and trotted off in the opposite direction. We managed to distribute all our flyers unmolested.

It couldn't have been but a day or two later when Pastor Eddington was strolling through one of the lots we had bought, and up drove our city councilman, jovial and friendly all of a sudden. He got out of his car and buttonholed the pastor. "Oh, I never intended to take your church's property," he said. "I wouldn't get in the way of God's work!"

Yeah, whatever. The pastor graciously accepted the councilman's gesture, and a little over a year later we would hold the grand opening ceremony for our new church.

Throughout construction of the church, which Pastor Eddington designed and built himself as the general contractor, Diane drilled into our heads that "We're not taking our issues across the street to the new building. We need to leave the envy and jealousy and rebelliousness right here."

Years of opposition from within the church had taken a toll on Diane. People often resented her direct nature and her truthfulness. She didn't hesitate to call attention to a person's hypocrisy, and some felt she came off as shrill. Pastor Eddington drew hard lines in his messages from the pulpit, and he led by the example of his life. But Diane was a prophetess, and like the prophets of old, she spoke the Word of the Lord to expose stubborn sin.

Her bluntness came through in the women's group she led at the church. Diane was known to get up in your face and ask her trademark question, "How are you and Jesus getting along?" A mealy-mouthed reply pretty much conveyed a "not-so-hot, ma'am" and opened the door wide for further personal queries.

At one of the women's meetings she blurted out my all-time favorite Dianeism: "Ain't no penis in the world worth going to hell for!"

Her experiences with evil spirits in South Dallas had convinced Diane that the devil's lies should be given no quarter. The light of truth must shine, regardless of what gets caught in its rays.

I was attending a women's meeting at church when the Holy Spirit told me to speak openly about my struggle with same-sex attraction. *Do I have to?* I asked God. *Can't I wait until I'm eighty?* By then, I figured, I just wouldn't care anymore.

But no, I heard the gentle voice of the Spirit telling me *now,* even though I had a career and a reputation to think about.

It had been only a few years earlier when I told Larry about my struggle. As soon as the words left my mouth, I started weeping, and I couldn't have asked for a more loving and understanding response. He held me close and told me it didn't matter what I did in the past; all that mattered was the woman God had made me, and this happened to be the wife he loved.

I summoned my courage and called Diane and made the same confession. To my surprise, she wasn't remotely fazed. Like Larry, she believed that Jesus Christ could totally transform a person's life, including her sexuality.

We filed into the church as usual on January 29, 2006. There was an opening prayer. A handful of praise songs. A solo. Nothing that presaged anything unusual.

By the end of the morning it would sink in that I'd witnessed something exceptionally rare. This particular morning was a blast of the Spirit of Truth, as the Holy Spirit is sometimes called in Scripture: a concussion wave that split the air for a second and was gone.

"Hell is real," Diane said, taking the podium to preach. "And somebody's going there."

As we digested those words, Diane started walking slowly down the center aisle, looking around her. At that distance, because of her failing eyesight, she can't recognize faces. She can see only vague, human-shaped blobs.

"If this house was full to capacity," she said, "and I asked, 'How many born-again believers in here?' Everybody would stand up."

She paused. The rhythm of her message shifted. "How many born-again believers *do* we have in here?" Everyone lifted a hand or signaled their presence somehow. Then she sprung the trap.

"All right. How many fornicators do we have up in the house?"
Silence.

"How many adulterers do we have?"

Not a word.

Just then, a woman, a visitor that day, set her Bible down and slowly rose to her feet.

Every set of eyes snapped her way. A sort of rustle went through the church house. I know I averted my eyes just as quickly—embarrassed. Nervous.

The woman was middle-aged—trim and stylish, well dressed. Someone who had it together, at least based on all outward appearances.

Diane noticed the woman from the corner of her eye as she walked past. "Bless God," she said, a slim note of surprise in her voice.

So much for the rhetorical questions—you know, the kind you're not supposed to answer. Truth was in the house.

"But see," Diane said, riding this wave of the Spirit, "the blessed part is, when you can admit to your sin, you're on your way."

She continued. "How many folks do we have up in here that are envious?"

By this time, the Spirit of Truth had hit us in the heart. As if there were springs in our knees, bodies popped up all over the sanctuary.

"How many people do we have here that's jealous?"

A whole row stood up in unison. I got up too.

"See, God is good...and I hope y'all are taking notice."

This went on, leading to an old-fashioned altar call, the kind where people repent of their sins, publicly if need be. At a moment like this there is no shame. The only goal is to get right with God.

The woman who was first to stand told the entire congregation that she had been in an adulterous relationship for some time. She was a faithful churchgoer in another part of town. Something, she said, had drawn her to this church today.

We would never see or hear from her again.

But that day the church family embraced her. There wasn't a scrap of haughtiness or judgmentalism; every one of us knew that we were guilty of at least one of the sins Diane had mentioned.

I guess we could have just said to ourselves, "Now, now, we've all done some bad things. Just quietly tell Jesus you're sorry, and try to do better next time."

But that Spirit of Truth was there, sending shock waves through the house. We had but two choices: Repent—which wasn't mere sorrow, or regret that you got caught, but a decision to turn away from sin. Or run.

Bible Girl

A year or two before I told Diane Eddington about my struggle with same-sex attraction, I had a dream in which I found myself in a New Orleans gift shop that displayed the voodoo accoutrements that are peddled to tourists, things like fetishes and masks and rag dolls to stick with pins. I was astounded to see that people treated these things as though they were quirky and cute.

In real life I had visited New Orleans a few times, and while I loved the food and the Old World vibe, I'd never been in a place where the demonic spirits seemed so evident. I could sense the presence of foul spirits all around me as I walked along Bourbon Street, immersed in the smells of urine, vomit, and spilled beer. To me, there was nothing curious or quaint about the vile gift shop in my dream. I felt like throwing up. Cringing inside, I thrashed my hands against my body as though I were scraping off slime, and then I bolted for the door. I ran away from the shop, hoping to escape that dark city. I was running down a sidewalk near a pleasant-looking brick church—*Get me outta here*—and outside it a preacher was shouting through a loudspeaker. His words went something like this: "It's okay to be gay and Christian. You've got to remember that God is love—he accepts you just as you are!"

I started running even faster, gasping for breath.

Just then a wooden cross toppled in front of me. I tripped over it and fell headlong, landing on my knees on rough concrete. I hit hard.

As I lifted my head, I realized I needed to get a grip. I couldn't run away from evil when it was all around me—there really was nowhere to escape to. Plus, I knew better than to turn tail and run, because I'd seen the power of Jesus crush demonic forces. I started praying on my knees, interceding through tears for the men and women caught up in homosexuality and for a church that could no longer tell the straight truth about sin. Then I woke up.

The dream stuck with me for years and was kicking around in my consciousness in 2006 when I came up with the idea to start a religion column at the *Dallas Observer.* The editorial staff had launched a news blog called Unfair Park (the title is a pun that makes sense to anyone from Dallas), and the column would be my contribution. I decided to call it Bible Girl, the first thing that popped into my head. Soon after my first post in late August, I found out that the *Observer's* parent company, Village Voice Media, had called all its lead editors to a company retreat in New Orleans.

Immediately I thought about the setting of my dream, which I had always believed was from God. I look at things simply when God speaks to me through Scripture or prophecy, and I concluded that God was calling me to take a public stand on same-sex attraction now that I had a suitable forum in Bible Girl. I took the dream to mean that I should make a statement about same-sex attraction before I went to the company retreat, which was less than a month away. Then I would have to face my colleagues in the alternative press, who were known for their liberalism concerning alternative lifestyles.

All of this kind of freaked me out. Much of my fear about revealing my past had melted away when I confided in Larry and Diane, but they loved me and cared about me. I knew I wouldn't get such a kind reception at the *Dallas Observer.* Though my bosses at Village Voice Media, Michael Lacey and Christine Brennan, had always respected my Christian beliefs, I had fleeting thoughts that if I wrote about my experiences with same-sex attraction, I might be labeled a bigot and a homophobe and lose my job. I was also concerned that people might ridicule my husband or harass my son.

I gave it a lot of thought, then decided to take a flying leap of faith. If my interpretation of the dream was off-track, I figured, God would just have to catch me.

Taking that leap is a little like dying. You don't know if you'll land on your feet or tumble into a chasm and never be heard from again. But God put something in me—faith—that compelled me to take those leaps again and again. I had decided years before that I would live for God and not for my own comfort or advancement. I continually fought against personal pride, and throwing myself off the precipice again and again helped me trust God and let go of selfish motivations.

I was surrounded by people at The Body of Christ Assembly who understood faith and the plunge of radical obedience. When you've left behind your old life and have no interest in going back, it requires fierce obedience to God. Half-steppin' submission to Jesus won't keep people free from drug addiction, depression, or sexual sin. I told Pastor Eddington and Diane that I was going to take a public stand on gay marriage, at that time the hottest issue in American Christianity. They pledged to support me without question. I was filled with love for the Eddingtons, a man and woman of enormous spiritual stature of whom the world thought nothing, even the church world. I was blown away that God had taken such delicate care in placing me under their guidance. I had learned this secret, that humbling yourself to godly leaders, whatever their faults might be, brought tremendous peace and protection. I could do crazy things in faith because I knew they'd pick me up if I crashed.

"There are more people for you than against you," the pastor prophesied to me. I found that hard to believe, since I knew my audience at the *Dallas Observer,* and it was made up primarily of readers who were decidedly hostile to people of faith. Pentecostal Christians were an object of particular disdain, and I didn't know of a single one working in the alternative press besides me. But I accepted my pastor's words. He and Diane and Dicloria laid hands on me and blessed me.

A few days later I received a press release from gay activist Mel White, well-known in Christian circles as a prolific author and former ghostwriter for evangelical icons such as Jerry Falwell and Pat Robertson. White came out in 1993 at Dallas's Cathedral of Hope, the largest gay congregation in the country. He later wrote about how he endured decades of "antigay" therapy, including prayer, exorcism, and electric shock, before he fashioned his own statement of faith: "I am gay. I am proud. And God loves me without reservation." White had just written a book, *Religion Gone Bad: The Hidden Dangers of the Christian Right*, and in it he argued that conservative evangelicals were engaged in a secret conspiracy to stir up the kind of hateful prejudice that gets gays killed.

I decided to interview White, and that's how he ended up in my seventh-floor office with its panoramic view of North Dallas. With the information from our conversation, I wrote a column, which was sort of a warmup for the flying leap. The week after my column on White, I planned to tell the alt-press world that God had healed me from same-sex attraction.

When White arrived for the interview, I didn't bother to tell him that I disagreed with virtually all the conclusions in his book. "When you hate what I am and whom I love," White wrote, "you hate me."

Nonsense. I can hate sin and love you. This means I can oppose what you stand for but care about you enough to pull you out of the thing that's killing you.

White probably made the logical assumption—that I was a typical alt-press writer who'd accept everything he said about homosexuality without hesitation. In the American media in general, mainstream or alternative, homosexuality and gay marriage are nonissues. In the alt-press, anyone who opposes homosexuality or gay marriage is considered a bigot, a hater, and a homophobe. I dutifully jotted down notes as White talked, then something weird happened. While we were sitting in my office, a freak thunderstorm rose up. Rain came shooting at the windows in horizontal streaks, and a lightning strike cut off electricity to the *Observer* building. He and I were sitting there in the dark, stunned by the force of this Texas supercell. We got up and stood in awe, looking out the windows. It was a strange moment, both of us oohing and aahing at the power unleashed by this storm. Then just as quickly as it came, the storm stopped, and the sun peered out. Though we were still in the dark at the *Observer*.

I found White to be an intelligent, engaging interview subject. I thanked him for his time, and off he went.

The storm would parallel precisely what I experienced. I wrote two columns for Bible Girl, the first on the gay-marriage issue, the second on my personal battle with same-sex attraction.

"In the book of Genesis," I wrote in the first piece, "God establishes marriage between a man and a woman. For an evangelical such as myself, that settles it: the Word is indisputably clear; I follow. I am not at liberty to construct elaborate circumventions." The column drew a muted response, though I was accused of being a bigot, as expected. Bible Girl was new and difficult to locate on the *Observer* Web site, and I hadn't even told my bosses that I'd launched the column. I figured they'd find out, and if they hated it, they'd let me know. Or just get rid of me.

Oddly enough, I didn't experience any jitters leading up to writing my big confession in the next column, that God had freed me from same-sex attraction. I just sat down on the couch in our living room one Wednesday afternoon and knocked it out on a laptop while my son watched cartoons. I was having fun.

> Today I will say that sexual orientation is a mystery. It does frustrate me greatly when evangelicals talk about "sexual preference." Hmm…let's see. Today I'll have a Wild Cherry Pepsi. Tomorrow I'll have a can of Squirt.

I kind of laughed inside when I noticed the sexual connotations of my choices of sodas. On I went, tapping away with two fingers.

> The truth is we are all born broken—so often in the area of sexual identity, something that touches the core of who we are and what we were created to be.
>
> That, I believe, is the authentic biblical view: born broken, children of original sin. Desperately in need of a savior—who

then tells us we must be "born again." Sexual brokenness takes so many forms: homosexuality, children who've been violated, the middle-aged man who frantically pursues younger women.

Most evangelicals and gays have this in common: they fixate on the question of whether homosexuality is a genetically ordained condition. The majority of evangelicals, of course, say it is not; most gays believe it is. There is intriguing but maddeningly inconclusive scientific evidence for each side of the argument. How you read it mostly reveals your preconceptions.

So, did I inherit depression? Did I inherit homosexuality?

Maybe, maybe not. As a follower of Jesus Christ, I say it doesn't matter. That's right—it doesn't matter.

I learned at The Body of Christ Assembly that it *doesn't* matter whether you inherited a predisposition to gamble, drink, or abuse drugs or sex. Whatever your problem is, if you acknowledge it as sin and look to Jesus to heal you, he will do it. Desperate people get delivered.

Saint Paul understood this. He wrote to the church in Corinth, a gang of loose-living former pagans, "Do not be deceived: Neither the sexually immoral nor idolaters nor adulterers nor male prostitutes nor homosexual offenders...will inherit the kingdom of God. And that is what some of you *were.*"

In the Bible Girl column, I wrote my own kicker: "Thank God for the past tense.

"I believe Jesus Christ has the power to totally transform a person's life. That used to be what evangelicals believed. Now they're so cowed by issues like gay marriage, so desperate to fit in, that they've grown faint of heart and faith."

That night my husband read my column draft and smiled. He gave me his blessing and told me to run with it. His strength amazed me. Not too many men would appreciate their wives writing about a struggle with sexual identity. My only hesitance in posting the column was in knowing that readers, particularly my sharp-tongued brethren in the alt-press, would speculate about my marriage. I didn't think it was appropriate to be tacky and triumphal and note that Larry and I probably had more good sex in a month than a lot of folks have in their lifetimes. "Well," I said to Larry that night, "people can say whatever they want about me, but that doesn't make it true." I'd already ruled out the possibility of posting an anonymous "testimony." At my church, if you believe it, you put your name behind it. We understood the power of a witness.

It's funny, because while I anticipated a vicious response to my second column, I didn't know which avenue the critics would take. Would they deny that I had been healed of same-sex attraction or deny that I'd ever experienced homosexual temptations at all? I tried to address that in the column: "I know some will read this and say I never was or still am. We're so wedded to preconceptions. Since you don't know me, all I can say is this: my experience is no more than it is, no less than it is."

The next morning, September 21, 2006, I fine-tuned my column, then froze for a moment before mashing the Send button. My piece, "The Mystery of Sexual Orientation," went to my blog editor, Village Voice Media film critic Robert Wilonsky. I sent the column to his e-mail and left the office hastily. I had a lunch appointment and was running late, true enough. But neither did I want to see my closest colleagues' reactions—not until I'd had a few minutes to collect myself. And to wonder if I'd still have a career in the alt-press at the end of the day.

When the Hebrew people were poised to enter the Promised Land with Joshua leading them, they stood on the banks of the Jordan River. This stream of displaced humanity was bunched up on the riverbank, with the river at flood stage. The people held babies in their arms, towing along the weak and the ailing and their few miserable possessions. The Lord had revealed his plan to Joshua, and it involved a step of faith on the part of the Levites, members of the priestly clan who were carrying the ark of the covenant. God told Joshua to have them go on and step into the Jordan. Come what may.

The Levites obeyed. We holy rollers call that faith.

As soon as their feet touched the water, the river parted. This rag-tag nation comprised of the tent-dwelling children of former slaves passed through on dry ground.

In my small way, I could relate. That moment I made a step of faith, even as I was driving to my lunch meeting, music blasting, the Holy Spirit swelled up within me. All my senses were alight—I felt exhilarated, strong, razor-sharp in thinking. If it resembled anything I'd experienced before, it was the manic highs of bipolar disorder, yet without the grandiosity and delusional self-focus. When I got back to the office after lunch and read the first few comments that had already been posted in response to my column, I found myself grinning stupidly.

One reader commented: "Beautiful!! I can totally relate. It was like hearing myself."

Another said: "Thanks for sharing, Bible Girl. Enjoy your life in the closet."

And a third: "When did Unfair Park become such a Bible-thumping blog? So uncool. And girrrrrrl…your problem was not being a lesbian; you were, and possibly still are, big-time psychologically imbalanced. Don't confuse the two of them. Take another holy shower and pray the LORD (who, by the way, is not male but female and also a LESBIAN) saves you."

I was undaunted, even by the following comment: "Did it truly never occur to you that your depression was linked to your near pathological need to deny your sexual orientation?"

Much later, the comments would devolve into curses, digs at my church and family, and crude speculation regarding which sex toys I might've preferred in my supposed previous life as a lesbian. But far from discouraging me, I got a kick out of my critics' seemingly desperate need to discredit what God had done for me.

For nearly two weeks I was filled with joy, so much that at times I found it hard to focus. I followed up those two columns with a couple of lame entries. I wasn't used to that kind of sustained joy, and it would take another year and a series of bizarre demonic attacks for me to figure out why.

For the time being, I just enjoyed the ride. Pastor Eddington was right: though the first wave of comments was mostly negative, defenders began to creep out of the woodwork. They backed me up by supporting orthodox Christian belief concerning the practice of homosexuality. Historic Christian teaching is that for two thousand years the body of believers has deemed it sin.

All over the country, the column was cited and discussed on blogs and comment boards, and Unfair Park registered some of its heaviest traffic to date. Somewhat to my surprise, my Village Voice bosses loved the column. This, they said, was truly alternative. I even got praise from one of my editor colleagues at the *Observer,* who said he didn't agree with me on anything but loved the writing. The column was well read, at least, and that was the goal.

The thrill of seeing the column vault to national prominence ended abruptly the following month when, during the time scheduled for the annual women's conference at church, the brothers invited a once-prominent speaker named Apostle G. to come and speak to them. I'd always enjoyed Apostle G., who used a brilliant sense of humor to make hard truths palatable. He was a down-to-earth guy, a former street tough, and though he had kind of disappeared from the black Pentecostal conference scene in recent years, I looked forward to seeing him again.

I sure wasn't ready for the message he'd come to bring. Pastor Eddington introduced Apostle G. at the women's conference and asked him to give a few "words," which is customary in black churches, and he proceeded to drone on for an hour, ignoring the order of service and the fact that many of our out-of-town guests had to leave that night. Not only was he dismissive of our schedule, he had the nerve to pitch what I could only describe as a pyramid scheme wrapped in the guise of a travel service. Mind you, this travel service might never be declared a pyramid scheme in Texas, which is lax in regulating questionable multilevel-marketing ventures. But it was clear to me that very few people who signed up to pay the monthly fees would ever benefit. Most disturbing, though, was the embarrassingly outdated information Apostle G. offered about the stock market and the state of the economy. I felt like he was taking advantage of my leaders and treating the rest of the congregation like ignorant ghetto folk. I was incensed— even more so when I heard that he'd made what I considered bigoted comments about Jews during a men-only session that Larry attended.

I walked past Dicloria Eddington, the pastor's sister, in the fellowship hall that day, and we just looked at each other and shook our heads. We couldn't believe this guest speaker had hijacked the women's conference. Everything in the conference was off-balance from that point. I couldn't understand the pastor's decision to offer this man a platform to pitch a business scheme we knew little about. Come to think of it, we knew next to nothing about Apostle G. himself except what we'd seen in his public ministry. Churches often embrace a national speaker on blind faith, assuming that his character lines up with his message.

I thought about that dark dream in the voodoo gift shop in New Orleans. The sickened feeling I'd had in the dream came over me again, and I had an urge to run away screaming. I stayed at the conference, but barely.

That night I had trouble sleeping. Apostle G. was scheduled to minister at church two times the following day, a Sunday, and I dreaded sitting through it. At one point I woke up and believed the Holy Spirit was speaking to my heart. I furiously scribbled words on a piece of scrap paper by flashlight. I knew I had to warn Pastor Eddington about this man.

In the morning I called the pastor and told him what I'd written down. He wasn't pleased, and his response to my concerns was unusually sharp. I hung up the phone, feeling like I'd been sucker-punched.

Apostle G. did indeed minister that Sunday, and what I heard wasn't nearly as bad as what I expected; he gave a decent exposition on financial principles, but in my mind, the damage had already been done the previous day. A dozen people or so, mostly visitors, had plunked down fifty dollars to sign up for the first month's subscription fee for the travel business.

The week after the conference I was despondent. I couldn't shake my reservations about Apostle G. and our pastor's tacit approval of the man's sketchy business scheme. I called Diane and unloaded my thoughts, and we ended up shouting at each other. When I realized what I was doing, I shut up. Agree with them or not, I had decided I would never disrespect my leaders.

I prayed to the Lord. "Was I really hearing from you?" I said. "Was it wrong for me to speak out?" I wrestled with these thoughts for several days. I talked to Larry, who'd seen the same things I saw in Apostle G.'s message but more or less shrugged them off.

With considerable agony, I decided that if Apostle G. moved his enterprise into our church, I would have no choice but to leave. My conscience wouldn't allow me to do otherwise. Larry and I were church elders, and I could not be part of what I believed to be an exploitative— if not fraudulent—business.

Diane had said one thing that offered me consolation: the pastor would consider all things before making a decision. He wouldn't act rashly. But I still found myself sitting on the edge of my bed one evening, praying with my face in my hands, rocking and sobbing. I hated the thought of ever leaving my brothers and sisters at The Body of Christ Assembly, the closest family I had known for sixteen years. I poured my heart into that ministry, and it looked like it could all end in heartache and loss.

As I prayed, I felt the Holy Spirit begin to swirl around me with a gentle presence. Even as I cried, a sense of peace started coming over me. I took a few deep breaths and dried my eyes. Then I spoke directly to God. I was ready to leave the church if need be, but I would do it right and go without bitterness.

"Lord," I said, "whatever you want me to do, I'll do it. If I never preach again, if I'm never a leader again, if I never enjoy my pastors' trust and esteem again, if you require me to walk away from everything I've worked for all these years, I will trust you."

What followed still perplexes me a bit. Right away I experienced tremendous peace, and at the moment I spoke those words, I relinquished any more attempts to influence Pastor Eddington's actions. I had made a decision from my heart to submit to his leadership, even though I thoroughly disagreed with having any association with Apostle G.

In this struggle over conflicting views of Apostle G., and the harsh words exchanged with Diane, I had surrendered my desire to control. God had appointed Pastor Eddington as my spiritual leader, and I would honor his decisions as long as they didn't cause me to violate my conscience.

Within months, the Holy Spirit would be released in my life like never before. And, thank God, we haven't seen Apostle G. since.

Sexual Abuse in the Church

"Guess what I just saw on the news," Diane told me on the phone. "A woman says Sherman Allen whupped her with a paddle during counseling, and she's suing."

Such an allegation didn't surprise her. Diane had heard things about Allen, a Pentecostal pastor, for years. A young woman she knew had been found running down the street partly naked trying to get away from Allen, who later would become a prominent Church of God in Christ pastor in Fort Worth. The earlier incident had been hushed up. In many black Pentecostal churches, people are warned to "keep your mouth off the man of God," regardless of what kind of life he lives. God will rebuke him, the teaching goes; all you need to do is go in your closet and pray. I always thought it was a sorry excuse for covering up certain leaders' sins.

Diane rejected the type of thinking that would excuse a leader's moral failings. Growing up, she saw the effect it had, with church leaders' hidden sins sprouting here and there like the fruit of invisible spores. We had heard Allen preach several times, and he was a mesmerizing speaker, a highly intelligent man who could dispense theology right alongside ghetto slang. When the spirit was high, he'd let loose from the pulpit with a sanctified scream: "Ahhhhhhhh!" He seemed to embody the new breed of Pentecostal preacher: sophisticated and successful, but true to his roots in the impassioned spirituality of black Pentecostalism. He had a reputation as a powerful prophet, dropping personal "words" about homes, cars, financial abundance, and fame. A retinue of bodyguards attended to his needs—often for no pay—and members of his church literally raced each other to the altar to present him with monetary blessings and demonstrate their devotion to him.

One thing threw me when I visited his church, Shiloh Institutional Church of God in Christ. I observed a good number of gay men in his congregation, and they were comfortable making a display of their sexuality. I recalled Diane's words, repeated many times over the years: if you're in sin and you know it, you shouldn't feel comfortable sitting up in church. Something—the Word of God, the presence of godly people—should "upset the devil's peace."

Within a week of the February 2007 news report, I was sitting with Diane in the conference room of the lawyers representing Davina Kelly, the woman who had sued Allen. I intended to write a follow-up story and had asked Diane to come with me because of her knowledge and experience in the black Pentecostal milieu. A young married mother of three, daughter of a Church of God in Christ pastor, she told how Allen had paddled her repeatedly on the bare butt, causing severe bruising. The beatings, she claimed, were a form of discipline for minuscule transgressions such as failing to memorize Scripture passages he gave her as part of a regimen of spiritual "counseling." Later, Allen allegedly initiated a sexual relationship and forcibly sodomized her. Another woman we spoke with that day detailed Allen's involvement in the occult, complete with statuary of saints that in one case faded in and out of view during a church service years earlier.

Carrie Drake began to weep quietly when she described how Allen beat her with wooden paddles when she was a teenager, and how her mother, a longtime Allen follower, refused to do anything to stop it. She miscarried within two hours of one such beating.

Both of the women had brought their complaints to local leaders in the Church of God in Christ, but the leaders did little to curb Allen, who was viewed as an up-and-coming figure on the Dallas–Fort Worth black Pentecostal scene.

That night I tossed and turned, severely agitated in my spirit. I had twenty years of experience as a reporter, and everything I'd seen and heard indicated that these women were telling the truth. The next morning, Diane and I compared notes, and she agreed that the women's stories seemed trustworthy. We also found that neither of us had been able to sleep. We were so angry that church leaders had known about these allegations for more than a decade but had allowed Allen to continue unchecked.

The talk of voodoo also rang true. I discovered that Allen came out of the Spiritualist church, an amalgam of Roman Catholicism, voodoo, and Protestant Christianity, with saints and hexes and root herbs and church services that rocked with the intensity of Pentecostalism. Allen reportedly obtained some of his prophetic insights by gazing into a crystal ball.

How Allen could have insinuated his way into the Church of God in Christ, an old and respected Pentecostal denomination that opposes any occultist practices, astonished me. But it wasn't long before I'd delve deeper and talk to people who had observed him using tarot cards, consulting seers, and lighting voodoo candles inscribed with such words as *Prosperity, Money,* and *Control.*

"Just know, Julie Lyons, that you need to stay prayed up like never before," the prophet told me as I nibbled on a stack of pancakes. Looking around the restaurant, I saw several people pretending not to listen but hanging on his every word. This prophet and former pastor, who had worked alongside Allen years earlier, delivered a warning that several others would repeat. "You really don't know what you're getting into. You have stepped into a very sinister and dark world of spiritual witchcraft."

In my investigative reporting I would hear that Allen "lived in sin" with a young woman for years while taking the pulpit every Sunday as a champion of holiness; solicited permission slips from parents to paddle girls in his church, sometimes ordering them to undress first; and sexually abused and threatened several women.

I told the prophet about a dream I had in which a large black hand reached around the edge of my front door. I was sitting in a chair in the hallway, watching all this in slow motion, unable to move. All I could say through clenched teeth was "Go away." The hand had somehow unlatched the door but couldn't go any farther. I willed myself to get up from the chair, grabbed my sleeping son from his bedroom, and ran out the back door.

The prophet interpreted my dream while Diane, a prophetess herself, listened in case a second layer of discernment was needed. "What the Enemy is trying to tell you is, I'm gon' come in here and come after you," he said. "In a sense it's a demonic warning. 'If you keep touching this I'm ashow you who you're really dealing with, because you don't know who's on the other side of this door.'

"But be not afraid," the prophet said in a loud, steady voice. I glanced at a table beside me and saw a woman stop with a forkful of pancake poised midair. "For I have overcome the world." He quoted Jesus' words to his disciples as he was about to be betrayed to the religious authorities and crucified.

I knew that God was speaking to me through this prophet, but it wasn't the kind of thing I'd share with my newsroom colleagues. I believed a spiritual assault was on its way, yet I never would have guessed what form it would take.

The first half of that year, when I spent many hours investigating Allen's alleged misdeeds and continued to write about deliverance from same-sex attraction in the Bible Girl column, I was subject to the weirdest series of demonic attacks I'd ever encountered. I was researching voodoo practices on the Web in my office one afternoon, and I physically sensed the whirling presence of demons manifesting around my PC. I felt them crowding me as I clicked through pages of voodoo accessories available from a store in New Orleans. The spirits were making me nauseated, and I cut short my reporting for that day.

The most infuriating thing happened in my bedroom. My husband and I had always enjoyed a highly satisfying sex life, and all of a sudden my body shut down. Its normal sexual functions died. I was angry at first, but after several weeks of this, I resigned myself to frustration. I recalled what Pastor Eddington taught, that "what Satan intends for evil, God will use for good" among those who obey, and an interesting result of this trial was that I became more sensitive and considerate toward my husband, since I found myself making love with little hope of obtaining any pleasure in return. I wondered if my body would ever go back to normal. And, you know, this wasn't exactly something I wanted to take in front of the church with a public request for healing prayer. I decided to trust God and just deal with it.

After ruling everything else out, I concluded it was some crazy spiritual attack. My body was perfectly healthy. My husband and I had a happy marriage, a loving son, a fiercely supportive spiritual family. I was thriving in the Word of God, and my body had never acted up like this before, even through a difficult pregnancy. You'll reach a point, Diane told me, where the Enemy hates it that you get up in the morning.

I had reached that point.

My body came back to life with a vengeance after six weeks of this (and not a few urgent prayers from my husband), and subsequent events did nothing but tick me off and make me more determined to get to the bottom of the Sherman Allen story. Especially when I met a woman the lawyers had ironically dubbed Joy. I sat in the office of a black Pentecostal church in Fort Worth, surrounded by somber-faced church mothers who wrinkled their faces in disgust when Joy told how Allen allegedly had raped her anally and vaginally with a three-foot wooden club. Though Allen was charged with aggravated rape in connection with the 1983 incident, Joy stopped cooperating with prosecutors. She claimed Allen told her he'd do the same thing to her daughter if she was stupid enough to tell anyone.

In the midst of recalling how he cursed at her and called her a bitch and a whore, and how the excruciating pain caused her to tumble from a bed onto the floor in her apartment, the woman moved from soft-spoken words to a high-pitched wail.

"Oh God, oh God, oh God, oh God...," she stammered.

At the end of the assault, Joy told us, the young preacher propped her up in front of the bathroom mirror naked and pried her eyes open so she was forced to look at her own face.

"God told me to do this to you," she recalled his saying.

My reporting on the Sherman Allen case would take me deep into the black Pentecostal subculture, where secrets about prominent leaders' immoral lives had been protected for years, yet many people knew exactly what was going on. I couldn't believe that godly men and women stood by silently while so many children and young people were violated. Sherman Allen hobnobbed with major players on the Pentecostal scene, and my Bible Girl columns became an unofficial sounding board for members of the Church of God in Christ. In fact, people sent in heartbreaking allegations about having been abused by prominent church leaders from all over the country.

But not everyone supported my investigative journalism. I was called a "demon," a "lezbo," and a "Judas" in public postings by church faithful, especially when I noted that I had been licensed as a missionary in the Church of God in Christ. And the strange spiritual attacks kept coming. I experienced a one-time bout of depression and a resurgence of same-sex thoughts, after six or seven years in which they were almost entirely absent. The thoughts stopped short of anything explicitly sexual, but they still creeped me out. I fought back the way my leaders taught me: I cast down every thought that "exalts itself above Christ."

"God didn't deliver you to allow you to go back into sin," Diane told me. "He's not going to let you fall."

Fall I did not, but by May 2007, weighed down with details of the most sickening sexual allegations I'd ever encountered in the church, I found myself bereft of all humor and obsessing whether anyone in the Christian world really lived right. I felt like I was plodding through deep sand, moving slowly, inexorably, into thick darkness.

I wish I could tell you why it happened when it did. I preached a message titled "Made in the Desert" about persevering through hardship and then traveled to Portland for a journalism conference in early June. While I was flying back, I felt the Holy Spirit doing something in my life. A current of spiritual energy seemed to radiate through me. It wasn't an overwhelming thing, but it lingered for hours.

The timing seemed so random: I was munching on snacks on the plane, doing nothing in particular, stopping occasionally to chat with my son. The spiritual energy wasn't accompanied by any great divine revelation.

When I returned to work, I had much more physical energy than before, so much that it affected my ability to focus. I needed less sleep and quickly lost weight. And I was filled with hope again. I began to experience joy—and this time it stayed with me. People in the church noticed I was a different person. "Something has changed in you," Mother Hall, the pastor's mother, told me one summer day. "It's like you're free."

I was praying one day, and the Holy Spirit impressed on me why all this was happening. *For seventeen years I refined you in the desert,* I heard him say. *Now I am getting ready to show the glory of Jesus Christ through you.*

I didn't know exactly what that meant. I dared not even think about it; it sounded far too lofty for a screwup like me. All I knew was that I'd never go back to the way things had been. While my circumstances were exactly the same, life inside me had changed forever.

The lawsuits against Sherman Allen were still working their way through the civil courts as this book went to press. The Church of God in Christ's presiding bishop, Charles E. Blake, suspended Allen from all pastoral duties soon after taking office in 2008. Allen responded by withdrawing from the denomination and renaming his church. He still leads a church, though his congregation has dwindled since the lawsuits made the news.

Broome Bobo, the Dallas-area law firm representing plaintiffs Kelly and Drake, has heard from numerous other women making similar allegations against Allen. I spoke to some of them when I was working as a reporter for the *Dallas Observer,* which took the lead in investigative reporting on the Allen case. Some of them had no interest in suing—they just wanted to make sure Allen wasn't allowed to abuse anyone else.

17

Supernatural Healing

I read Dawn's e-mail, and I knew she was sinking. I remembered enough about depression to notice that shift to the melancholy, followed by concentric waves of self-assault. I got in my car and headed over to her house. I didn't call until I was halfway there, because otherwise I knew she would have sent me back home.

Dawn was the mother of Conor's best friend, and she and I had passed each other in the halls of our children's Christian school for more than two years before speaking to each other. Both of us were shy and extremely busy with work. I noticed Dawn because she seemed apart from the affluent families at the North Dallas school, and not just because she was one of the few black parents. From a lifetime of feeling like an outsider in my own way, I thought I could relate. We became close friends after meeting at a bunch of play dates, bound together by our passion for the Word of God.

The first time we had lunch together near the large hospital where Dawn worked as a physician and medical-school faculty member, she told me how she'd been born with sickle cell disease, an incurable and usually fatal condition caused by a DNA mutation that is prevalent among blacks. The red blood cells of a person with this hereditary disease sometimes contort into sickle shapes and become clogged in the body's small blood vessels. When this happens, Dawn told me, the pain is excruciating, so much that the contractions of childbirth seemed like nothing to her by comparison.

Dawn experienced such terrible pain as a child that she frequently prayed for God to kill her. She grew up in an extremely poor South Texas family, with virtually no access to medical care, and the disease wasn't even diagnosed until she joined the army as a teenager. (She received a medical discharge after a severe sickle cell attack during basic training.) Among her childhood memories is lying in bed in the squalid shack that she and her mother and brother shared, twisting in pain during sickle cell crises and fantasizing about her funeral and the relief death would bring.

As an adult, Dawn had been hospitalized numerous times, twice a year on average. She had nearly died on at least four occasions. There wasn't much the doctors could do except pump narcotics into her or administer blood transfusions when little oxygen was making its way to her organs.

When I received the e-mail from Dawn in September 2007, she was deep into a sickle cell pain crisis. Those first ripples of pain can bring on a sinking feeling that extends beyond the physical. She rated her pain at 3.5 on a scale of 5, a probable sign that she'd be on her way to the hospital within a day or two. This was a frightening prospect in Dallas, where Dawn had been treated shabbily on several occasions by hospital personnel who assumed she was a drug addict scamming to get heavy-duty narcotics. They didn't snap to it until they discovered she was a doctor herself.

Confronted with a dear friend in pain who was fading into despair, I had to make a decision. Be a chicken when it comes to prayer for physical healing, like I'd been most of my life, or gather up the faith I possessed and take another flying leap. I made a decision to stay with Dawn and pray until things got better, or take her to the emergency room. Whichever came first.

On the twenty-minute drive to Dawn's house I surveyed the effects of the Holy Spirit's recent work in my life. The joy was still there, and here I was taking another step of faith under circumstances that would have exposed the coward in me just a year earlier. But now I could no longer look past a sister's suffering. I wouldn't duck and run from pain. A surge of faith had compelled me to take new risks.

One was praying for physical healing. Growing up in a doctor's

house, I was always immersed in talk of the natural causes and consequences of illness. My dad, a dermatologist, would calmly correct the
mistaken notions and crazy correlations his patients came up with: "I
ate a Snickers bar—*and then I got this pustulating wart!*" Having been
raised in that environment, it was tough for me to develop a realistic
faith in supernatural healing—until I experienced it myself.

It started with my son's crummy brown goldfish, which he won in
2005 in the Ping-Pong toss at his school carnival. Conor was thrilled
with his prize, and like several other suckers at the school, we walked
out of a pet store with a sixty-dollar aquarium starter kit. Two weeks
passed before the goldfish—dubbed Swifty—developed a nasty case of
fin rot. The creeping crud corroded the fish's extremities to the point
where all he had left for fins were jagged nubs and a single slender bone
in place of a tail. Then even the bone fell off.

We pumped this antibiotic stuff into Swifty's tank, all in an effort
to spare Conor's tender heart. But it didn't seem to help. Finally, with
Swifty scudding around feebly at the bottom of the tank, looking like
a goner, I suggested to my son that we pray. So the boy and I got down
on our knees and laid hands on the fish tank, and we prayed that God
would heal Swifty. I managed to keep a straight face.

Not too far in the back of my mind was this thought: *If I can't believe
that God will heal a goldfish, my faith really is pathetic.* Swifty didn't sprout
a tail while we knelt there, but over the course of several days he
improved significantly. He developed an appetite, and his fins started
growing back—then his tail. Suffice it to say that Swifty is now a three-
and-a-half-year-old goldfish with a rippling tail and a full set of fins. The
drab brown fish even turned a dazzling gold color at some point.

That, I believe, was the kindergarten test of my faith. The real deal
happened to me a year later, in June 2006, when a visiting evangelist
at my father's church prayed that I be healed of chronic Achilles ten-
dinitis, a condition I'd had for three years. Actually, he prayed three
times. I was the last person in the prayer line, and as I waited I cringed
while the evangelist prayed for a lady's leg to be lengthened. "Line up
with God's Word!" he barked. "Line up!" he said within earshot of the

whole congregation. Memories of a disgraced Dallas faith healer flashed before me—a dude who was supposedly caught on camera faking healings that looked a lot like this. I knew God *could* heal me. But would he? I found myself repeating the conflicted words of a man from Jesus' day: "I do believe; help me overcome my unbelief!"

When the evangelist came to me, I mentioned my sore ankles, the result of exercising without shoes and ignoring the pain. He crouched down, touched them, and briefly prayed. "Line up! Line up!"

He looked up at me. "How does it feel?"

I told him I could only figure out whether something had happened by walking down some stairs. For whatever reason, my ankles were at their shakiest going down stairs. So I stepped onto the carpeted stage and descended a few stairs. "They're still sore," I said, "but they're better than they were."

The evangelist wasn't satisfied. He prayed two more times. Each time, I felt less pain than before. Finally, I decided not to monopolize the man's time anymore.

My ankles do seem better, I thought on my way to my dad's house. But when I climbed the stairs to my bedroom, I could feel twinges of pain.

A weird thing happened as I lay in bed that night. I felt a sensation of heat in my ankles. I suspected it was the Holy Spirit; I'd heard of things like this. My faith level blipped ever so slightly.

The acid test came in the morning. I knew what I had to do, but I was a little reluctant—didn't want to be disappointed. Finally, I pressed my index finger against the Achilles tendon on my right foot, the really bad one. I felt nothing. I traced with my finger a tendon as supple as a thick rubber band.

Three years of pain: gone in the morning.

I guess you could say I had to see it to believe, but whatever the case, I no longer was satisfied with my sorry level of faith for physical healing. I asked God to change me, to increase my belief.

When I walked in the door at Dawn's house, she was sitting on the floor in dim light, clutching a heating pad to her chest. She was rocking slightly, the same thing she'd done as a child to distract herself from the pain.

She stared at me blankly. There was nothing to say.

"What do you want God to do?" I asked. I couldn't have thought of a dumber question.

"I want to be healed," she said.

I felt my faith shudder. I rambled on about this and that for a while and asked a bunch of lame questions, which she answered patiently, still rocking. Then I read some scriptures on healing, more to boost my faith than hers.

I was stalling for time. I knew this was the point where my belief so often faltered. It's the same struggle for most Christians. Are we going to pray for a miracle, or will we mumble platitudes about God's "sovereignty"—basically, how he does whatever he wants, whenever he wants to—to cover over our lack of faith?

Just then Larry called on my cell phone. I handed the phone to Dawn, and he prayed for her healing. I couldn't hear his words, but I picked up his steadiness, his confidence, his faith. I pulled myself together.

After he hung up, I sat next to Dawn, placed my hands on her shoulders and prayed. Actually, I prayed and prayed. I could feel the surge of the Holy Spirit's presence—his anointing—in and around me. A thought drifted by about the saints in the old black Pentecostal churches, who had no balm but prayer. When they appealed to "Doctor Jesus," they meant it just like that. He was their only Physician. No wonder so many of them testified of miracles in their time.

After several minutes of prayer, I got a sense from the Holy Spirit that I should place my hands on Dawn's upper chest. When I did that, she and I felt exactly the same thing: my hands, or the place where I'd put them, or both, became noticeably hot. Heat was radiating through that area of her body, where she was experiencing the worst pain.

I know I prayed about her childhood memories, of lying alone, writhing in extreme pain, feeling forsaken by God. Dawn, in fact, wouldn't make a commitment to Jesus until she was twenty-one. I also prayed against the demon of depression.

Dawn told me the pain had started to recede. By the time I went home perhaps two hours later, she told me she felt great. The melancholy was entirely gone, and the pain resolved completely within two days, much faster than her usual recovery time.

For the first time in two days, Dawn was able to sleep. I knew God had acted through our prayers and faith. Larry and I had taken a risk, because of our love and concern for Dawn.

I made a decision that night never again to shrink away from healing prayer. I had been healed myself, and I knew the joy of God's healing touch. So why would I hesitate to pray that he would heal someone I love?

Why people don't get healed as often as we want them to, I don't know. But I resolved to do what I could: pray. And pray and pray, if need be.

18

Love Is the Conductor

Every day at work I immersed myself in reporting and writing on the Sherman Allen case, and at night I came home to a husband who prayed for my mind and spirit to be cleansed of the junk I had come into contact with that day. When you are investigating a story involving a man's years of abuse against innocent women and children, plus the introduction of demonic religion into the church, it starts to weigh on you spiritually.

Three or more times a week I would drive to South Dallas to go to church. It was a welcome transition from my weekday work environment, which had become increasingly hostile. I held dual citizenship in radically different worlds, the cynical newsroom contrasted with a congregation that expected God to show up and make himself known. The effect was jarring.

Each week I wrote a new Bible Girl column, and each week I got whacked in the head by a shovel when the reader comments rolled in. They didn't hold back in their criticism of me and my beliefs. Many of them expressed in the most vulgar terms how incensed they were that a devout, theologically conservative Christian had been given space to write on the Web site of an alternative newspaper.

The irony is that I wasn't the right-wing evangelical they were picturing. I had never fit in all that comfortably among white evangelicals, even in my youth. I had always gagged on the phoniness, hypocrisy, and indifference to the spiritual issues with which people struggle. How could evangelical churches judge liberal Christians for not taking God and the Bible seriously and then belittle Pentecostal Christians for taking God *too* seriously? Pentecostals take God at his word and fully expect him to work supernatural wonders in the here and now. A certain strain of evangelicals argues that God discontinued giving believers the more spectacular spiritual manifestations—such as the gifts of tongues, prophecy, healing, knowledge, or miracles—when the last apostle died. And it seems that the evangelicals who don't subscribe to that line of thinking simply get too busy with other things and push the supernatural to the fringes. But if God and his work aren't supernatural, what are they?

Now that two decades have passed since I last was a member of a white evangelical church, I realize I judged those churches too harshly. I have strong feelings about a lot of things, and sometimes the gray gets lost on my black-and-white scale. But I stand by my statement that it's wrong for evangelical Christians to portray Pentecostals as the lunatic fringe for believing *too much* in God and his power. That has never made sense to me.

Everybody wants to fit in and belong to something bigger than themselves. If you have children, you see this tendency in the way kids love to spend time with their friends. It explains why we join civic organizations or political movements. We want to make a difference in the world, and we seek a place where we can join forces with other people who share our commitments.

And there are people who spend most of their lives looking for a place where they can belong. I spent more than thirty years searching for just this. Even in church, as eager as I was to find a spiritual home, I was frustrated in my attempts until I started attending The Body of Christ Assembly. I was white and female, and this small, inner-city black Pentecostal church was the first place I ever felt I was accepted for who I am. Eighteen years later, the people of this church are my home and family. Finally, loving and being loved by these Christians, I was no longer an oddity or an outsider.

Today we are still a small congregation, with perhaps sixty-five active members, including children. In some ways the lack of numerical growth is frustrating, since Christians tend to measure success by the number of butts on pews. My friends and relatives continue to ask: "Well, is your church growing?"

I keep the real answer to myself, because I don't expect people outside The Body of Christ Assembly to get it. The congregation isn't growing in size at a rapid rate, but the individuals in the congregation are growing. They are getting to know God better, they are growing in their ability to live like Jesus—rejecting sin and embracing righteousness. And they are growing in their trust of God, knowing that he loves them and will take care of them. They are not chasing after Christian celebrities or spiritual fads, and that says a lot to me.

I look at Monique Morgan-Edwards, a South Dallas native who raised seven children, much of the time as a single parent. Her oldest child, LaQuasha Johnson, is an engineer for a multinational firm and a summa cum laude college graduate. Monique's two oldest boys are on scholarship at Southern Methodist University, and another son accepted a full ride to Episcopal School of Dallas, one of the most prestigious private academies in the area. Her three youngest children, triplets, excel in academics and athletics, and all her kids are recog-

© Robert Conner, DFW Digital Photography

Monique Morgan-Edwards (right), known as a prayer warrior,
with her daughter, youth minister LaQuasha Johnson

nized for their excellent character. In Monique I see the effects of God's blessing on a family, the result of years of perseverance in the Word of God.

Monique is a tenacious prayer warrior. If you have to get a prayer through in a hurry, you call Sister Monique. Her own struggles have cultivated compassion, and she is someone who always has my back. All I have to do is look her way, and she can tell if I'm going through a rough time. I don't even have to ask her to pray. She just does it.

"The world would look at my situation and say I'd never make it," she told the church recently. "They could point to all the black-family statistics. I thank God, because he wrote a new statistic. He has changed my mind, he has changed my heart. I'm a single mother, but I'm a praying mother. There is nothing I should want for, because Jesus is the man of the house."

There are others who can recount stories like this; I couldn't possibly tell them all. South Dallas is dotted with households that experienced the healing of Jesus Christ through Pastor Fredrick Eddington's ministry.

One time a visiting evangelist prophesied to the pastor and Diane that while the church may not be big, the people who stuck with it would be saved people. What he meant is that phonies and frauds wouldn't be able to hang at The Body of Christ Assembly, but that the truly saved people would welcome the Word of God even when it hurt, and they would persevere. I couldn't think of a greater measure of success than that. I was reminded of Jesus' words, that we are to make disciples of all nations. He didn't say anything about filling the rolls with large numbers of church members. When I drive to my son's private school in affluent North Dallas, I pass numerous large churches with beautifully designed campuses. There are times I have to suppress an attitude, especially when my brothers and sisters have to reach deep into their pockets to come up with our church's monthly mortgage payment. The disparities between north and south, rich and poor, white and black, seem so immense, and I don't understand why so few of my peers see the genuine riches I do at The Body of Christ Assembly and the extraordinary strength I see in my spiritual father and mother.

What many Christians miss, and what many nonbelievers don't recognize, is that the spiritual life is not a solitary way of life. Being an individualist and getting by on your own don't cut it. God never intended for us to walk this Jesus road alone. God refers to his followers as a kingdom and a family. Saint Paul describes Christians being joined together in a spiritual body. Each of us has little meaning or purpose outside the context of our place in a functioning family of believers.

Many people of my generation shop for a better church like you might trade in an old car for a newer or more luxurious model. The flit from church to church, never forging intimate relationships with other believers, never experiencing the blessing of submitting to pastoral leadership, never grasping what it means to have sisters and brothers who share your burdens and fight alongside you. As spiritual kin we laugh together, break bread together, pray together, study God's Word together, suffer together, cry together. I rejoice when a sister or brother rejoices; I mourn when one mourns. They do the same for me. Joy is greater when it is shared, and pain is diminished when others share it with you.

A spiritual family teaches you how to love like you should and shows you how to endure hardship. Loving my sisters and brothers brought about a deeper healing in me, going to the root of my fear of rejection. When I took the initiative to love others before they loved me, God poured more of his love into me and made my heart secure.

Love, I discovered, is the conductor of Holy Ghost power, like a platinum wire from heaven to the soul. I preached a message on that. "The *only* thing that counts," Saint Paul wrote, "is faith expressing itself through love."

I've learned that if you want to pray and get results, start loving people like Jesus did.

My friend Dawn once asked me a series of probing questions, trying to figure out why I seemed uncomfortable around some of the white people we both knew. Had I developed some strange bias against them? I didn't think I had, but I had noticed that many well-meaning white Christians tend to see blacks as abstractions. And I do have to guard against becoming angry with my white peers in the faith for not trying harder to bridge the color divide in American Christianity. Their tendency to objectify color takes some interesting twists.

Too often, for example, white Christians view black Christians, particularly Pentecostals, as being innately spiritual, as if spirituality comes naturally to black people because of their ethnic or racial heritage. Whites seem to think that blacks have an elemental connection with primitive religious practices best suited to their supposed childlike beliefs. And white people are too easily impressed with the passion and emotion of worship services in black churches. Whites are awestruck by black expressions of religiosity, and they don't see beyond the smoke and mirrors when a black church traffics in a religious show, with fabulously tight choirs, loud preaching, and a choreographed call-and-response of shaken hankies and hallelujahs. It's easy to identify the spiritual emptiness of a staid, tradition-bound white church. But there can be just as much emptiness, spiritual impotence, and hypocrisy in an energetic black church. It's just that the black church is a lot more interesting.

Though The Body of Christ Assembly is in a part of Dallas that most people consider the ghetto, you seldom hear that word used in my church. Nor would you hear people giving sensational testimonies about reaching out to "the gang members and the drug dealers and the prostitutes." Whenever I hear talk like that, it strikes me as dishonest. I doubt that any of the people who talk about ministering to the downtrodden as a way to encourage bigger donations actually develop lasting and equal relationships with any of the individuals behind those labels. At The Body of Christ Assembly, we have ministered to people who were involved in gangs, drugs, and prostitution. But they are people—individuals with complex personalities and intricate backstories. They have hopes and dreams and accomplishments, and their lives consist of more than throwing gang signs and selling crack. Furthermore, once a person has turned his or her life over to Jesus Christ, God makes that individual a new person. The former person ceases to exist, and we don't spend a lot of time talking about her. We say you're a new creature in Christ, so much so that when my sisters talk about their past lives, it's difficult even to imagine I'm talking to the same people they're describing. My closest friends think the same of me, when I describe what a selfish brat and general head case I used to be.

Yeah, there are things about black Dallas that still irk me. It seems like the television is on 24/7 in many of the homes I visit, even when we're praying. I've just resigned myself to it. And I don't understand black Texans' predilection for barbecuing every piece of animal matter inside the house—or why the chicken thighs frequently turn out pink and slimy next to the bone. (*Parboil,* I hear my mom saying. *Parboil.*)

I'm a Midwesterner, and maybe that's why I don't care much for Southern cooking, whether it's the black or white version. To me, black-eyed peas taste like dirt. And the smell of fried catfish turns my stomach. I have assimilated to some extent, and I meekly take my place with a Styrofoam plate in the church potluck buffet line. But one thing Diane taught me was to be myself in a culture that was different from my own.

My son accomplished that feat effortlessly. When he was four and the sole white kid participating in the church's Black History Month play, he got the only role that would work for a white kid. Likewise, my husband was given the role of the devil in a recent Christmas play. (It really happened.)

At a dress rehearsal for the black history play, the narrator was standing in the pulpit doing his best preacher's voice as he recited Martin Luther King Jr.'s "I have a dream" speech. When he got to the part about "one day right down in Alabama little black boys and black girls will be able to join hands with little white boys and white girls," that was Conor's cue. He started walking up the aisle holding hands with Diamond, the pastor's granddaughter.

When he got to the front, he stopped and screwed up his face. "I'm not white," he said. "I'm pink!"

Everyone burst out laughing, and Conor didn't have a clue why.

At four, my son hadn't learned to identify himself with a category of people called white. He attended a largely black church, of course, and only last year did he discover that Auntie Di (Diane) and Auntie Mo (Sister Monique) were really not his aunties by blood. (Now he probably wonders why they were given the authority to spank him.) You'd think he would have noticed at some point that almost all his relatives were white. And maybe he did, maybe he didn't. We never talked about it at home.

Larry and I didn't classify people by color in our son's presence, and the result was interesting. He viewed the world in a different hue altogether. People were just people, identified by their roles—like "Big Pastor"—or the color of their clothing.

I observed how, in social interactions—in places such as the grocery store, the mall, the doctor's office—Conor would make eye contact equally with black and white people and engage in natural conversation. I noticed as well that a lot of white children *don't* do this. Somewhere along the way they've picked up from their parents a sense of otherness concerning blacks, and—like their parents—the children hesitate to push beyond it. You sense the wheels turning within, a young mind recognizing difference and feeling the discomfort of not knowing how to process it.

Certainly some of this is rooted in prejudice, but the lack of meaningful contact with people of other races plays an important role too. Larry and I let go of our grandiose notions about being a force for racial reconciliation years ago, and we simply became holy rollers, sisters and brothers in the black Pentecostal church. I don't spend a lot of mental energy examining the questions of race, and I don't consider myself a deep thinker on the subject. To me, the problem is simple. Prejudice is a sin, and I know of only one way to deal with sin: repent. When you face your sin honestly, God will take you on a process to become entirely free from it. For me, that meant forming intimate friendships with a few black women who are roughly my age. We discovered something, and that is that the bond of the Holy Spirit—a love that is rooted in God's power—is much stronger than the bond of blood. Taking that as the foundation of our friendship, my dear sisters and I have forced one another to peer beneath every layer of complexity in our own attitudes toward race. "As iron sharpens iron, so one [woman] sharpens another"—that's what the Word of God says, and that describes precisely the nature of my friendships with Diane and Dawn.

I am thankful that my son will probably bypass the lengthy process of getting loosed from the evil of racial prejudice and all that accompanies it. Conor didn't even learn that there were negative associations with a person's skin color until he reached kindergarten in a mostly white school. He has grown up comfortable in two cultures, yet as Diane has pointed out to me, he is uniquely himself. He doesn't try to pretend he's black; he is noticeably white by culture as well as color.

It took years for me to lose all my race-related assumptions and frame of reference. I knew something had changed in me when I no longer saw black people as emblems but as Sister Diane, Sister Dawn, Sister Monique, and Sister Valoria—people I knew intimately. We hurt one another's feelings sometimes and have learned to quickly say we're sorry. We spank our kids in the ladies' rest room, get annoyed with our husbands, and argue the merits of Williams versus Popeye's fried chicken. (Popeye's spicy, thank you.) We can talk for hours about the Bible, but we also talk about how the First Lady (Diane) manages to work into an inordinate number of sermons the fact that she and her husband have it going on in the bedroom.

One day Dawn, who joined The Body of Christ Assembly a few weeks after we prayed for her healing, pointed out that all my closest friends are black. I hadn't thought about it much, since by that time being around black people had become my comfort zone. Every now and then my mind wanders during a church service, and it occurs to me that I am sitting in a church full of black people. Or sometimes when I'm standing outside the church, pocket Bible in hand and dabbing sweat off my face, a woman will look at me like I just stepped off a green flying saucer. It suddenly dawns on me that I am probably the only white person for blocks. I tend to forget that I'm a novelty.

Somewhere along the way I got lost in love for my sisters. I have two friends, Diane and Dawn, who have become closer to me than my natural family. Dawn and I joke that if we ever cease to be friends, one of us would have to be "taken out" because we know too much about the other. She decided it would be me, because she earned a marksman rating in the army, and all I had was a couple of crummy National Rifle Association merit badges from Bible camp.

So my closest friends are black. I don't know if that's a good thing or a questionable thing. Maybe the most I can say is it is nothing in particular. They are the individuals who own a huge place in my heart, and that is all.

Spiritual Warfare
in Africa

At The Body of Christ Assembly, we call ourselves a Holy Spirit–led church, which means we're used to the unexpected turn of events. We might stop in the middle of a Sunday-morning service and file outside the church in a long line, singing a hymn and embracing people as we pass them in the street, offering to pray with them right there. Why? Because God told us to. We're accustomed to unexpected visitors, strange happenings, and odd, divinely orchestrated appointments. Like the day in 2006 when another South Dallas minister introduced Pastor Eddington to an African visitor. Diane, Larry, and I met the man soon afterward. Was he friend, freak, or foe? I ran through the options, having encountered a fair share of all three over the years.

Masters Ndimande was a young, English-speaking pastor from Botswana, in Southern Africa. He claimed God had sent him to the United States to enlist help for his people. He arrived with only a few hundred pula, the currency of Botswana, in his pocket and discovered he couldn't exchange it for dollars. By the time we met him, he had bounced from pastor to pastor, and no one quite knew what to do with him. He was reduced to living at a Salvation Army shelter and taking free meals at a soul-food restaurant.

Pastor Eddington always received a brother in ministry, and he was moved by Pastor Masters's account of the troubles in his country, where nearly half the adult population is HIV positive. Seventy-five percent of the adults in his congregation, he estimated, are infected with the AIDS virus. Masters, a Zulu from South Africa who is married to a dignified

Motswana (a person from Botswana) named Fona, had started a project for AIDS orphans in Gaborone, the capital of Botswana, and he was seeking financial help from American Christians. He called his church and his ministry Echoes of Joy.

Pastor Masters—that's what everyone called him at home—spoke well of his wife, who had stayed behind with their infant daughter. "I am the husband of one wife," he said, pulling out a photograph. After spending time with Pastor Eddington, Masters decided he wanted to establish a connection with our church. He invited us to send a ministry team to Botswana.

For a few years we had to put him off, since we were preoccupied with finishing our own church-building project and getting on our feet again financially. Pastor Masters kept asking. He wasn't interested only in money, which we sent; he wanted something else. He wanted us to bring the message of holiness.

I crack up every time I watch the video that captured our arrival in Africa. It portrays The Body of Christ Assembly ministry team exactly as I've known them all these years: a fun-loving group, not inclined to take themselves too seriously or wear the burden of ministry like a hair shirt. Their attitude underscores my own belief: ministry should be fun. Jesus' yoke is easy. Serving God's people in Holy Ghost power has its share of heartaches, for sure. But that's only part of it. Serving God's people brings joy—unforgettable joy.

On July 10, 2008, we gathered late at night at Dawn's house in Johannesburg, South Africa, where she had relocated with her husband and sons. The Americans from The Body of Christ Assembly were so happy to get there after thirty-six hours of travel that we filled her heavily secured housing compound with hoots and loud talk and laughter. Larry jumped into her freezing-cold swimming pool, displacing a heap of water. It was winter in that hemisphere, and the video shows his pale body steaming as he pulls himself out of the water. Then Diane, who automatically shifts into a series of poses whenever anyone pulls out a camera—"I'll make your picture look good," she'll say—offers greetings from the 'hood.

"Helloooo," she says on the video with a flutter of the hand and a head waggle. "What-e-ver." Pastor Eddington is hovering behind his wife, trying to get his handsome face in the picture. Dawn stands beside them laughing, with a do rag and rollers in her hair. I held the camera, and I was laughing so hard I was choking.

The next morning our ministry team, plus Dawn and her sons, loaded into a Toyota truck and Dawn's little green Renault and drove the five hours to Gaborone. Our escort was Binoy Oonnunny Baby, an Indian immigrant who had settled in Botswana, got saved while running an import-export business, and had since given it up to devote his life to helping children who live on the streets of Gaborone. Pastor Eddington tends to butcher people's names, and a visit to Africa took this habit to new heights. He insisted on calling our guide Brother Carbon. If you're wondering how he derived "Carbon" from the man's name, I'm not surprised. The members of the ministry team never figured what random association from the recesses of our pastor's mind had birthed that one, but it stuck. Among The Body of Christ Assembly team, our guide was forever after known as Carbon.

While we passed Beware of Baboons signs along the two-lane highway through South Africa, I thought about the verse of Scripture the pastor had asked us to focus on. "For our struggle is not against flesh and blood," he told us, quoting from Ephesians, "but against the rulers, against the authorities, against the powers of this dark world and against the spiritual forces of evil in the heavenly realms."

We were about to experience firsthand the literal truth of that verse.

Each team member would take part in revival meetings with groups of Batswana, and we had no program whatsoever. The Holy Spirit had told Pastor Eddington that we should be open to whatever God directed us to say or do. Not long after we arrived in Gaborone, we found that our ghetto training in Dallas had perfectly equipped us for the unexpected message we'd take to Botswana.

Bishop Fredrick Eddington prays with Mavis Segomoco Boshwaen, a minister in Gaborone, Botswana

Just like in South Dallas, people were always checking us out to see if we were for real. The Batswana were similarly tentative, and it was difficult to penetrate their reserve. After days of long revival meetings in a frigidly cold church, we felt like we hardly got to know them. But in Gaborone we ran across the same spirits—holy and otherwise—that we find in South Dallas, and at the end of our journey I began to see the real implications of Pastor Eddington's scripture. We were tempted to turn our anger against people rather than the *real* perpetrators of evil: agents of darkness in the spirit world. We were engaged in a life-or-death battle against a concentrated force of evil. Even in the worst days of violence-torn, drug-infested South Dallas, we had never encountered such an army of demons.

The first night of the revival meetings saw a sparse crowd, maybe sixty people, in Pastor Masters's church in west Gaborone. We arrived at the church—which appeared to be a former factory—toward the end of the exuberant praise service, and as soon as we entered the building, the praise team shifted to a slow, somber version of an American worship song. That pattern would persist for the next couple of nights; we never quite figured it out. Dawn and I were relieved later in the series of meetings when the Batswana filled the sanctuary with warm, lilting, polyrhythmic praise, complete with a hand-wiggling dance that I never could master. It was bitterly cold in the unheated, concrete church building that first night, while the Batswana sat stoically on white plastic chairs as a visiting bishop preached.

I was about to learn much about sin—even flagrant sin—and repentance, miracles, and power in the spirit realm. I thought about Jesus' comments after the crowds began following him everywhere, when he realized that for many, his miracles were more attractive than the God who performed them. Jesus said that an evil and perverse generation always looks for signs. But the miraculous signs weren't the point. All he had to offer, he said, was the "sign of Jonah."

If you're looking eagerly for a dramatic sign, Jonah's won't quicken your pulse. Jonah had the simplest possible message for the people of Nineveh: "Yet forty days, and Nineveh shall be overthrown." No remedy was offered; no promises of prosperity and greatness or even a reprieve from promised destruction if the people chose to repent of their sin. Surprisingly, the pagan king of that "great city" responded in the only appropriate way: he repented. He put on sackcloth and humiliated himself before his own people. No ifs or buts, just abject sorrow over the city's sin. The people repented as well, "from the greatest of them even to the least." Even cattle, goats, and sheep were clothed in sackcloth by order of the king and his court.

That, I discovered, is the sign of Jonah: *repentance,* which means turning your back on sin and embracing a new way of life.

In six days of revival meetings held in Gaborone, we did, in fact, see God perform signs and wonders. But we were looking for signs of real repentance. Every revival of lasting significance from the eighteenth century to our day has been marked by men and women throwing off sin in face-to-the-floor repentance.

In Botswana, the people seemed meek and loving in a not particularly demonstrative way, but we had all learned not to base our impressions on outward behavior. We wanted to know what was going on in their hearts, and God would reveal it to us in the starkest terms.

It happened in benign enough circumstances. The ministry team had gone to a primary school where one of Pastor Masters's church members worked. The faculty wanted to meet our pastor and pass on their personal prayer requests. We put Conor and Dawn's sons in the back of Carbon's truck and drove to the school, then crowded into a tiny break room. Pastor Eddington spoke a few words about the privilege of teaching children, and then the teachers and staff, mostly women, forwarded their requests hand to hand on crumpled bits of paper. The pastor promised to pray over them.

The next night the team gathered in a hotel room, ripped at pieces of grilled chicken with our fingers, and opened the written prayer requests. I starting reading, sitting up in bed. The very first request left me speechless.

"Please pray that God will bless my marriage," one teacher wrote, and I paraphrase. "I am supposed to get married in the fall, and my fiancé is an alcoholic. We have been living together for two years, and I have two children. I have been saved for eleven years now. I want to serve the Lord with all my heart. Please ask God to do something about his addiction. Also, I have financial problems, and my sister and uncle are sick with AIDS."

I pulled out another scrap and read. Then another. Then perhaps two dozen more. All but a few told a similar story. Sinful relationships, illness, financial difficulties, plus the frequent refrain that "I love God with all my heart" and want to get closer to him. In other words, as Diane put it, "Bless my mess."

Diane just shook her head. She thought about the empty religion we so often encountered in the church world. "I always wondered," she said, "if people pray and praise so hard like we see all the time, why aren't they in better shape spiritually?"

We had our answer. It's the same answer in Botswana as in South Dallas or the Wisconsin town where I grew up: hidden, unrepentant sin, with a gloss of religiosity to obscure it.

On day three, we were facing a group of about twelve male pastors and preachers, three women in ministry, and a handful of women who sat in the back, some of whom our pastor had prayed for the previous night.

Diane, Dawn, and I arrived late, after the men had started talking about ministerial issues. I could tell that the workshop had devolved into serial monologues from two or three men who felt compelled to offer their opinions on every question. There didn't seem to be a whole lot of listening going on.

Finally, Pastor Masters, who stood patiently at the front with a microphone in his hand, closed that part of the session. He turned things over to Diane, who got up and spoke a few words about living a godly life. She spoke in such an authoritative way that no one dared challenge her, though we'd already grasped that women held a marginal place in some of the churches here. We hadn't heard a single woman's voice so far during the revival meetings, excluding the voices of the praise-team members, even though at least 70 percent of the attendees were women.

While Diane spoke to the group, I felt the Holy Spirit begin to energize me. I fidgeted and shifted in my seat. God was speaking to my heart, and it was difficult for me to remain calm.

As Diane wrapped up, I reached for Dawn's hand. "Pray for me," I said. She nodded.

I was bracing myself for speaking what the Holy Spirit was telling me to say to these pastors and church leaders. As planned, Diane called me up before taking her seat. I gave a little introduction, that it was an honor and privilege to take part in the conference. "I humble myself before you," I said.

Then I abruptly ended the introduction. "The spirit of prophecy is upon me," I said. I heard a reflexive amen or two.

I noticed that my right hand, holding the microphone, had begun to shake. Afterward Pastor Masters would demonstrate how much it was shaking—like I'd been scrubbing a dirty pot. I was just barely aware of it.

The Holy Spirit prompted me to walk to the back of the room, where several women were seated apart from the ministers' tables. I knew I needed to stand there while I spoke.

"I've noticed something in this conference," I said. "The men are doing all the talking." I repeated myself two times, the last in a whisper. "The men are doing all the talking.

"Yet among the women, everywhere I go—I can't ignore it—I discern tremendous hurt, desperation, and pain. The Holy Spirit has put a question in my heart. 'Men of God, why is there so much confusion about sexual immorality in this country?' You who speak, who stand in the pulpit, why is there so much confusion?"

The room had gone completely silent.

"We may not hear the women's voices," I said. "They may not be doing any of the talking. But I recall the words of God when Cain had slain his brother Abel—the blood cries out from the ground."

I crouched on the concrete and pointed down. I measured each word. "The blood...cries...out...from the ground."

I stood up again, without looking at the people's faces. I thought about saying more, about offering consoling words as a means of closure. I sensed that I should not.

Dawn would tell me later that everything about me changed while I prophesied—my voice, my countenance, even my color. "It's like you're hearing something on the inside," she said. "You're talking or listening to someone, but it's no one we can see. You're there but you're not there."

When I stopped speaking, the room was still silent.

Years ago Diane had told me that I had the spiritual gift of prophecy. That means the Holy Spirit sometimes gives me words to speak that pinpoint a situation, a need, or a biblical truth that needs to be emphasized right then.

I had gathered from the teachers' prayer requests that Botswana's culture was male-dominated. And in a different way that I can't explain, I picked up in my spirit that these women were hurting terribly. I didn't know why just yet, but we'd soon come face-to-face with the evil spirits behind the anguish.

20

Watching Hell Break Loose

That night things started busting loose. Pastor Eddington preached, and though my memory of his sermon is sketchy, I know he stressed repentance from sin. I heard the words *adultery* and *fornication* mentioned repeatedly. I don't recall too much of his message, because everything was eclipsed by what followed.

After preaching for maybe twenty minutes, the pastor stepped down from the podium onto the lower level of Pastor Masters's church. The church had two floor levels, with one about five feet higher than the other. The pulpit and praise team and visiting preachers were on the higher level, where a drummer banged away on a snare drum and two mangled cymbals. When the pastor leveled off into a holy-roller hum, singing his message in a rhythmic cadence, the drummer and keyboardist followed behind him with their slightly off-kilter version of a black-church shout beat.

On this night there was a packed house, with about 125 people crammed into the room. As Pastor Eddington's words resounded in the sanctuary, stuff started breaking out all over the lower level.

So much happened so quickly that it threw me off balance. I was in a daze for a few moments, reeling from sensory overload. Then I stepped onto the floor and prepared to pitch in. Pastor Eddington was already down there, laying hands on people and praying. Diane remained on the upper level, where she extended her arm toward the lower floor and prayed. From her vantage point and with her vision, the things that were unfolding around me must have looked like pandemonium. I was sucked into a scrum of surging, staggering bodies.

I had seen this happen before in South Dallas—though never on a scale like this—when the Holy Spirit's presence would bring about extreme agitation. Demons would manifest, coming forth and making themselves known after being stirred up and exposed by Jesus' probing Spirit.

When this happened in Gaborone, Pastor Eddington commanded the demons to leave in the name of the Lord Jesus Christ and by the power of his blood. A phalanx of blue-clad ushers from Pastor Masters's church would act as catchers if the person with a demon looked like he or she might fall. Most of the time they did fall, sometimes without anyone touching or laying hands on them. At least the Batswana are typically small, slender people, making them easier to catch. Back in South Dallas I've sometimes found myself the only line of defense between the floor and a 250-pound woman who's toppling backward.

In Gaborone, Dawn and I caught our share of falling bodies.

As Pastor Eddington continued praying and laying on hands, people kept falling to the floor, often lying there writhing and screaming. The noise was sometimes deafening, with the shrieks and groans of women who were manifesting demons and the male ministers swarming around them, barking and shouting at the spirits in English and Setswana. Closer to the dusty concrete floor, where I spent most of my time praying for women who had fallen out, it was quieter. Or at least it seemed that way as I focused on each individual soul.

I saw one woman fall out, and then the pastor prayed for her again because he discerned that the demon hadn't left. He had the woman stand up, and he laid hands on her while I stood behind her. Suddenly I got smacked in the face, and my glasses went flying as the young woman slammed into my arms and chest before wilting and falling to the floor. Larry was standing nearby, and he said the woman had more or less catapulted at a forty-five-degree angle. The physical strength these demons conjured up astonished me. I saw movements that no person could replicate using only his natural strength: abrupt leaps, rapid rolling, turbocharged thrashing.

When a woman fell, I would get down on the floor and plead the blood of Jesus and pray in tongues. I began to notice a phenomenon: several of the women appeared to lose consciousness, though you could see their eyeballs twitching and rolling beneath the lids. The women would lie rigid, limbs stiff and bodies taut. But after a while their stomach muscles would tense up and their chests would start to heave. They'd arch their backs and move in what resembled a sexual rhythm for minutes at a time, and if you'd speak in their ears, they would seem not to comprehend.

After observing this a few times, I asked Bishop M. what was causing it. Bishop M. was a respected elder minister from Zimbabwe with a gentle spirit, and he'd settled near Gaborone to pastor a tent church. He explained that it was evidence of "the spirit of lust and anger combined."

I moved on to someone else, still on the lower level, which I called "the pit." Just then a minister bent down and spoke in my ear, telling me that two Satanists had entered the church to disrupt the meeting. At that moment Pastor Eddington was praying for one of them, a short woman in her early twenties with long braids pulled back on either side of her unsmiling face.

As the pastor prayed, a demon rose up in the young woman. She screamed and plunged to the ground, where she flailed her limbs and rolled around. Word had spread that she was a practitioner of witchcraft, and an aggressive mood seemed to sweep the ministers in the pit. Several of them gathered around her and took turns yelling at the demon to come out, while others held her down as she tossed about.

Dawn was standing off to the side, shaken by all the noise and commotion, and she recalls feeling sorry for the young woman, who appeared as though she were being tortured in soul and body. More than once the girl was helped to her feet, and the ministers would have another go, hollering, "Get out, get out!" as she fell again. One of the women ministers whispered to Dawn that the girl had been used in satanic rituals by her grandmother, and she wasn't able to speak the name Jesus.

By then the pastor had worked his way back to where the young woman lay on the floor. When he heard this story, he announced: "She will speak the name Jesus by the power of the Holy Ghost." He then asked her to say Jesus. The girl would move her mouth, then abruptly stop.

Pastor Eddington called Dawn over. Dawn is never quick to speak, and Pastor Eddington believed that a gentle, quiet-force approach was needed to help the woman. "Minister to her until she says Jesus," Pastor Eddington said. "Speak to her like a mother."

Dawn stood beside the girl, speaking into her left ear. She told me later what happened. "God loves you so much," she had said. "He doesn't want you to suffer anymore. He doesn't want you to be bound up. He wants to be your Father. He wants you to experience joy and peace."

For many minutes, Dawn spoke to the young woman in reassuring tones. Two times she stopped and asked the girl to say Jesus. It seemed like she wanted to say it—her lips would begin to move—then she'd freeze. "I can't," she'd say.

Dawn continued to speak of God's love. "You can say Jesus," she said. "You will be set free."

She stopped a third time and asked the young woman to say the name. She heard a single word in a miniature voice: "Jesus." Dawn wanted to be sure.

"Say it again," she told her.

"Jesus. Jesus," the girl replied, slightly louder. Dawn smiled and made eye contact with the pastor.

She felt the prompting of the Holy Spirit to approach the girl differently now, simply to love her. She wrapped her arms around her and held her. The girl began weeping. Dawn sensed that she had never experienced this kind of love before. "Release her, restore her," Dawn prayed. "Heal her—give her peace. Give her joy."

By now Dawn was weeping too. She held the girl in her arms for twenty minutes or more, while Pastor Masters's wife, Fona, plus an evangelist named Philda Kereng, and I gathered around to support Dawn and the young woman in prayer. This was the image that stuck with me that night, of Dawn, who was about a foot taller than the girl, towering over her as they embraced. I found symbolism in it, the power of God's love overwhelming the darkest demons.

When Dawn finally released the girl, the noise in the room had diminished to a hum. Above us the worship team launched into a joyful chorus about rain—spiritual rain. The people around us joined in dancing and singing.

Right around this time we saw lightning flashes through the upper-level windows. The next thing we knew, rain was pouring onto the metal roof and trickling though cracks into the sanctuary and onto our heads. The people seemed momentarily stunned; in eight years, Pastor Masters would explain, rain had not fallen in Gaborone in July.

On Sunday morning the men and the boys from our group drove off with Carbon to preach in Bishop M.'s faded yellow tent in a village called Mogoditshane. I thought about how happy Conor and his two friends, Dawn's sons, were in Botswana. It was as though they were born for this journey. They had been chased by vervets (African monkeys) on the hotel grounds, played in the dirt, hunted for lizards, ate greasy doughnuts for breakfast, and rode in the back of a pickup truck, making faces at the mommies while we signaled frantically for them to keep their limbs inside the truck bed. I was so used to urban Dallas, where you're as vigilant as a crackhouse lookout and never trust anyone when it comes to your kids. Botswana had little crime, and people went about their business, including driving, at an amiable pace. Here our boys could be boys, free to roam and investigate things, now bouncing along in the back of a truck.

I had brought Conor to Botswana with a little trepidation, because I didn't know what we'd encounter. But I saw that he fit in with no problem. Even during long services every night in a frigid church, the three boys would settle into a corner and talk and play quietly, or wrap themselves in a blanket and doze off while a nightmare tableau from a Bosch canvas unfolded in front of them.

Later I asked Conor if he knew what was going on in the services.

"Demons," he said, fiddling with his Spy Gear dart shooter. And that was that.

As the boys drove off with the men that morning, Diane, Dawn, and I made our way to Pastor Masters's church, where Diane had assigned me to preach. After the exhilarating Setswana praise—no sad, slow American songs this time—I stepped behind the pulpit and launched into my message, speaking bluntly about fornication and cohabiting, the Batswanas' polite term for what we in South Dallas call "shacking."

"Would you defile your natural father's house?" I asked the audience. "Would you come and have sex in the church?" My message was interpreted into Setswana.

"Our bodies are the temple of the Holy Spirit," I said. "If we wouldn't think of defiling the house of God, this physical structure of steel and concrete where God doesn't actually live, why would we defile the temple where he *does* live?"

Most of the congregants were young, probably in their twenties, and they watched me intently but silently. The quietness unnerved me. I could feel my courage flagging. When I opened the service for prayer, I made a muddled appeal, and just then Pastor Diane stood up, walked toward me, and took the microphone. I felt like I'd been rescued from a sea of stony faces.

Diane has a sort of magisterial presence, developed through years of forcing herself to speak the truth when few want to hear it. Her vision has deteriorated in the last three years, and she tends to look at people slightly askew, as though she were looking right through them. Which, in fact, she is. Dawn calls her "the blind lady who sees."

Diane summoned Fona and stood her in front of the congregation. "What you need is a spiritual mother," Diane said, "to help you walk in holiness." Then she called the single women to come to the front of the room for prayer.

She began laying hands on them, and one by one the stoic faces cracked. Women started falling, wailing. A young woman next to me pulled her knees against her chest, circled her arms around her legs, and wept. Later I'd find out she'd had a child out of wedlock with a "man of God," and now this man would not marry her or support the child.

At one point Pastor Masters rose and asked for the microphone. He called a woman by name, and when she came to the front, I winced. It was the same woman whose conflicted prayer request we'd read two nights earlier. I could tell she was bracing herself.

Masters looked her in the eye. "You must change your ways," he said evenly. He asked Diane to pray for the woman. Diane laid hands on her and prayed. Immediately the woman dropped to the ground. Diane didn't miss a beat. "You don't need to fall out," she told the woman. "You need to repent."

Diane gestured to the ushers. "Get her up," she said.

The female ushers struggled to raise the woman, who was much taller than they. When the woman stood, Diane prayed and the woman dropped to the floor again.

Once more the ushers helped her up. "You need to repent publicly," Diane told the woman. "We're helpers one to another. If you repent publicly, your sisters will help you be accountable." I heard a rising wail, like something ragged escaping from the woman's soul. She sank to her knees. "I repent!" she yelled. "I am so sorry—forgive me!"

She began sobbing, her cries interspersed with words spoken in Setswana. She held her arms tightly to her side as her body arced with each sob.

Diane observed her with peripheral vision for a moment, then nodded. Satisfied, she moved on. She called the single men, and they lined up in front of her. They were far fewer than the women. "I see where the problem is," Diane said, alluding to the culture of promiscuity in Botswana.

She asked all who wanted to be married some day to move forward, so God could prepare them for that step. Then she started laying hands on the men.

One small man was shuddering with each word he spoke. It was obvious the Holy Spirit had settled on him and was ushering each of Diane's words right to his soul. She hadn't even reached him in the line to pray for him when he dropped to the ground without being touched.

21

The Night Demons Raged

That night Pastor Eddington called a solemn assembly at Masters's church. All the pastors and preachers—perhaps thirty in number, mostly men but with a sprinkling of women—knelt together on the upper platform as Pastor Eddington, who by now was being called Bishop Eddington, prayed to commission them into ministry. He called for unity, something sorely lacking in a country where many of the pastors were fighting to survive, and he led them through a prayer of repentance for their contentiousness and lack of cooperation.

During the prayer one woman stood out. Roughly dressed and slightly unkempt, she had what I could only describe as a darkened countenance. Like a goat among bleating sheep, she didn't seem to belong. I got a strong sense of spiritual incongruity. Later I'd find that Pastor Eddington was picking up the same vibe: *What is she doing here?*

At the risk of appearing to pick on one of the few women in the group, the pastor called her out. "You have been buffeted about, succumbing to temptations and getting involved in things you have no business being involved in," the pastor said into the microphone. His voice had a firmness, an edge I had seldom heard in the eighteen years I had known him. "Who is your covering?" he asked.

The woman didn't give a straight answer. She said she had tried to find "covering," which is a spiritual leader, a mature Christian to encourage her and hold her accountable.

"You can't do this on your own," the pastor said. "You need help."

The woman mumbled something in reply, diverting her eyes.

The pastor's response was uncharacteristically sharp. "Did you listen to anything I said?" Pastor Eddington wanted the preachers and pastors to realize that repentance from sin was a requirement for them as well as the members of the congregation.

We helped administer communion, squares of bread and a sweet, pale purple drink that had probably never been in the presence of a real grape. Diane was sitting off to the side, and the Holy Spirit warned her that Satan would do something to disrupt the solemnity of the occasion. Sure enough, just a few moments into Pastor Eddington's prayer for communion, we heard a muffled groan in the back. The next thing I saw was two heels and striped tube socks looping up in the air, followed by a loud splat. An older woman had upped and flipped backward in her chair and was now rolling on the floor, moaning indecipherable words in the deep, strangled Hollywood demon voice. No one on the platform even moved.

I went to where the woman lay and noticed a young pastor bent down to her face, mumbling into her ear. The woman thrashed about on the floor with considerable force, rolling over my foot. Nothing, however, disrupted the communion service. The ministers went to the lower level to serve communion to the packed congregation. The pastor preached a few words on repentance, then waded into the lower level to start praying again. And just like the events of the previous night, demons started making their presence known. The first time a demon audibly manifested, Diane said to herself, "It's starting up again."

Pastor Eddington worked his way through the crowd, laying hands on the men and women who inched toward him. Sometimes he would single someone out and prophesy, giving them a "word" about sin or school or relationships. Every time, he prayed and prophesied differently. He'd get in a spiritual zone, and afterward he'd remember few faces or words spoken.

When he laid hands on one thin young woman, a demon took control of her. While she was under the influence of that spirit, she tried to bolt out the door, and as she pedaled her legs, she dragged four or five men and women along with her. I had noticed by now that this was a recurring tactic; in the gospel of Luke we hear of a man possessed by many demons that would continually drive him, naked, into desolate places, even causing him to break the chains that kept him from hurting himself and others. I knew from my own experience that this is how demonic oppression works: the spirits pull you into a lonely place so they can torment you without interference. Away from the love, support, and protection of your sisters and brothers, you're road kill.

One aggressive young minister prayed for another skinny girl, and she fell out. Then he walked away, mission accomplished. As she lay there, she started doing the chest heaves I'd observed earlier. I pleaded the blood of Jesus, then I gestured to my husband. "It's still there," I said. The demon hadn't left—it was playing possum. The girl appeared to be asleep and was mouthing nonsensical syllables, "Na...na...na..." I was getting weary, and I was relieved to have my husband there. He crouched down and ordered the demon to get out in Jesus' name. By calling on the Holy Spirit, he broke the power of curses on the girl's life while she rose to her knees and heaved and shuddered, head bobbing.

When I was praying for this girl, the Holy Spirit showed me another part of the equation: many of these girls had been sexually violated. A spirit of lust could be transferred from the rapist to the victim if the woman wasn't under the protection of the Holy Spirit. Many of these girls had been raped, exploited, and abused.

It took about twenty minutes of concentrated prayer before the demon was cast out. I made note of what happened as the presence of the Holy Spirit overtook her: The chest heaves and convulsive movements stopped completely, and the girl began to breathe normally. She nodded her head in response to some of the things Larry said. A peaceful spirit now held sway.

Too many times, though, the young women who were prayed for that night went down to the floor with a demon and got up with a demon. A few of the ministers seemed overly interested in making a show of stabbing their fingers at the demons and screaming for them to get out, but they didn't follow through till the end. To me it resembled a sexual conquest: The ministers would do their thing, get bored, and walk away, scanning the crowd for another opportunity for public spectacle. Meanwhile the woman would be left on the cold concrete to be tormented another day by the same spirit she arrived with.

Down in the dust with girls and young women, praying in tongues for them and understanding only a little of what I was seeing and hearing, I was struck by the fragility of these women. It was very cold in the church most nights, and the women had pulled together whatever they could in the way of clothing to erect a flimsy barrier against the chill. One girl had wrapped a bath towel around her skirt that was shed amid the convulsing. Many covered themselves in blankets. I would see the women in the same sweaters, sweatshirts, and jackets night after night. A turn on the floor would coat them in dust.

I couldn't help but notice the worn shoes, the faded sweaters, the crude hair weaves, these ineffectual attempts to wear something that imparted dignity. Yet the overall impression was of the meanness of life and our human inability to conceal our spiritual nakedness. Some of the women had scars on their faces, and again I picked up in the Spirit the agonized state of many souls.

I found myself getting angry at injustice, angry at men. Diane had always warned me of the dangers of getting into self while you're ministering. Quicker than you can detect it, your spiritual discernment is replaced by natural observation and personal biases. None of these things conduct the power of the Holy Spirit. I had to make a concerted effort to turn my thoughts to the real enemy—Satan. I hated his guts for what he'd done to these women.

When the skinny girl got up, I saw her face for the first time. She couldn't have been more than fifteen years old. I embraced her, and I refused to let her go. I was too tired to carry on a conversation, plus she didn't seem to understand much of what I said anyway. As the crowd started filing out the doors that night, I took off the gold Celtic cross I always wore and clasped it around her neck. "Every time you see this," I said, "I want you to remember how much God loves you."

It's all I could think of to do. She didn't say a word; she just smiled.

22

The Scourge of Immoral Leaders

The next day, Diane, Dawn, and I sat next to the deserted hotel swimming pool, huddled together under a wool blanket. We sipped hot tea while Diane recited the testimonials she had heard so many times from holy rollers while she was growing up. "'I've been saved all day, and no evil have I done...'" She paused for a moment. "You lie!"

"How about this one?" she continued. "'I woke up this morning with my mind stayed on Jesus.'" Dawn and I waited for the rejoinder. Diane was laughing now.

"I know you woke up some mornings with something on your mind besides Jesus!"

Me? I woke up with my mind on Sugar Babies, the exquisitely sweet candies that one can find only in certain American mom-and-pop stores. Dawn and I, in fact, had squirreled away a slightly melted box of Sugar Babies that I'd brought from home. We stored it in her hotel-room safe to keep it away from the kids, who had their own candy, or so we reasoned. Dawn felt only the slightest twinge of shame when we had to summon the hotel security to open the safe after I messed up the combination. I wondered what the guard thought when he opened the door and found no jewelry, no cash, no laptop—just a half-eaten box of Sugar Babies. Dawn tipped him generously, and off he went to solve the next crisis involving rich foreigners.

Our time in Gaborone was winding down, but we could take some satisfaction in our work there. We had preached the difficult message that God had sent us to deliver.

We saw our boys in the distance, playing contentedly in the mud on the hotel grounds. I could hear their voices ringing out in the cold afternoon air. Our conversation turned to the meetings and the fact that we'd had very little time to mingle in informal settings with the people. We had been whisked immediately out the door after each service, with ushers fetching our bags and Bibles; Pastor Masters said it was their tradition, a way of showing respect for visiting ministers.

Diane discerned a spiritual purpose. "God set it up that way," she said. "He didn't want us getting 'common' with the people. We'd have a hard time staying faithful to the message of repentance if we mixed." She thought of her childhood days in Talco, Texas. If the Holy Ghost moved with power during a revival meeting, the people were taught to hold the pleasantries and maintain a reverent silence. In the same way, she said, a move of repentance in Botswana shouldn't be followed by vacuous chitchat.

Soon we were joined by Pastor Eddington, Larry, and a visitor, one of the African pastors. We talked about the scarcity of money in the churches in Botswana and how many of the ministers hoped that our pastor would become their spiritual father, their bishop. It was clear that, for whatever reason, these ministers lacked trust in one another. In fact, later that day we would hear disturbing information about the moral failures of some of the ministers who had participated in the conference.

Pastor Eddington didn't react when he heard these things; he already knew about some of it from private counseling sessions. Larry, Diane, and I were shocked. Stuff like this was happening all the time in American churches. A week didn't go by without word of a pastor's indiscretions and his church's attempts to hide it, but it still never failed to disappoint us.

Dawn, however, looked like she'd been punched in the gut.

That night Pastor Eddington shared his own story with the audience, telling how he'd gone from drug-addled schizophrenic to man of God, faithful husband, successful builder and businessman.

"That's why I preach the power of God," he told the crowd. "That's why I know there is nothing too hard for God. That's why I know God is a great deliverer, because of what he did for me."

After each phrase he would pause for the interpreter, but they were so in synch by now that what we heard was an unbroken stream of preaching. On this fifth night of the revival the people were expectant, even joyful; gone was the stoicism we'd observed the first two nights. Their body heat had even managed to warm the sanctuary just a bit. Many of the same men and women returned night after night, including the woman preacher that the pastor had rebuked, the lady who'd publicly repented, and the demon-possessed girl who had finally said "Jesus."

"A crazy person don't serve God!" the pastor shouted, rumbling into a cadence. "A crazy person don't live right!"

He swept his arm across the platform, gesturing to the men and women on the lower level, some of whom had been saved, baptized in the Holy Spirit, and delivered from demons in the past few days. "This is that which was spoken by the prophet Joel," he said, repeating Saint Peter's words to the crowd at Pentecost: " 'And it shall come to pass in the last days, saith God, I will pour out of my Spirit upon all flesh: and your sons and your daughters shall prophesy, and your young men shall see visions, and your old men shall dream dreams: and on my servants and on my handmaidens I will pour out in those days of my Spirit; and they shall prophesy.' "

"I am here tonight because Jesus is alive," the pastor said. "The people in Botswana got something that is greater than sickness, greater than poverty, greater than death, greater than the Enemy.... You know how to pray, you know how to praise, you know how to shout, you know how to call on his name!"

Many in the congregation were standing and clapping. Pastor Eddington called to the front all who needed prayer for God's help in breaking out of seemingly impossible challenges. This time, as many men as women approached the front. The pastor stepped down among them, praying and prophesying. People fell out, but only a few demons manifested this night, and the ones that did were quickly dispatched, as though the darkness were being gradually rolled back. The pastor had been laying hands on people for a while when a drama began to unfold on the opposite side of the lower level, where Larry and I were standing.

T., an Asian immigrant who'd been baptized in the Holy Spirit two nights earlier, was moving toward the back of the pit, his eyes popping out. The way he held his arms in front of him, he looked like the zombie in Michael Jackson's "Thriller" video. He began shouting above the din in an authoritative voice: "The power of the Holy Spirit! The power of the Holy Spirit!"

He was under the influence of a spirit, but I didn't know whether it was the Holy Spirit or something else. All eyes turned to him as he charted a vector to the far corner of the room. There an older woman was standing by herself. T. was headed straight for her, but his eyes were fixed in the distance.

"The blood of Jesus!" T. called out in that stentorian voice.

By now the woman realized she was standing in his path. She was oddly dressed, in a hooded track suit with unmatched shoes. She put her hand on her hip. At one point she thrust an index finger at him. She did her best to look nonchalant with this Asian man shouting and coming straight at her.

"Why are you here?" T. thundered. "What have you come here for?"

"What do you mean?" the woman asked, somewhat defensively.

This was starting to look like a dicey encounter. Brother Carbon got up and wrapped his arms around T., and in a few moments Pastor Eddington intervened. He took the woman aside and spoke with her privately, and attention turned to the few demons manifesting here and there around the room. I lost track of T., who had melted into the margins of the crowd.

At the end of the service the pastor pulled the woman and T. together at the front of the room. Then he called for Diane, and I walked her down the concrete stairs. He didn't want the service to end on a note of confusion, he said, and he knew that Diane's presence had a way of flushing out the truth. T. was still under the influence of a spirit, and when the pastor asked him a question, it seemed as though he were struggling with all his might to extract the answer from his natural mind.

"Do you know this woman?" the pastor asked.

T. looked at her searchingly. He was trembling. He answered tentatively, slowly: "I don't know you."

The woman shrugged. "I'm your next-door neighbor," she said.

"She's your next-door neighbor?" the pastor asked T.

T. leaned back against the concrete stage, still staring at the woman. He let out a small shriek—"Aah!"—and bent backward on the platform. He looked as though he'd been momentarily overcome by God's Spirit. When he came to his senses, he said quietly, "Yes, she is my neighbor."

The woman, it turned out, led a ministry for young women in Gaborone. The pastor believed she had come to the revival meeting in disguise, looking as though she were a woman off the street. She was, indeed, T.'s next-door neighbor—though they seldom if ever spoke to each other. Earlier in the service, the pastor found out, T. had accidentally brushed up against the woman. She told the pastor and Diane she'd drawn a circle around her feet and made a vow: if any man crossed the circle, he would die.

As Diane and I discussed what had happened, it started to become clear. Just two nights before, T. had been filled with the Holy Spirit at the revival. Larry and the pastor had independently prophesied the same thing to him: because of his servant heart, God was going to bless him. Because he had been generous to others, God was going to be generous to him. The purpose was that he be a blessing to the ministry.

Meanwhile, the woman, by her own admission, was devising curses against people. That night at the revival service, she couldn't possibly have been operating in a clear conscience. And like the woman minister the pastor had confronted the night before, T.'s neighbor wasn't accountable to any other leader. "Our walk with Christ really depends on our accountability," Diane said to us. "It's obvious that just saying you're accountable to God is not enough."

When T. had asked the woman "Why are you here? What have you come here for?" it was the voice of the Holy Spirit exposing a woman who purported to be a minister of the gospel but was pronouncing curses on people. When the import of T.'s words struck me, I shuddered inside.

"I don't know you."

That was the Holy Spirit speaking. If the woman didn't belong to God, whose was she?

At the final night's service, Pastor Eddington preached, prophesying a brighter future for Botswana, while we met in darkness. The electricity had gone out in west Gaborone, and we alternated between candlelight, feeble power from a generator, and pitch blackness. It didn't seem like the pastor noticed. With or without a microphone or house lights, he carried on as though he had his own source of light.

The pastor asked those who had been saved or baptized in the Holy Spirit during the revival to come to the front. The former witch stood there; her countenance had completely changed, and that night I heard her loudly singing praises to Jesus.

The service ended in dancing and raucous praise, with people rising to their feet while those who had been delivered of evil spirits collected their jackets and flip-flops from wherever they'd been scattered in the fray. The American visitors—the pastor, Diane, Larry, me, Dawn, and our three sons—were ushered through a crack in the sliding metal doors to the cool outdoors. Our work was finished.

When we got to the hotel around midnight, we were hungry. Larry and the pastor went on a late-night chicken run with Brother Carbon. While they were gone, Dawn came to the room. She was disturbed about something, and at first she didn't want to say why. We sat on the bed and prayed. We asked God to search our hearts for any offensive thing, to line us up with his heart.

Dawn's discomfort had been building, because most nights she sat in the pit with the boys and was able to observe things the rest of us didn't. This final night of the revival she was so unsettled by what she saw that she put a jacket over her head, retreated to a corner, and prayed.

What Dawn had seen was some of the African pastors lighting on the women like lions to the attack. They'd lay hands on them and appear to push them over, forcing them to be "slain" in the Spirit.

Something was off about it all. Dawn felt that some of what she saw was fake, that a few of the ministers were trying to one-up one another. She saw one evangelist walk up to a woman in the crowd and have a conversation with her while our pastor prayed elsewhere. Then the evangelist stepped up to the front of the pit. He called up the same woman—"Let's go," he said—and aggressively laid hands on her and, almost as if on cue, she launched into the gyrations of the demon-possessed and fell out.

To Dawn it looked like a set-up, a show. He was calling attention to himself, not to God's power to deliver people from evil.

On another night I saw the same evangelist glance around him before praying for an obviously ill person, as though he were gauging its value as spectacle. Before he prayed he led the person to the front where the two of them could be seen by everyone.

"Is it me?" Dawn said. "Is this just my unbelief? Is something wrong with me?"

"No," I said. "I think the Holy Spirit showed you these things. I saw some of this too, but maybe I'm too concerned about being liked. I didn't want to say anything."

There was more. Dawn was distressed by all the yelling at demons, the obvious torment these women were suffering—and why was it that only women seemed to get demons cast out of them? What about the men?

And then there was the report we'd heard about a couple of the ministers leading immoral lives. Yet if these things were widely known, why were those ministers allowed to pray for vulnerable, desperate young women in the assembly?

At the end of that last night Dawn had seen one of those ministers talking to the girl who'd been delivered from witchcraft as though he were counseling her. The sight of it frightened her.

"I wanted to run over to her and say, 'Don't talk to him,'" Dawn said. "'Don't let him get too close to you. Some of these men are wolves —they're predators.'" Then she said to me: "We're leaving now, and I worry that the women will be left unprotected. Many of these girls experienced a spiritual rebirth. I fear for them."

After we'd talked awhile, Larry got back with the chicken. Now I was deeply disturbed myself and recapped our conversation. I took some comfort from his calmness, and I trusted and hoped that God would help us find a place of peace.

As Dawn went back to her own room, Larry asked if she'd arrived at some resolution. "No," she said and shut the door.

I couldn't sleep that night. I knew God had given me a prophetic gift; he'd called me to be a messenger of his truth. But I had witnessed some of the same things Dawn had seen, and I said nothing. What was wrong with me? Had a dose of false religion dulled my ability to see right and wrong? Had a little immersion in the titles, the protocol, the egos, and ambitions of the ministerial crowd clouded my conscience?

In the morning I tried to read the Bible, but I found no comfort there. My mind was racing; I was too distracted to pray. I did ask God for one thing—that I would have an opportunity to speak to my leaders.

That, in fact, is how I had left things with Dawn. "We have to trust that God knows how to protect his sheep. And I know the pastor and Diane. I'm certain they're aware of some of these things. The [African] pastors asked Pastor Eddington to be their bishop, and we've got to believe that God will give him wisdom as their leader."

I had to drop off something at the pastor and Diane's hotel room that morning. I told them about some of the things I'd seen and that I was uneasy about leaving brand-new believers in the hands of ministers who appeared to have mixed motives. As I had suspected, the pastor was wrestling with many of the same issues. And even though Diane—with her failing eyesight—couldn't see what Larry and Dawn and I had observed, she had picked up static with her spiritual antennae.

First of all, the pastor pointed out, we didn't know for certain that what we'd heard about the ministers' immorality was true. But more important, the pastor had discerned enough spiritual darkness that he had led all the pastors and preachers in a public prayer of repentance, followed by communion. He had actually counseled in private one of the ministers whose actions so disturbed me, and the man "cried like a baby," the pastor said. The man hadn't denied that he needed to get right with God.

Was the repentance genuine? Only time would tell; we had to allow that time. "Produce fruit in keeping with repentance," John the Baptist warned the crowds who flocked to him. Repentance will always show proof. If God does something inside you, it will produce evidence externally.

Since the pastor was now the bishop of Gaborone, the new spiritual father to several of these ministers, he would begin the process of getting to know them as sons. He would continue to preach and counsel holiness. He would make clear his expectations. He would correct them as necessary. Or, as happens more often, the men and women who disdain accountability would simply leave.

I headed back to South Africa and eventually South Dallas with a garment bag full of dusty skirts and stories that were already sounding surreal—even though I'd seen it all myself.

We took a seven-hour "scenic route" back to Johannesburg. Brother Carbon would get into impassioned conversations with Larry and Pastor Eddington, and then he'd speed up, slow down, and veer dangerously close to the other side while the women followed in Dawn's car. I was coming down with the flu; six nights in a freezing cold church hadn't helped. But I was still analyzing the things I'd seen, and for a few hours the bad seemed to overwhelm the good. I obsessed about the thought of predator preachers devouring the vulnerable women.

I felt for a moment like throwing up. "I'd rather have a witch outside the door of the church," Dawn had told me the night before, "than the wolf *inside*."

I couldn't have agreed more.

As Diane and Dawn reminisced about growing up in rural black holy-roller churches, talking about the sounds of foot stomping, washboard, and beaten tambourines, about tarrying services and shouting and the best smothered chicken they'd ever had in their lives, and the way the old aunties steered them away from questionable dishes at the church potluck with a single syllable—"mmm"—I pulled myself together. I felt like I'd seen the very best and worst Christianity had to offer. Many times it seemed as though we were whipsawed between elation and utter disillusionment. Ironies and incongruities abounded; Pastor Eddington had been elevated to bishop in Gaborone, yet we were going home to a small church in the inner city where we'd soon get hit with a massive electric bill amid 107-degree heat.

My leaders preached and lived the truth, that much I could say. Some people developed an appreciation for it; a few even grabbed it and wouldn't let go. Most, however, shrugged and walked away.

On the twisting, mostly empty road back to Johannesburg that evening, Diane pulled out the business card of the woman T. had confronted during the revival meeting. "I don't want it," she said, thrusting it toward me in the front seat.

Now, I am the First Lady's fixer. That is my job, and I don't take it lightly. I am her eyes, her hands, her feet. So I wasted no time rolling down the window and tossing it outside. It was a classy, laminated thing, so it's probably still lying in the red dust somewhere between the Botswana border and Joburg.

I didn't have to ask Diane why; I knew exactly how she felt. On this very long journey we had begun and we had ended with the same sentiment: All we want is the real thing. A real Jesus, a real relationship with God, a real change in our lives.

Driving back to Johannesburg, following Brother Carbon's swerving trail, I thought of what Diane had told me, words she'd adopted from Jesus' warning about the lonely walk of righteousness. Her words had become my refrain. "The road to holiness is narrow," she would always say, "and you only find a traveler every now and then."

23

My Life as a Holy Roller

Eighteen years ago I was a single woman in my midtwenties, engaged to be married, and hungry for spiritual reality. Today I am forty-five, married, a mother, and amazed by the way God has shown up in my life.

Back when I was working the cops beat for the *Dallas Times Herald*, I was regularly thrust up against the worst of humanity. I saw in bloody detail the effects of Satan's influence, the damage and destruction that take their toll on wrongdoers, innocent bystanders, and the families who love either the perpetrators or the victims. By now you have read my story, and you know that God and Satan are as real to me as the alarm going off in the morning. I would despair with this knowledge if I wasn't certain that God has the upper hand.

The idea of God was not new to me in 1990 when I headed to South Dallas in hopes of finding a feature story that merited front-page treatment. Jesus and I had been distant acquaintances for years, and I knew from my childhood that there were Christians who took God and prayer and the power of the Holy Spirit seriously. It's just that I had never had a full-on, life-changing encounter with such people and their right-beside-you God until I started attending The Body of Christ Assembly.

I have stuck with this one church for nearly two decades, which, if you're not a regular churchgoer, is more of an accomplishment than you might think. The truth is, I have been tempted on several occasions to leave. One time many years ago I stomped out of the sanctuary right after Sunday school ended, deeply offended about something. Pastor Fredrick Eddington's sister, Dicloria, chased after me and leaned in my car window, doing her very best to pull me out of a sulk. I listened, and I got over myself.

So many people have prayed for me, spoken "words" to me at exactly the right time, and picked me up when I was falling—none more so than my husband, Larry. Let's just say it's tough to go through God's refining fire that I described in this book. Very tough.

Honestly, if I had known how tough it was going to be when I first stepped into The Body of Christ Assembly as a worshiper, I would have run in the opposite direction. But here we are, Larry and me. Humbled, most definitely. Scarred even. But standing as members of a loving community, with a faith made strong in the desert.

When you "make it through," as the old saints like to say in the Pentecostal church, you realize you're an entirely different person from when you started. Everything that isn't godly, that isn't right, shrivels up and falls off along the way. You are left with a life that is far different from the one you started with. It's a transforming experience.

I am far from perfect—way far. But I am no longer the selfish, hardheaded, moody, and undisciplined person I was when I began this journey. I'm not sure exactly how and when all this changed. It just did. I might not have been supernaturally delivered from a crack-cocaine addiction, but I can testify to another act of God: the miracle of a transformed life.

It astonishes me that God took someone with a deep wound of rejection from childhood and made her strong enough to stand amid withering attacks as the writer of Bible Girl. My critics were very public, very personal, very vulgar, and came from outside my newspaper as well as within. At times I laughed at the ridiculous ferocity of my enemies and the crazily contradictory nature of their arguments. It struck me how God had chosen damaged goods—me—and appointed the most unlikely leaders, a preacher and a blind prophetess from a small black church in the ghetto, to stand with me every step of the way. Up in the heavens, this must be someone's idea of funny.

But that's just like the Jesus I know. He came to "heal, deliver, and set free," as Pastor Eddington so often says, and I'm so glad this Jesus saved me.

For someone who used to suffer badly from depression, it is a miracle in itself that, in the eighteen months since June 2007, I have experienced more joy than in the previous forty-four years of my life. At times I feel absolutely giddy. I'm already a squirmy person, and joy makes me fidgety and full of energy.

With the joy comes love. I remember going bowling with the kids from the church in the summer of 2007 and being amazed by the overwhelming love I felt for them. I just sat there and basked in the wonder of loving someone else. All of a sudden I wanted to run for Jesus, serving him with abandonment. I looked around my world and everything seemed to be moving in slow motion, so I just started ripping and running.

My friend Dawn and I walked door to door in the streets of South Dallas, evangelizing and praying for the lost, the broken, and the sick. Used to be I only went along for the ride when the church witnessed in the community. I felt like the only white person for miles, and there were times when I probably was. I just didn't care anymore. The Holy Spirit was stronger inside Dawn and me than whatever we encountered out there—or, as they say in deep South Dallas, "out theya."

I'd gotten to the point where all I wanted to do was take the gospel and walk it through the streets. And I took that literally: As we walked we were taking Jesus wherever we set foot. We were packing the Holy Ghost. We were reaching out to a community that was hurting, offering as the only lasting solution the love and care of God. For each willing person we came across, we offered to pray. Since the love of God was with us, the power of God would show up when we prayed. People would weep. Children would become joyful. The old and young would set aside their disappointments and talk to us, asking questions and sharing their experiences with us.

Those days were perhaps the most wonderful I've experienced in my life.

As I write this I am on the eve of another journey to Botswana and South Africa. When I get back, I'll be out on the streets of South Dallas again. I can't wait.

There is a three-word distillation of all I learned from my leaders at The Body of Christ Assembly: holiness or hell.

Holiness has become a musty old word, a sort of discredited concept in the Pentecostal church. The idea of holiness, meaning God-likeness, had lost its flavor around the time it was reduced to a code for acceptable dress and myriad prohibitions against everything from watching movies to playing football. Like Saint Paul said in his writings, these admonitions—do not touch or taste—hold no power over sin. And how often we'd seen that played out in little churches where the women were "being holy" by shunning makeup and jewelry but the preacher was sleeping with multiple church members, sometimes women, sometimes not. The scenario was so common in black Pentecostal churches it was almost a joke. I could understand why so many young people who grew up in that tradition wanted nothing to do with church or with God when they came of age.

I grew up in churches where holiness wasn't taught in any practical sense; it really wasn't an expectation. It was seen as an automatic thing—a legal label of sorts, based on the biblical teaching that Jesus had provided justification for sin *once and for all*—or it was thought of as some otherworldly state we'd never attain. Pastor Eddington believed differently. He taught that we would have victory over sin in this life on earth, and that it should be easier for a Christian *not to sin* than to commit sin. I'd never heard that before, but now, when I opened my Bible and studied for myself, I saw this concept everywhere.

"The man who says, 'I know [Jesus],' but does not do what he commands is a liar, and the truth is not in him," Saint John wrote. "But

if anyone obeys his word, God's love is truly made complete in him."
Love and truth, truth and love—the pillars of holiness. It's just hard to
understand why some people respond to the message and some don't,
why some are healed and some continue to suffer. Or why an addict will
weep bitter tears at the altar and then walk outside the church doors
only to end up back on crack a few days later. If I figured it out at all,
I saw that God's power and grace were always there, but you had to be
desperate for them.

Desperate enough, Diane would say, to make a choice: holiness or
hell.

Where Are They Now?

One of the greatest blessings in Pastor Fredrick Eddington's life in the last few years was the privilege of baptizing his father, Herthen Eddington Sr., who gave his life to Jesus Christ late in life. He apologized to Fredrick for how he treated him as a child. Pastor Eddington took his father on vacations and enjoyed many good times with him, and Eddington Sr. doted on his grandchildren and great-grandchildren, whom he loved dearly. He passed away in 2008.

Sherman Allen still pastors a church in Fort Worth. I wrote extensively about the Sherman Allen case for the *Dallas Observer*, and my reporting can be found in the archive at www.dallasobserver.com as well as under the category "Bible Girl" on Unfair Park, the *Observer*'s award-winning news blog.

The story I wrote on the 1990 bathtub shooting in South Dallas, "The Girl Who Played Dead," can also be found in the *Observer* online archive.

Most of The Body of Christ Assembly people mentioned in this book are still members.

We call Catherine Johnson "Mother Johnson" at the church, and she is one of the intercessors—the prayer ladies.

Chris and Yolanda Edwards are rocks of strength at the church. They both teach Sunday school.

Monique Morgan-Edwards and her children are mainstays at the church. Her beautiful married daughter, LaQuasha Johnson, was licensed as a youth minister in 2007. LaQuasha preaches uncompromisingly about holiness.

R. L. and Doris Spencer handle many responsibilities at the church, and Sister Spencer witnesses in the community and prays for residents in nursing homes. Both of them are church ushers.

Mother Alice Hall still lives in South Dallas. She is known at the church and in her family for her generosity and kindness.

Missionary Lola Hines preaches occasionally and is one of the church's honored mothers. She retired two years ago from her longtime job at a bomb factory, where the blood of Jesus Christ protected her through many accidental explosions. Her sister, Missionary Genetta Brown, is also retired and lives with her husband in West Texas.

As I mentioned, Dawn relocated in late 2007 with her husband and sons to South Africa, where she participates in several ministries with a Johannesburg church. She accompanies the members of our church who go on mission trips to Botswana. She has lived in good

Missionary Lola Hines, one of the church's
honored mothers

health the last two years, but we are waiting in faith for her total, permanent healing from sickle cell disease.

Evangelist Dicloria Eddington left The Body of Christ Assembly in 2007 after many years of service. She now ministers in another Pentecostal church.

We see Queen Victoria Curlin at the church occasionally. She still tells people how Jesus delivered her from crack cocaine.

Swifty the goldfish is alive and getting too big for his tank.

My husband and I live in Southwest Dallas with our son. Larry finds jobs for people with disabilities through one of the church's subsidiary ministries, and he dreams of ministering in parts of the world where Christians are suffering persecution. Our son considers Africa his favorite place in the world.

Acknowledgments

All the events described in this book are real. I obtained my information from personal observation, multiple interviews, news reports, and public documents.

While I have made every effort to present accurate information, some dates and facts were difficult to pin down, and I have attempted on my own to resolve conflicting accounts. I take sole responsibility for any errors.

There are no composite characters in *Holy Roller*. In every instance in which I cite a full name, it is the person's actual name. Two individuals, Dawn and Frederica, are identified only by their real first names. The names of some individuals who played a minor part have been changed.

I owe a tremendous debt of gratitude to Pastor Fredrick L. Eddington Sr. and Copastor Diane Eddington, leaders of The Body of Christ Assembly. Not only did they sit through hours of interviews, but for eighteen years they have served lovingly and patiently as my family's spiritual leaders. Not once did they try to impose their own spin on this story. I am thankful for how they've loved me all these years. But what stands out even more is their unflinching commitment to truth. I love you, Pastor and Diane. May God continue to bless you richly.

Two dear friends provided constant support throughout the writing of this book and graciously handled what I confess were a series of meltdowns. I thank you from my heart, Diane and Dawn. I couldn't imagine being blessed with two more wonderful friends.

My mother, Joanne Cutting-Gray, PhD, read most of this manuscript and offered invaluable suggestions and moral support. Thanks, Mom.

My father, Dr. James Schuster, and his wife, Carla, steadfastly prayed for me and supported this project from the beginning. They have also offered aid at crucial times to The Body of Christ Assembly, financially and otherwise, and we consider them part of the church family.

My grandmother, Emily Gray, was always ready to listen and pray. Thank you for encouraging me to write.

I am indebted to my brothers and sisters, past and present, at The Body of Christ Assembly, who submitted to interviews or provided information for this book. These individuals are, in alphabetical order: Veronica Banks; Missionary Genetta Brown (Diane Eddington's aunt); Queen Victoria Curlin; Dawn; Anthony Eddington (Pastor Eddington's brother); Copastor Diane Eddington; Evangelist Dicloria Eddington; Pastor Fredrick L. Eddington Sr.; Gregory Eddington; Chris Edwards; Yolanda Edwards; Alice Hall; Christopher Hines; Missionary Lola Hines; Catherine Johnson; Ingra Johnson; Martin Johnson; Elder Larry L. Lyons Jr.; Monique Morgan-Edwards; Doris Spencer; R. L. Spencer; and Pamela Wright.

Some of the material in this book was adapted from Bible Girl columns that I wrote for the *Dallas Observer*. It is used with the permission of Village Voice Media, the *Observer*'s parent company. I want to thank my former bosses, Michael Lacey, Christine Brennan, and Andy Van De Voorde, as well as blog editor Robert Wilonsky, for supporting the Bible Girl concept even though they undoubtedly disagreed with many things I wrote. Their commitment to investigative reporting and truly alternative journalism shines in an age of media homogeneity.

I am grateful to the man and women of God who prophesied into my life concerning this book: Copastor Sandra Gardner, Prophetess Janice Mixon, the Reverend Cynthia Pfeffer, Evangelist Joyce Terrell, and Pastor Bill Thompson. Thanks for obeying the Holy Spirit.

My editor, Ron Lee, and my agent, Greg Daniel, saw the potential in *Holy Roller* and managed to extract it. Thank you for believing in me.

My son, Conor, cheered me up many times while I worked on this book. For a while at least, he won't have to ask, "Mama, why are you always staring at the computer?"

Most of all, I want to thank my wonderful husband, Larry, for standing with me all these years and encouraging me to be the woman God intended me to be. There is no way I could have done it without you. I love you dearly.

Notes

Chapter 1

17 "I found the girl who'd survived by playing dead": Updates on the victims from the Bathtub Massacre are included in Julie Lyons, "The Girl Who Played Dead," *Dallas Observer,* July 17, 2003, www.dallasobserver.com/2003-07-17/news/the-girl-who-played-dead (accessed October 15, 2008).

Chapter 2

18 "Now I lay me down to sleep": This traditional prayer, with origins in the eighteenth century and published in *The New England Primer,* has been recited at bedtime for more than two hundred years.

Chapter 3

30 "Saul, Saul, why do you persecute me?": Acts 9:4–5.

30 "Something like scales fell from Saul's eyes": Acts 9:18–19.

33 "Women were prohibited from wearing pants": Some Christians adhere to a literal interpretation of 1 Corinthians 11:5–10 and require women to have their heads covered in church by either a hat, a scarf, or long hair. Most Pentecostal Christians today, however, view Saint Paul's requirement as culturally specific to his time.

Chapter 4

44 "Jesus' followers waited in the Upper Room": See Acts 1:4–5.

44 "old things passed away; all things became new": See 2 Corinthians 5:17, KJV.

45 "The things that occurred during the White Oak revivals": To read more about this, see the New Testament book of Acts.

46   "I'm saved and I know I am": "I'm Saved and I Know I Am,"
      public domain.

47   "He sanctified me with the Holy Ghost": "What He Done for
      Me," public domain.

47   "searches our hearts" and "intercedes for us": Romans 8:26–27.

49   "Jesus, I'll never forget, when away down in Egypt land": "Jesus,
      I'll Never Forget," public domain.

50   "when you made a commitment to Jesus, you were a new per-
      son": See 2 Corinthians 5:17.

Chapter 5

56   "Bishop Smith licensed Fredrick as a pastor to start a mission
      church": Though Fredrick Eddington was credentialed as a pas-
      tor in the Church of God in Christ and remained under the
      oversight of a denominational bishop for many years, the church
      he founded, The Body of Christ Assembly, would always be
      independent of the denomination.

58   "No one who puts his hand to the gospel plow and looks
      back...is fit for service in the kingdom of God": See Luke 9:62.

59   "if they keep quiet, the stones will cry out": Luke 19:40.

Chapter 6

66   "Go away from me, Lord": Luke 5:8.

72   "What are words worth? What are words worth?": Chris Frantz
      and Tina Weymouth, "Wordy Rappinghood," *Tom Tom Club,*
      copyright © 1981, Sire Records.

75   "All who draw the sword will die by the sword": Matthew 26:52.

75   "I have hardly ever seen a man die so entirely submissive to the
      will of God": Dietrich Bonhoeffer, *The Cost of Discipleship* (New
      York: Macmillan, 1963), quoted in "Martyrs in the History of
      Christianity," www.religion-online.org/showchapter
      .asp?title=1570&C=1474 (accessed November 29, 2008).

76   "If your right eye causes you to sin, gouge it out and throw it
      away": Matthew 5:29.

76   "Cheap grace is the deadly enemy of our Church": Bonhoeffer, *Discipleship,* 45.

76   "Cheap grace means the justification of sin without the justification of the sinner": Bonhoeffer, *Discipleship,* 46.

77   "pledge of a good conscience toward God": 1 Peter 3:21.

Chapter 7

81   "The B-I-B-L-E, yes that's the book for me": "B-I-B-L-E," public domain, www.dltk-bible.com/biblesong.html (accessed November 29, 2008).

85   "a world of evil among the parts of the body": James 3:6.

88   "Jesus loves me this I know, for the Bible tells me so": Anna Bartlett Warner, "Jesus Loves Me," in Susan Warner, *Say and Seal,* J. B. Lippincott, 1860. The tune we have today is modified from Anna Bartlett Warner's version and is public domain.

Chapter 8

97   "plucking the donations out of donor envelopes and throwing the prayer requests in the trash": Scott Baradell, "Robert Tilton's Heart of Darkness," *Dallas Observer,* February 6, 1992.

Chapter 9

102   "be holy, because I [God] am holy": Leviticus 11:44.

103   "In the beginning was the Word, and the Word was with God": John 1:1.

104   "Whatever you bind on earth will be bound in heaven": Matthew 16:19.

104   "If you hold to my teaching, you are really my disciples": John 8:31–32.

105   "a Word from God that applies precisely to the *here and now*": It is eyeopening to see how Jesus and the writers of the New Testament handled Scripture. They broke every known interpretive rule, at least those that are taught today in evangelical seminaries. They plucked a fragment from the Old Testament here, a verse

there, even combining phrases to make an argument or express a new twist on an old truth. Conservative scholars will say that Jesus and the apostles were special cases; God authorized them to pick and choose and create a new theology. Plus, you ain't them, so don't try this at home. I agree, to a point. But we're missing a deeper insight—that Scripture is a living entity.

105   "from death to life": John 5:24.

106   "They overcame him by the blood of the Lamb": Revelation 12:11.

106   "Faith cometh by hearing, and hearing by the word of God": Romans 10:17, KJV.

Chapter 10

109   "God inhabits the praises of his people": See Psalm 22:3, KJV.

109   "Jesus on the main line, tell him what you want": "Jesus on the Mainline," public domain. Lyrics available at www.lyrics freak.com/r/ry+cooder/jesus+on+the+mainline_20120160.html (accessed November 29, 2008). To hear an interesting vocal rendition of this song, see the Joseph Spence album, *Glory* (Rounder Records, 1990).

114   "Gerasenes demoniac": To read the entire story, see Luke 8:26–39.

115   "For the grace of God that brings salvation has appeared to all men": Titus 2:11–12.

116   "No one who lives in him [Jesus] keeps on sinning": 1 John 3:6.

116   "Holy! Holy! Holy!": See Revelation 4:8.

116   "transformed into his likeness": 2 Corinthians 3:18.

119   "He will baptize you with the Holy Spirit and with fire": Matthew 3:11.

119   "You will receive power when the Holy Spirit comes on you": Acts 1:8.

Chapter 11

120   "principalities, against powers, against the rulers of the darkness of this world": Ephesians 6:12, KJV.

124   "the last shall be the first, and the person who is greatest is the one who serves": See Matthew 20:16, 26.

125   "The gifts and callings come without repentance": See Romans 11:29, KJV.

Chapter 12

136   "Weeping may endure for a night, but joy cometh in the morning": "Weeping May Endure for a Night," public domain.

Chapter 13

145   "God is no respecter of persons": Acts 10:34, KJV.

145   "Offer your bodies as living sacrifices": Romans 12:1.

146   *"guide you into all truth"*: John 16:13.

149   "I die daily": 1 Corinthians 15:31, KJV.

149   "press toward the mark for the prize": Philippians 3:14, KJV.

Chapter 15

162   "When you hate what I am and whom I love...you hate me": Mel White, *Religion Gone Bad: The Hidden Dangers of the Christian Right* (New York: J. P. Tarcher / Penguin, 2006), 48.

163   "God establishes marriage between a man and a woman": Julie Lyons, "The Slippery Middle Ground on Gay Marriage," Bible Girl, the Unfair Park blog, *Dallas Observer,* September 13, 2006, http://blogs.dallasobserver.com/unfairpark/2006/09/the_slippery _middle_ground_on.php (accessed October 18, 2008).

163   "Today I will say that sexual orientation is a mystery": Julie Lyons, "The Mystery of Sexual Orientation," Bible Girl, the Unfair Park blog, *Dallas Observer,* September 21, 2006, http:// blogs.dallasobserver.com/unfairpark/2006/09/the_mystery_of _sexual_orientat.php (accessed October 18, 2008).

164   "Do not be deceived": 1 Corinthians 6:9–11.

164   "I believe Jesus Christ has the power to totally transform a person's life": Lyons, "Mystery of Sexual Orientation."

165　"I know some will read this and say I never was or still am":
Lyons, "Mystery of Sexual Orientation."

Chapter 16

172　"She miscarried within two hours of one such beating": Carrie
Drake and Davina Kelly are named plaintiffs in separate lawsuits
against Sherman Allen. Their allegations against him are con-
tained in pleadings that are part of the public record. See *Carrie
Drake v. Sherman Clifton Allen, Shiloh Institutional Church of God
in Christ, Inc., Church of God in Christ, Inc., John Doe 1, John
Doe 2, John Doe 3,* Cause No. 342-227529-07, 342nd Judicial
District, Tarrant County, Texas, Plaintiff's Original Petition,
pages 1–12. See also *Davina Kelly and Darian Kelly v. Sherman
Clifton Allen, Shiloh Institutional Church of God in Christ, Inc.,
Church of God in Christ, Inc., John Doe 1, John Doe 2, John Doe 3,*
Cause No. 236-222319-07, 236th Judicial District, Tarrant
County, Texas, Plaintiffs' Original Petition, pages 1–9.

173　"lighting voodoo candles inscribed with such words as *Prosperity,
Money,* and *Control*": These and many other allegations against
Sherman Allen, as well as the lawsuits that have been filed against
him, were reported in several articles I wrote for the *Dallas
Observer.* They also were reported widely in the Dallas–Fort
Worth news media. For more of the background, see the follow-
ing: Julie Lyons, "Sherman Allen Gets Spanked," Bible Girl, the
Unfair Park blog, *Dallas Observer,* May 10, 2007, http://blogs
.dallasobserver.com/unfairpark/2007/05/sherman_allen_gets
_spanked.php; Julie Lyons, "Pentecostal Preacher Sherman
Allen Turns Out to Be Reverend Spanky," *Dallas Observer,*
February 20, 2008, www.dallasobserver.com/2008-02-21/news/
pentecostal-preacher-sherman-allen-turns-out-to-be-reverend-
spanky; Melody McDonald, "Lawsuit Accuses Pastor of Abuse,"
Fort Worth Star-Telegram, February 10, 2007, www.religion
newsblog.com/18393/sherman-clifton-allen-2; and Michael
Grabell, "FW pastor suspended after rape accusations," *Dallas*

Morning News, May 12, 2007, www.dallasnews.com/shared
content/dws/dn/religion/stories/DN-fwpastor_12met.ART0
.North.Edition1.42f1253.html.

174 "For I have overcome the world": See John 16:33.

Chapter 17

181 "I do believe; help me overcome my unbelief!": Mark 9:24.

Chapter 18

187 "we are to make disciples of all nations": See Matthew 28:19.

188 "The *only* thing that counts...is faith expressing itself through love": Galatians 5:6.

190 "We say you're a new creature in Christ": See 2 Corinthians 5:17.

191 "one day right down in Alabama little black boys and black girls": Martin Luther King Jr., taken from his speech "I have a dream." A transcription of this speech is available at www .usconstitution.net/dream.html (accessed January 16, 2009), and a video of this speech is available at http://video.google.com/ videoplay?docid=1732754907698549493 (accessed November 29, 2008).

192 "As iron sharpens iron, so one [woman] sharpens another": Proverbs 27:17.

Chapter 19

196 "For our struggle is not against flesh and blood": Ephesians 6:12.

198 "sign of Jonah": Luke 11:29.

198 "Yet forty days, and Nineveh shall be overthrown": Jonah 3:4, KJV.

198 "from the greatest of them even to the least": Jonah 3:5, KJV.

201 "the blood cries out from the ground": See Genesis 4:10.

Chapter 21

212 "in the gospel of Luke we hear of a man possessed by many demons": See Luke 8:26–39.

Chapter 22

217   "This is that which was spoken by the prophet Joel":
       Acts 2:16–18, KJV.

223   "Produce fruit in keeping with repentance": Luke 3:8.

Chapter 23

229   "these admonitions—do not touch or taste—hold no power
       over sin": See Colossians 2:20–22.

229   "The man who says, 'I know [Jesus],' but does not do what he
       commands": 1 John 2:4–5.